The Global Impact of Religious Violence

The Global Impact of Religious Violence

Edited by

ANDRÉ GAGNÉ, SPYRIDON LOUMAKIS,
AND CALOGERO A. MICELI

WIPF & STOCK · Eugene, Oregon

THE GLOBAL IMPACT OF RELIGIOUS VIOLENCE

Copyright © 2016 André Gagné, Spyridon Loumakis, and Calogero A. Miceli. All rights reserved. Except for brief quotations in critical publications or reviews, no part of this book may be reproduced in any manner without prior written permission from the publisher. Write: Permissions, Wipf and Stock Publishers, 199 W. 8th Ave., Suite 3, Eugene, OR 97401.

Wipf & Stock
An Imprint of Wipf and Stock Publishers
199 W. 8th Ave., Suite 3
Eugene, OR 97401

www.wipfandstock.com

PAPERBACK ISBN: 978-1-4982-8305-2
HARDCOVER ISBN: 978-1-4982-8307-6
EBOOK ISBN: 978-1-4982-8306-9

Manufactured in the U.S.A.   OCTOBER 17, 2016

Contents

List of Illustrations | vi
List of Contributors | vii
Introduction: Religion and Violence on the Global Scene | ix

1. Tyranny of Political Correctness and Religious Violence | 1
   André Gagné

2. Apocalypses and Superhero Mythology | 13
   Jennifer Tacci

3. The Common Good Gone Bad | 39
   Costa Babalis

4. Genocide and Religion in Rwanda in the 1990s | 47
   Spyridon Loumakis

5. Discourse of Sacrifice | 84
   Marion Achoulias

6. Is There Such a Thing as a Radicalized Brain? | 114
   Marc-André Argentino and Dalia Sabra

7. Religion and Violence: Rethinking the Role of the Biblical Scholar in the Contemporary World | 134
   Calogero A. Miceli

8. Secularized Theology and the Propensity for Violence in the Modern State | 154
   Derek Bateman

9. The Global Impact of Religious Violence | 167
   Hector Avalos

List of Illustrations

Figure 1: Front page of *Kangura* 26 (November 1991). Courtesy of Montreal Institute for Genocide and Human Rights Studies, Concordia University (Montreal, Quebec). http://migs.concordia.ca/links/documents/KANGURA_26-November_1991.PDF | 64

Figure 2: Front page of *Kangura* 3 (January 1991). Courtesy of Montreal Institute for Genocide and Human Rights Studies, Concordia University (Montreal, Quebec). http://migs.concordia.ca/links/documents/KANGURA_3_INTERNATIONAL.PDF | 65

List of Contributors

Marion Achoulias is a PhD student and part-time faculty member in the Department of Religion at Concordia University (Montreal, Quebec).

Marc-André Argentino is a PhD student in the Department of Religion at Concordia University (Montreal, Quebec).

Hector Avalos is a professor of Religious Studies at Iowa State University (Ames, Iowa), U.S.A.

Costa Babalis holds an M.A. in Theological Studies from Concordia University (Montreal, Quebec).

Derek Bateman is a PhD student and part-time lecturer in the English Department at Concordia University (Montreal, Quebec).

André Gagné is a tenured Associate Professor in the Department of Theological Studies at Concordia University (Montreal, Quebec).

Spyridon Loumakis is a PhD student and part-time faculty member in the Department of Religion at Concordia University (Montreal, Quebec).

Calogero A. Miceli is a PhD student and part-time faculty member in the Department of Religion at Concordia University (Montreal, Quebec).

Dalia Sabra is an M.A. student in the Department of Psychology at Concordia University (Montreal, Quebec).

Jennifer Tacci is an M.A. student in the Department of Theological Studies at Concordia University (Montreal, Quebec).

Introduction

Religion and Violence on the Global Scene

André Gagné, Spyridon Loumakis, and Calogero A. Miceli

This volume originated from a conference on the theme of "Religion and Violence" that was held at Concordia University on June 16th, 2015. The majority of papers presented at the conference and subsequently included in this book are by graduate students from different backgrounds of research all of whom interacted with Professor Hector Avalos's (Iowa State University) work in some way. The event was to honor and underline the significant research done by Avalos on the topic of religious violence. The following publication is an extension of this recognition to Professor Avalos for the impact of his research in fields of religious and scriptural studies, and their relation to violence.

Religious violence is a timely and relevant subject which scholars of religion and scriptural studies urgently need to address, and even more so now that many feel its effect on a global scale. Among the most current examples of the global impact of religious violence is seen in the struggle with Islamist radicals. In the past two years, the terror attacks in St. Jean-sur-Richelieu, Ottawa, Paris, Baga, Beirut, Brussels, Istanbul, Bagdad, Orlando, Dhaka, Nice, Würzburg, and Ansbach just to name a few, clearly demonstrate that religiously motivated violence has become a worldwide phenomenon.[1] In many cases, these attacks have been claimed by the so-called Islamic State (IS, ISIS or ISIL). The group's salafi-jihadism[2] now transcends the Middle

---

1. For some of the reasons why Jihad is now a global phenomenon, see Fawaz A. Gerges, *The Far Enemy: Why Jihad Went Global* (Cambridge: Cambridge University Press, 2005).

2. Concerning the global expansion of Salafism, see Roel Meijer (ed.) *Global Salafism: Islam's New Religious Movement* (Oxford: Oxford University Press, 2013).

East, and one should not be surprised, in light of Mustafa bin Abd al-Qadir Setmariam Nasar's influential book entitled *Global Islamic Resistance Call* (Da'wat al-muqawamah al-islamiyyah al-'alamiyyah), which appeared online in 2005.³ In his work, Nasar, who is better known as Abu Mus'ab al-Suri, teaches that, "Terrorism is a religious duty, and assassination is a Prophetic tradition," and speaks of the righteous terrorists, the Mujahideen (those engaged in jihad), as "terrorists toward their enemies, God's enemies, and his weak servants."⁴ Al-Suri expounds on portions of the Qur'an (Al-Anfāl 60, Al-Baqara 217 and Al-Tawba 12) in order to convince and call his readers to the duty of jihad.⁵ Nasar also believed that since 9/11, old models of operation, which emphasized "secret – regional – hierarchical organizations," needed to be replaced by what he called "Individual Terrorism Jihad."⁶ Mujahideen can now engage in guerilla warfare and small resistance units operating individually from another, in order to have the enemy collapse under pressure. For al-Suri, the entire world is now the jihadists' battlefield.⁷ Islamists can, therefore, carry out religiously inspired terror acts on a global scale since those who wish to fight can do so in their own countries or from anywhere else.⁸ This is believed to be much more efficient than on the home front.⁹ Islamism is but one of the most obvious examples of the globalization of religious violence. Articles in this book examine other groups, actors, and geographical regions, as well as other factors that play a role in the proliferation of religious violence on the global scene.

Let us now turn our attention to the contributions of this book. The first article, penned by André Gagné, sets the stage as to why scholars should discuss issues surrounding religious violence in the public sphere. Gagné laments the current mood of political correctness when it comes to violence and religion, and cites several examples where racist allegations are made toward people who criticize Islam. According to Gagné, Islamic identity and

3. See the English translation of the core of al-Suri's *Global Islamic Resistance Call* by Brynjar Lia, *Architect of Global Jihad. The Life of Al-Qaeda's Strategist Abu Mus'ab al-Suri* (Oxford: Oxford University Press, 2014).

4. See *Architect of Global Jihad*, 383–385.

5. For more on the idea of Jihad and its definition in Islam, see David Cook's masterful book, *Understanding Jihad. Second Edition* (Oakland, California: University of California Press, 2015).

6. *Architect of Global Jihad*, 367.

7. See Gilles Kepel, *Beyond Terror and Martrydom*. Translated by Pascale Ghazaleh (Cambridge: Harvard University Press, 2008), 165.

8. See André Gagné, "Global Terrorism: A new age of unpredictability." *OpenCanada.Org.* July 28, 2016. https://www.opencanada.org/features/global-terrorism-new-age-unpredictability/

9. *Architect of Global Jihad*, 369–370.

culture have now become racialized to the point where those who critique the Muslim religion are often accused of "Islamophobia." When it comes to religious violence, people usually understand what violence is, but scholars seem to have a more difficult time defining religion. Gagné agrees with the definitions provided by Avalos and Geertz which emphasize the idea of belief and way of life which presupposes the existence of empirically unverifiable forces and/or beings, or what Geertz calls transempirical powers or beings. It is also unfortunate, according to Gagné, that the media minimizes the place of scholars in explaining religious violence in this day and age. Why do media outlets prefer conducting interviews with politicians, social workers, and security experts instead of academic experts on the study of religion on current events related to religiously inspired violence? Can the reason be that scholars of religion and scriptural studies are also caught up in political correctness, not willing to admit that violence does sometimes result from religious thinking?

In the subsequent essay, Jennifer Tacci guides us through the marvellous world of superheroes, religious violence, and apocalyptic thinking. Buildings violently attacked leave a lasting trauma on communities for certain, Tacci tells us, but are there any "superheroes" that can protect the United States from disasters such as 9/11? Although what we now call *Ground Zero* has been a popular tourist attraction over the last decade and a half, it is also a landmark for the rise of secular apocalypticism. According to this post-9/11 idea, religion is such a crucial factor in modern violence that it has the potential to destroy life on our planet. Tacci also points out, in her contribution, that secular apocalypticism is just one of the many cultural responses to the traumatic events of 9/11. Taken from there, she poses a crucial question: If a comic book writer can question the relevance of superheroes after an event like 9/11, could a scribe pose similar questions about God in the aftermath of an event like the destruction of the Second Temple in Jerusalem in 70 CE? Why is apocalyptic thought important in the context of religious violence? Apocalypticism, according to Tacci, is an ideology that can sometimes stimulate religious fanaticism. Tacci warns us that apocalyptic texts can at times serve to perpetuate feelings of hate and violence even by those who were not part of the actual tragedy. At the end of her contribution, she remarks that the danger lies not in the literature or the art that is created, but rather in the authority that is ascribed to them.

In a short essay,[10] Costa Babalis examines the idea of the "common good," explaining how such a notion has too often been turned into po-

---

10. Costa Babalis's essay is a slightly expanded version of an oral presentation planned for, but not presented at, the colloquium "Religion, Violence, and the Ethics of Biblical and Religious Studies," held at Concordia University (Montreal, Quebec,

litical and religious hegemony, and sometimes for the benefit of religious extremists. Giving examples from the Crusades (1095–1291 CE) and other religiously motivated wars, such as the Thirty Years War (1618–1648 CE), Babalis shows how the "common good" is also appropriated by religionists and rhetorically used in light of competing interests. Avalos' theory of scarce resources serves as the basis of Babalis' arguments as he clearly recognizes the distinction between empirically verifiable resources and those that have been created through religious thinking. In conclusion, Babalis notes that religions have the unfortunate tendency to generate violence when they exploit the ambiguity between the physical and spiritual realms.

Spyridon Loumakis takes the reader a few decades back, in the Great Lakes region of Africa, and more specifically in Rwanda, where a state-authorized, time-efficient, and group-perpetrated genocide was committed amidst civil war, great fear, and anger. This genocide, however, was never studied in modern scholarship for its religious component, as it is, in general, rarely done in state-authorized violence. Loumakis argues that religious violence goes beyond religious texts and authorities; it can be found ingrained in a society that justifies and accepts horrible actions such as those committed during genocide. Loumakis combines first-hand witness accounts of victims and perpetrators, judicial records, media reports, International Human-Right fact-finding work, and "traditional" historical evidence of political propaganda in order to study the Rwandan genocide. Though all of the evidence does not paint a single unified narrative, it does bring to the surface an emphasis on religious aspects that have so far been neglected in research. In other words, what role did religion play in the minds of those committing such atrocities or in those treated like animals that were brutally beaten to death, slaughtered without discrimination of sex and age, and butchered with machetes and knives? How could these actions by Christians against Christians be justified under God's assumed omnipresence and omniscience? In his conclusion, Loumakis calls for an expanded use of Avalos's scarce resource theory in order that scholars may go beyond sacred texts and their "right" interpretation. The words and deeds of the actors and participants of the 1994 Rwanda genocide reveal that reading the Bible and claiming its understanding can be quite irrelevant. Before all, a religion is experienced in everyday life, even during genocide, having more often to do with their vague invocation or with general claims tentatively based on a shared religious background that people should have in a certain culture.

Canada) on June 16th, 2015.

Another aspect of religious violence is the one inflicted on non-human animals. This is what Marion Achoulias addresses in her compelling piece on sacrificial discourse, religious studies, and violence against animals. In her essay, Achoulias rightly challenges the anthropocentric scholarly tradition found in most research on violence. She notes that responsible scholarship takes the problematization of violence very seriously, and is concerned with all its victims, even those who differ from humans. Violence against animals affects all layers of society and not only the fundamentalist religious faction; this is why Achoulias sees very few differences between the religious and the secular when it comes to violence. Among many other things, this essay seeks to understand whether or not there are any historical and semantic connections between ancient animal sacrifice and today's mass slaughter of animals. Achoulias's work shows that religion, economics, and other ideologies can sometimes dangerously interconnect. In the end, are we not all participating in a contemporary manifestation of the sacrificial principles of the past, at the individual and societal levels?

"Is There Such a Thing as a Radicalized Brain?" is the thought-provoking question that Marc-André Argentino and Dalia Sabra pose from the outset of their contribution. In order to examine the ways in which young adults become radicalized, Argentino and Sabra look at some possible genetic, biological, and neurochemical causes which could be at the root of violent behavior. They show, for example, how neural pathways in the brain have proven to be highly correlated with aggression, and that hyperactivity can be linked to impulsive aggression. Similarly, the plasticity of an individual's brain can be a factor of violence or even just poor decision making, especially when most adolescents are not yet cognitively fully mature. Is human behavior solely pre-determined by people's genetic makeup or is there something more beyond our heritable genetic identity that can possibly make people violent, aggressive, radical, or extremist? In order to answer these questions, Argentino and Sabra utilize the results of a recent experiment, which examined the cognitive and neuronal foundations of religious belief and suggested a link between beliefs and well-known brain networks. Thus, the reader is invited to take into serious consideration the theory that religiosity, or religious cognition, likely emerged as a unique combination of several evolutionarily important cognitive processes (e.g. social cognition, language, logical reasoning). Therefore, Argentino and Sabra argue that their call for a multi-disciplinary approach encompasses biological, sociological, psychological, philosophical, and environmental factors. Religious beliefs and ideologies, psychological, and environmental factors, as well as genetic makeup should be considered together in the examination of radicalization, terrorism, and religious violence in general.

In his essay, Miceli interacts with Hector Avalos's *The End of Biblical Studies* and uses this as a launching point as he reconsiders the role of the contemporary biblical scholar. The central focus of the essay questions whether or not the biblical scholar should promote or disavow the value of the Bible and other religious writings. After outlining the various positions, Miceli advocates a neutral stance whereby he petitions that biblical scholars explain the historical significance and relevance of biblical texts for ancient as well as modern believers without either promoting continued use or disavowal of such endeavors. For Miceli, the biblical scholar should strive for some form of scholarly detachment from the object of study. However, the author finds some instances when the proposed position should be foregone. Miceli insists that in cases where biblical and religious texts are used to justify, promote, or incite violent actions then biblical scholars have a social responsibility to step in. When religious texts are used for violence the author argues abandoning the neutral stance in favor of a position that decries such actions. Overall, Miceli's paper puts forth a novel position with respect to how biblical scholars, and religious scholars more generally, should position themselves. His work adds yet another voice and alternative position in the continued discussions about the future of the field of biblical studies.

Derek Bateman's contribution focuses on the acts of violence that are sanctioned by either religious or state authorities. He tries to discern if and how such acts of violence differ in kind for the twentieth and twenty-first centuries. He also demonstrates that the dichotomy between religious and state violence is more problematic than we are ready to accept. For example, is absolute freedom an empirically verified resource for which one should kill? Are Western governments' references to the protection of national interests as a justification for acts of violence verifiable? Is the suspension of the operation of law and the subsequent power of decision maker to represent the state more rational than any religious claims? Is the state able to present empirically collected data to argue their reasons to engage in violence when they proclaim that the sustainability of the nation is in jeopardy and that, accordingly, action must be taken? Is the "faith" of liberal humanism in human progress resulting in universal peace and harmony nothing but another (secularized) version of the Christian belief in providence? And if it is one more version, then is it still sustainable that our ethical humanism demonstrates "fairness" in matters of violence? Is the "belief" in a utopian universal peace sustainable through rational and verifiable arguments? Bateman invites readers to rethink secular acts of governmental violence to maintain some of the above-mentioned "resources" as predicated on an unstable premise, which is promoted as an absolute right that incontestably allows for violent reactions if perceived to be threatened. In the end, he proposes that we should readjust our understanding of unverifiable scarce resources that religions generate when the limits of verifiability within the secular/political paradigm can also be observed. For Bateman, scarce resources, such as freedom and democracy, when perceived as being threatened by alternative political or religious ideologies, are verifiable only through the shared indoctrination of a social system that insists on a concrete understanding of what those resources constitute.

The volume ends with an article by Hector Avalos who offers a critique of each contribution, in dialogue with his research on religious violence. Avalos returns to key ideas found in his work, which were discussed throughout the volume. In addition, he highlights the originality of the present volume: scholars of these essays avoid what Avalos calls the "religionist" trap, where the role religion sometimes plays in violence is often minimized or overlooked. Avalos also notes the novelty that most essays were written by a younger generation of scholars, interested in examining religious violence from new perspectives, such as comic books, non-human animals, and cognitive science. After reviewing each contribution, Avalos ends his essay with a list of issues that still need to be clarified in the future study of religion and violence: causality in understanding violence as a result of religious factors or of non-religious factors; defining clearly what is meant by "religion"; and something that has characterized his own work throughout his academic career: the place of activism in scholarship.

The editors of this present work wish to thank all of the contributors for their participation in this important book, as well as all those who presented at the conference but were unable to contribute to this publication. We are also grateful to the Concordia University Departments of Theological Studies and Religion for their partial funding of the conference "Religion, Violence, and the Ethics of Biblical and Religious Studies" held at Concordia University in Montreal on June 16th, 2015. This book was made possible as a result of such an event. Finally, we are happy to dedicate this volume to Professor Hector Avalos for his contribution to the study of religious and scriptural studies in relation to religious violence.

Montréal, Québec, Canada
August 2016

1

Tyranny of Political Correctness and Religious Violence

André Gagné

THERE IS CURRENTLY A need for more scholars of religion and scriptural studies to speak on the rapport between religion and violence in a globalized world. Since 9/11, politicians, security experts, and even academics have been reluctant to attribute certain atrocities to religious thinking. Some purposefully avoid using the expression "religious violence" because they believe there is an "'abuse' of religion for the purposes of committing and justifying violence," or that "violence does not immediately originate from the various holy books or religious traditions."[1] It is a way to somehow avoid attributing violence directly to religion. To partially disculpate religion, people simply recast "religious violence" as "violence in the name of religion" or even try to rule out the notion of "religion" from the equation.[2] The basis for some of these arguments is that "religion" should be understood as a Western construct, comparable to capitalism, liberalism, or Marxism for example. The problem with this approach, as we will see, is that it does not take into account how people engaged in what is considered to be "religious violence" actually understand their own actions. Scholars who complain about the colonialism of the West[3] can also become colonialists[4] if

---

1. See for the example the recent comments by Heiner Bielefeldt, UN Special Rapporteur on Freedom of Religion or Belief since 2010: Waind and Bielefeldt, "The 'Dangerous Misunderstanding' of Violence."

2. See for example Armstrong, *Fields of Blood*; Cavanaugh, *The Myth of Religious Violence*.

3. The strong critique of colonialism by the West embraced by current scholars derives from Said, *Orientalism*. Scholars have noted problems with aspects of Said's work; see Ibn Warraq, *Defending the West*; Proudman, "Disraeli as an Orientalist," 547–568.

4. Bruckner, *La tyrannie*, 149–160.

they attribute intentions foreign to those who actually engage in violent actions. A recent research paper also stresses the idea that one should not deny the possibility that ISIS fighters have religious motivations for their actions:

> Based on past debates about radicalization and the intersection between belief and jihadist recruitment, it seems likely that at least some observers will conclude from these documents that ISIS and its recruits are cynically using religion or that the phenomenon really has nothing to do with religion. However, such a conclusion would be unwarranted based on the evidence available, and takes a far too simplistic approach to understanding the complexity of the Shariah and Islamic knowledge in general. The relative weakness of someone's knowledge of the Shariah does not necessarily say much about how religious they are or want to be. For one thing, a depth of knowledge of the Shariah is not particularly common for observant Muslims, and it is in many ways a construct of outsiders to think that it should be. . .Limited knowledge of an area of Islam traditionally left to dedicated experts says little about the contours of individual religious belief; if anything, it reflects our own projections onto others about modernity and education. . .we should not discount the role that faith plays in motivating the decisions of ISIS recruits, a faith that may not be dependent on specific religious knowledge or that may actively discount certain interpretations over others, even if these recruits do not think highly of their own learning in the Shariah.[5]

As an example of this, it has been well attested that the establishment of the so-called Islamic State was founded on the religious apocalyptic worldview of its shadow leader Abu Ayyub al-Masri, after the death of AQI's (Al-Qaeda in Iraq) Abu Mas'ab al-Zarqawi in June 2006.[6] As an expression of Zarqawi's desire to establish a caliphate, Masri went along with this idea fervently nourished by his own apocalyptic mindset and his belief in the imminent coming of the Mahdi, an end-time Islamic savior.[7] The apocalypticism espoused by Masri led to catastrophic policy making and was sharply critiqued by certain jihadist groups in Syria and Iraq, as well as by some leaders of al-Qaeda. They considered some of Masri's actions as contrary to Islamic doctrine. Both sides used aspects of the same tradition in order to legitimize

---

5. See Lebovich, "How 'Religious' are ISIS Fighters?"

6. See William McCants's careful analysis of the first phase of IS: McCants, *ISIS Apocalypse*.

7. For more details on Apocalypticism in Islam, see Cook, *Contemporary Muslim Apocalyptic Literature*; Filiu, *L'Apocalypse dans l'Islam*.

their actions. Masri's apocalyptic mindset could also be found in Islamic Scriptures, mainly the *ahadith*, despite the fact that some opposed his ideas and interpretations of the tradition. In any case, this so-called caliphate is the result of religious belief.

Since 9/11, it has been difficult to address the issue of violence with respect to Islam, and the recent surge of Islamist groups, such as ISIS, Boko-Haram, Al-Shabab, and others, has made things even worse. Despite these difficulties, some scholars of religion have engaged in the academic study of religious violence.[8] Muslims and ex-Muslims in North America, Europe, North Africa, and the Middle East[9] have also been speaking out against Islamism, even if they encounter strong opposition from politicians, artists, and even scholars. In the aftermath of the recent terror attacks in Europe and elsewhere, it is quite surprising that very few scholars of religion and scriptural studies have been at the forefront of *public* discussions surrounding religion and violence.[10] In the West, there are notable exceptions, especially in France, where some intellectuals and scholars[11] have been publically engaged in confronting religious extremism and finding solutions to the growing problem of radicalization among youth. But, even in such instances very few specialists, if any, trained in religious studies and/or scriptural studies have been consulted on such relevant questions related to their field of research. It is partially in response to a lack of engagement from scholars of religion and scriptural studies that a colloquium on religious violence was held at Concordia University in Montreal in 2015. The responsibility that is incumbent on scholars to explain how religion and violence are sometimes related has been noted by Hector Avalos in the past:

> As an academic scholar of religion, it is my responsibility to analyze how religion may contribute to the detriment or well being of humanity based on verifiable facts and reason. For the same reason, in order to make any progress in ameliorating the

---

8. For example, Juergensmeyer, *Terror in the Mind of God*; Avalos, *Fighting Words*; Rennie and Tite, *Religion, Terror, and Violence*; Juergensmeyer et al., *The Oxford Handbook of Religion and Violence*; Gleaves and Kristó Nagy, *Violence in Islamic Thought*.

9. In the case of Islamism, see for example Raza, *Their Jihad*; Ibn Warraq, *Defending the West*; Nawaz, *Radical*; Hirsi Ali, *Infidel*; Hirsi Ali, *Heretic*; Sansal, *Gouverner au nom d'Allah*.

10. According to Tite, scholars of religion studying sacred violence need to be engaged as public intellectuals; see Tite, "Sacred Violence," 3–10.

11. For example see Kepel, *Quatre-vingt-treize*; Kepel, *Terreur dans l'Hexagone*; Onfray, *Penser l'Islam*; Finkielkraut, *La seule exactitude*.

problem of violence, one has to confront violence in each religion in a frank manner.[12]

This is what I believe to be an important role scholars have to play in today's world. Avalos is correct when he says that certain scholarship can sometimes be irrelevant.[13] This is why students preparing for graduate work—Masters or PhD—should be asked "why?" they wish to pursue such an endeavor. This is especially true when it comes to the Humanities, where the prospects of a university career can be challenging.[14] Students need to ask themselves *why* they wish to research on a particular topic, to what end, and what is at stake? Since university professors—and in some cases graduate students—are financially funded by the state, how are they accountable for their research and teaching? In what concrete way can they contribute to the betterment of society and provide solutions to the ills we currently face? As a scholar of religion one has an ethical responsibility. We cannot just simply sit in our offices and shut ourselves out from the world into an ivory tower. Noam Chomsky's famous quote sums up quite well what a scholar should do: "It is the responsibility of intellectuals to speak the truth and to expose lies."[15] There are all sorts of reasons for which scholars do not engage themselves in more relevant work, but most of the time these reasons are related to one's career. Scholars can sometimes be afraid of making waves, especially if they are seeking tenure and this, up to a certain extent, can be understandable. Generally speaking, however, when it comes to matters of religion and violence, some scholars would rather simply not engage in what they would see as a contentious issue, convinced that those who study religions and/or their sacred Scriptures should be somehow sympathetic toward its practitioners. But, as Russell McCutcheon aptly says, scholars of religion are critics, not caretakers; they are not in the business of promoting any particular religious faith.[16] This brings me to an important aspect of the topic I wish to address, that of *political correctness* and its relation to racism and religion.

---

12. Avalos, *Fighting Words*, 28–29.
13. See for example Avalos, *The End of Biblical Studies*, 17–25.
14. See Jaschik, "The Disappearing Humanities Jobs."
15. Chomsky, "The Responsibility of Intellectuals."
16. See McCutcheon, *Critics not Caretakers*.

Political Correctness, Racism, and Religion

What is political correctness exactly? It is, essentially, the practice of being careful not to use speech and/or engage in actions that could offend a particular group of people. Such actions are closely related to current debates about freedom of speech or liberty of expression. One reason why I focus on this issue is due to the recent wave of denial of free speech in certain American universities—I am quite sure that we are also on the verge of facing these kinds of restrictions in Canadian universities as well. I cite two examples: Two years ago, Brandeis University cancelled their plans to bestow an honorary degree to Ayaan Hirsi Ali—a former Muslim and Dutch parliamentary who now fights for women's rights—because of her critical views on Islam. A petition signed by several student groups forced the administration to back down; all this in the name of political correctness.[17] As with people who critique Islam, she was labelled an Islamophobe. A few months after this event, comedian Bill Maher faced the same kind of opposition, when some 4000 students tried to prevent him from giving a commencement speech at Berkeley, also because of his views on religion, especially Islam. Thankfully, the university did not back down and Maher was able to give his address.[18] A few weeks prior to this controversy, Ben Affleck had lashed out against Maher and Sam Harris on national television, for what he considered were bigoted and racist remarks due to their harsh criticism of Islam.[19] People can sometimes be labelled as bigots and racist toward Muslims,[20] but is critiquing an ideology the same as being racist? Islam is not a race; rather, it is a belief and cultural system, as well as a religious and political worldview.[21] If criticizing Islam is racist, then the same should be true for Christianity. No one thinks that Christians are a race, even if Christians themselves have early on constructed their identity using racial imagery, and truly conceived themselves as a race.[22] The problem might be due to the fact that the Islamic identity has become racialized, and this in turn has produced a form of cultural racism.[23] Muslims are now strictly characterized in terms of their ethnicity instead of their beliefs.

17. Pérez-Peña and Vega, "Brandeis Cancels Plans."
18. O'Connor, "UC Berkeley Stands by Bill Maher."
19. Robinson, "Furious Ben Affleck."
20. Can it be that what is perceived as racism against Muslims should more precisely be labeled Arabophobia?
21. Concerning Islam's political worldview, see Cook, *Ancient Religions, Modern Politics*; and more recently Hamid, *Islamic Exceptionalism*.
22. See Buell, *Why This New Race*.
23. Meer and Modood, "Refutations of Racism," 335–354.

There seems to have been a mixing of race and religion in what is now called Islamophobia.[24]

This being said, people in the West are quite critical of Christianity and Judaism. We might ask why it should be different for the Islamic tradition. The common reply to this question is that Muslims are a minority in the West, they should therefore not feel stigmatized, but rather be welcomed. People should definitely not stigmatize any minority, but criticizing religion and culture is about challenging ideas, beliefs, and ways of life to see if they can hold up to scrutiny. The unfortunate reaction to criticism of Islam is that people either censor the debate, cry "Islamophobia," or label someone as a colonialist, rather than peacefully debating their own point-of-view. Those who see criticism as the expression of a colonialist mentality argue that the West considers itself superior to the rest of the world. Here, I must concur with Bruckner's assessment that the current political, social, and economic landscape of Europe—especially in places like France, Belgium, and Germany—show that these societies "loathe" their colonial past; they literally "hate" themselves for it, as they constantly wallow in guilt, shame, and on-going remorse.[25] According to Bruckner, this self-hatred and guilt is what has created the current atmosphere of political correctness in the West. Colonial nations should clearly amend for the wrongdoing, turn the page (or in religious terms "repent"), and focus on the future.

Now a society that shies away from criticizing ideas, worldviews, or beliefs for fear of hurting people's feelings could be manifesting another side of colonialism, since it is treating people as being inferior; incapable of coping with opposition, just like children who need to be protected and shielded from external forces. Islamophobia means "fear of Islam," that is, fear of the Islamic religion. Therefore, one can ask who is truly Islamophobic? Is it those who critique Islam or those who are unwilling to say anything for fear (phobia) of the consequences?

One of the critical questions one needs to ask with respect to Islam or any other religion is how some of its practitioners can generate violence? First, one must attempt to adopt a working definition of "religion." Some scholars are apologetic of religion, refusing to see it as a possible cause for violence. Social ills (like poverty, lack of education, exclusion, war, etc.) are for many the sole reasons people would engage in violence. We certainly agree that religion is not responsible for all the violence in the world, but does this mean that religion cannot sometimes be part of the problem?

---

24. For an analysis of the historical uses of this term, see Bravo López, "Towards a Definition of Islamophobia," 556–573.

25. See Bruckner, *La tyrannie*.

Westerners tend to ignore that for most individuals, religion, culture, and society are entwined. In many cases, religion fashions culture, which in turn weaves social ties between people. It might be somewhat of a surprise, but specialists of religion still struggle to define religion. The tendency in the scholarly world is to stress upon the idea that religion—when understood from a historical perspective—has very little to do with belief, but it is rather about engaging in the right practice (orthopraxy over orthodoxy). Even if this is partly correct, one cannot dismiss belief, since sacrifices, prayers, or other rituals were done as a consequence of belief. People thought—and still do—that they could appease or call upon the favor of supernatural entities. All this was done for the betterment of one's personal condition or that of their group or society. One of the clearest definitions of "religion" is that of Armin Geertz, for whom religion is to be understood as "a cultural system and a social institution that governs and promotes ideal interpretations of existence and ideal praxis with reference to postulated transempirical powers or beings."[26] This definition is similar to that of Avalos who understands religion as "a mode of life and thought that presupposes the existence of, and relationship with, unverifiable forces and/or beings."[27] Now, when recent examples of violence are followed by the Takbir,[28] then one cannot simply discount the role of religion in specific violent actions. Scholars like to debate on whether "true" religions (be that Judaism, Christianity, and/or Islam) can be violent or not. Trying to identify what is "true" from "false" religion is to fall into the trap of essentialism. One thing needs to be clear: people who act violently in the name of their god and/or religious ideology do not care if specialists think this is not "true" religion or even not religion at all. Scholarly mind games will not make that daily reality go away! But political correctness is felt even more in the public and political realms.

Political Correctness in the Public and Political Spheres

This is something I constantly witness firsthand, especially since Quebec and the rest of Canada have been targets of terror attacks and that a good number of youth have been radicalized. I am astonished to see how media, in general, carefully avoids speaking about religion when comes to specific acts of violence. Those in the media generally prefer interviewing politicians, security advisors, psychologists, and/or social workers when it comes to terror attacks and radicalization. Very few religion scholars, if any, are

---

26. See Geertz, "Definition as Analytical Strategy," 471.
27. Avalos, *Fighting Words*, 19.
28. The Takbir is the Arabic: Allahu Akbar (God is great).

involved with or invited by the press. Why is this so? Are religion and scriptural studies scholars declining invitations due to political correctness or fear? Can the reason be that religion specialists are thought to be irrelevant when it comes to public concerns? Why are scholars of religion not at the forefront of discussions about terror attacks, radicalization of youth, ISIS, the Middle East crisis, and many other related issues? Maybe the media—and people in general—do not care much about what scholars have to say, believing that such violence does not have anything to do with religion? This is reminiscent of Omar Mateen's father who stated that his son's crime against the LGBT nightclub in Orlando on June 12th, 2016 had nothing to do with religion.[29] The idea that "religion has nothing to do with it" is also commonly expressed by influential politicians in the West, such as United States President Barack Obama who often avoids using the words "radical Islam" for fear of stigmatizing the Muslim community, or the recently elected Canadian Liberal government which took quite some time to recognize ISIS as a genocidal group, even after the E.U., the U.K., and the U.S. have not hesitated to do so.[30] One politician even went so far as to say that ISIS was simply a "criminal organization with a religious veneer on it."[31] Of course, the stubbornness of politicians who refuse to clearly name the problem does not change the fact that groups like ISIS legitimize their actions on religious grounds. Colonialism is also at work when one believes to know more about the perpetrators' own intentions than the reasons themselves provide.

What is hitting us closer to home, especially in Montreal, is that the city is sometimes seen as a breeding ground for radicalization. In the past few months, there has been a significant number of Montreal youth who have to gone to Syria to join ISIS or were planning to do so.[32] The Quebec Liberal government has been extremely slow in devising a plan to counter radicalization. At first it did not wish to recognize that there was a problem. The Quebec Premier said that fundamentalism was a choice and that nothing could be done to prevent it! This is quite a defeatist attitude; just another way for the government to avoid establishing policies by fear of losing political capital. The mayor of Montreal finally decided to spearhead the current fight against radicalization in collaboration with the provincial government. The ultimate goal was the establishment of a counter-radicalization center.

29. Grimson et al., "Orlando Nightclub Shooting."

30. The Canadian government finally accepted the report on this issue by the UN commission in June 2016.

31. Hall, "Criminal Organization, Religious Extremists?"

32. Unknown, "Up to Six Teens."

The center opened its doors in March 2015.[33] As for the counter-radicalization plan to be adopted, the Security and Justice Minister of Quebec was proud to announce that her government had set up a strategy comprised of four main axes: action, prevention, detection, and co-existence. Unfortunately, in her neatly packaged rhetorical speech, she failed to identify (or admit) the true crux of the problem: that is, extremist religious ideology.[34] Another surprising fact was that education was missing from the equation. It is also interesting to note that such a program lacks teaching or education about religions. Teaching or educating people about religions should not be catechetical in nature. It is not teaching religion, but rather it is teaching people *about* religions. The educational program should offer critical thinking skills to understand religions from a historical perspective, taking into account their political and social development and impact through time. The only way to de-radicalize individuals is to deconstruct the erroneous ideologies that feed their destructive worldviews.

The reality is that better security and policies are insufficient to deal with radicalization and terror attacks. We need to target the ideology; this means that education has to be at the forefront of debunking dangerous and harmful ideas. Violence does not only emerge from one religion; rather, it can be seen throughout several religious traditions, time periods, and a variety of literary sources. We all need to acquire a critical perspective to fight against what has allured several of our youth down a perilous path. Our common goal should be to work toward a better society.

---

33. For more information on the center, see the website of the "Centre for the Prevention of Radicalization Leading to Violence," https://info-radical.org/en/.

34. Gagné, "Education."

Bibliography

Armstrong, Karen. *Fields of Blood: Religion and the History of Violence.* New York: Knopf, 2014.

Avalos, Hector. *The End of Biblical Studies.* Amherst, New York: Prometheus Books, 2007.

———. *Fighting Words: The Origins of Religious Violence.* Amherst, New York: Prometheus Books, 2005.

Bravo López, Fernando. "Towards a Definition of Islamophobia: Approximations of the Early Twentieth Century." *Ethnic and Racial Studies* 34 (2011) 556–573.

Bruckner, Pascal. *La tyrannie de la pénitence: Essai sur le masochisme occidental.* Paris: Grasset, 2006.

Buell, Denise K. *Why this New Race: Ethnic Reasoning in Early Christianity.* New York: Columbia University Press, 2005.

Cavanaugh, William T. *The Myth of Religious Violence.* Oxford: Oxford University Press, 2009.

"Centre for the Prevention of Radicalization Leading to Violence." 2015. https://info-radical.org/en/.

Chomsky, Noam. "The Responsibility of Intellectuals." *New York Review of Books.* February 23, 1967. http://www.nybooks.com/articles/1967/02/23/a-special-supplement-the-responsibility-of-intelle/.

Cook, David. *Contemporary Muslim Apocalyptic Literature.* Syracuse, New York: Syracuse University Press, 2005.

Cook, Michael. *Ancient Religions, Modern Politics: The Islamic Case in Comparative Perspective.* Princeton: Princeton University Press, 2014.

Filiu, Jean-Pierre. *L'Apocalypse dans l'Islam.* Paris: Fayard, 2008.

Finkielkraut, Alain. *La seule exactitude.* Paris: Stock, 2015.

Gagné, André. "Education should be at the Heart of Quebec's Anti-Radicalization Plan." *Montreal Gazette.* June 12, 2015. http://montrealgazette.com/news/quebec/opinion-education-should-be-at-the-heart-of-quebecs-anti-radicalization-plan.

Geertz, Armin. "Definition as Analytical Strategy in the Study of Religion." *Historical Reflections/Reflexions Historiques* 25:3 (1999) 445–475.

Gleaves, Robert and István T. Kristó Nagy, eds. *Violence in Islamic Thought: From the Qur'ān to the Mongols.* Edinburgh: Edinburgh University Press, 2015.

Grimson, Matthew, et al. "Orlando Nightclub Shooting: Mass Casualties after Gunman Opens Fire in Gay Club." June 13, 2016. http://www.nbcnews.com/storyline/orlando-nightclub-massacre/orlando-nightclub-shooting-emergency-services-respond-reports-gunman-n590446.

Hall, Chris. "Criminal Organization, Religious Extremists? Words Matter when it comes to ISIS." February 4, 2016. http://www.cbc.ca/news/politics/isis-chris-hall-1.3432664.

Hamid, Shadi. *Islamic Exceptionalism: How the Struggle over Islam is Reshaping the World*. New York: St. Martin's Press, 2016.

Hirsi Ali, Ayaan. *Heretic: Why Islam Needs a Reformation Now*. Toronto: Knopf Canada, 2015.

———. *Infidel*. New York: Atria, 2008.

Ibn Warraq. *Defending the West: A Critique of Edward Said's Orientalism*. Amherst, New York: Prometheus, 2007.

Jaschik, Scott. "The Disappearing Humanities Jobs." *Inside Higher Ed*. June 6, 2016. https://www.insidehighered.com/news/2016/06/06/new-study-documents-long-term-losses-new-humanities-faculty-jobs.

Juergensmeyer, Mark. *Terror in the Mind of God: The Global Rise of Religious Violence*. Los Angeles: University of California Press, 2003.

Juergensmeyer, Mark, et al., eds. *The Oxford Handbook of Religion and Violence*. Oxford: Oxford University Press, 2013.

Kepel, Gilles. *Quatre-vingt-treize*. Paris: Gallimard, 2012.

———. *Terreur dans l'Hexagone: Genèse du djihad français*. Paris: Gallimard, 2015.

Lebovich, Andrew. "How 'Religious' are ISIS Fighters? The Relationship between Religious Literacy and Religious Motivation." April 2016. http://www.brookings.edu/~/media/research/files/reports/2015/07/rethinking-political-islam/other-essays/andrew-lebovich_final-3.pdf.

McCants, William. *The ISIS Apocalypse*. New York: St. Martin's Press, 2015.

McCutcheon, Russell T. *Critics not Caretakers: Redescribing the Public Study of Religion*. Albany, New York: State University of New York Press, 2001.

Meer, Nasar and Tariq Modood. "Refutations of Racism in the 'Muslim Question.'" *Patterns of Prejudice* 43:3–4 (2009) 335–354.

Nawaz, Maajid. *Radical: My Journey out of Islamist Extremism*. Guilford, Connecticut: Lyons, 2013.

O'Connor, Lydia. "UC Berkeley Stands by Bill Maher Amid Commencement Speech Controversy." *Huffington Post*. October 30, 2014. http://www.huffingtonpost.com/2014/10/30/berkeley-defends-billmaher_n_6078000.html.

Onfray, Michel. *Penser l'Islam*. Paris: Grasset, 2016.

Pérez-Peña, Richard and Tanzina Vega. "Brandeis Cancels Plans to Give Honorary Degree to Ayaan Hirsi Ali, a Critic of Islam." *New York Times*. April 8, 2014. http://www.nytimes.com/2014/04/09/us/brandeis-cancels-plan-to-give-honorary-degree-to-ayaan-hirsi-ali-a-critic-of-islam.html?_r=0.

Proudman, Mark F. "Disraeli as an Orientalist: The Polemical Errors of Edward Said." *Journal of the Historical Society* 5:4 (2005) 547–568.

Raza, Raheel. *Their Jihad. . .Not My Jihad!* Ingersoll, Ontario: Basileia, 2005.

Rennie, Bryan and Philip L. Tite, eds. *Religion, Terror, and Violence: Religious Studies Perspectives*. New York: Routledge, 2008.

Robinson, Wills. "Furious Ben Affleck Blasts Bill Maher and Guests On-Air after they Claimed Islam is the 'Motherload of Bad Ideas' and Compared Religion to being in the Mafia." *Daily Mail Online*. October 5, 2014. http://www.dailymail.co.uk/news/article-2780960/It-s-gross-s-racist-Ben-Affleck-clashes-guest-Bill-Maher-talk-claims-Islam-motherload-bad-ideas-host-compares-religion-Mafia.html.

Said, Edward, W. *Orientalism*. New York: Vintage, 1978.

Sansal, Boualem. *Gouverner au nom d'Allah: Islamisation et soif de pouvoir dans le monde arabe*. Paris: Gallimard, 2013.

Tite, Philip L. "Sacred Violence and the Scholar of Religion as Public Intellectual." Pages 3–10 in *Religion, Terror, and Violence: Religious Studies Perspectives*. Edited by Bryan Rennie and Philip L. Tite. New York: Routledge, 2008.

Unknown, "Up to Six Teens from Montreal, Laval Might Have Joined Jihadists in Syria." *Montreal Gazette*. February 26, 2016. http://montrealgazette.com/news/local-news/three-montreal-laval-teens-might-have-joined-jihadists-in-syria.

Waind, Jon and Heiner Bielefeldt. "The 'Dangerous Misunderstanding' of Violence in the Name of Religion." February 16, 2016. https://www.opencanada.org/features/q-dangerous-misunderstanding-violence-name-religion/.

2

Apocalypses and Superhero Mythology

The Scars of Crisis and the Remnants of Outbursts between Reality and Imagination

Jennifer Tacci

In 1987, Will Eisner created a graphic novel about the life and death of a city building, simply entitled *The Building*. The story explores the collective psychic memory a building can leave behind when it is destroyed; a topic that, in its simplicity, can seem silly to some.[1] In the first pages, the reader is confronted with a landmark that is destroyed and replaced by a new and much more modern building. Over the image of the torn down building, Eisner writes in the empty space where the building once stood: "One day the building was demolished, leaving in its place an ugly cavity and a residue of psychic debris."[2] Construction workers have obviously torn down the building that Eisner is addressing. The reader assumes that the reason for the demolishment is capitalism at its best. The writer expresses his sadness over the removal of the building, which he describes as callous, admitting that he feels that the building "had a kind of soul."[3] In hindsight, after an event such as that which took place on September 11th, 2001, Eisner's expression of sorrow no longer seems silly, but rather prophetic:

> I know now that these structures, barnacled with laughter and stained by tears, are more than lifeless edifices. It cannot be that having been part of life, they did not somehow absorb the

---

1. Eisner, *The Building*, 6.
2. Ibid.
3. Ibid., 4.

radiation from human interaction. And I wonder what is left behind when a building is torn down.[4]

When landmarks are purposely knocked down it can be disheartening. But, seeing buildings violently attacked leaves a lasting trauma on communities. It is easy to be insensitive to buildings and people's personal attachments to landmarks when they are intentionally demolished. After all, we know that buildings are lifeless edifices. Eisner's tale of psychic residue left behind after a building is demolished and the idea that structures can hold memories or even ghosts is a popular focus of many horror stories.[5] Psychic residue, boarders on the paranormal, superstitious, and supernatural until, the focus moves away from fiction, and turns to a real historical event that touches on the collective memory such as 9/11. The memory of the destruction of the World Trade Center and Eisner's ideas about buildings absorbing the radiation of human interaction and the question of what is left behind when a building is torn down is abruptly relevant. The violent attack on these buildings and the immense loss of life at this site cannot help but make these buildings more than just lifeless man-made edifices. Suddenly, Eisner's graphic novel that had nothing to do with the loss suffered on 9/11 has new significance and importance. His reflection on the rapid replacement of people and buildings feels predictive: "And I wonder what is left behind when a building is torn down."[6] What we now call Ground Zero has been a popular tourist attraction over the last decade and a half since the demolition of the World Trade Center. People from all over the world travel to the site in order to see, touch, and feel the site where almost three-thousand people lost their lives. Eisner's graphic novel, published fourteen years prior to 9/11, demonstrates how a text can be reutilized in order to comfort a generation in the midst of crisis and also shows how interpretation depends on the life setting of current audiences.

In his article, "Explaining Religious Violence: Retrospects and Prospects," Hector Avalos describes 9/11 as a watershed date for the study of religion and violence. The author explains that since then: "the quantity of books on the topic proliferated greatly."[7] Avalos points out that 9/11 caused Westerners to feel more threatened by religious violence and caused schol-

---

4. Ibid.

5. For some examples see some of the best-selling and popular films: *The Amityville Horror* by Jay Anson (1977) adapted to film in 1979 and again in 2005, Stephen King's *The Shining* (1977) adapted to film in 1980, and Dennis Lehane's *Shutter Island* (2003) adapted to film in 2010.

6. Eisner, *The Building*, 4.

7. Avalos, "Explaining Religious Violence," 137–146.

ars to embark on a mission of understanding the link between religion and violence. 9/11 has been one of the most inescapable dates in recent history. This date and the related events have not only changed American culture, but have also impacted much of the world:

> At its heart, 9/11 was a religious event. This assertion applies to both the causes and the consequences of the attacks. The central issue for the attacks was a serious increase in religiously motivated violence throughout the previous decade. The attacks have had effects that have reverberated across many dimensions of human life...on politics and war, economics, the law, the media and arts, and psychology and education. When evaluating the human impact, our spiritual responses and coping methods are the most immediate and fundamental of these various areas.[8]

In his analysis on post 9/11 theories, Avalos discusses the rise of "secular apocalypticism, which believes religion, is such a crucial factor in modern violence that it has the potential to destroy life on our planet."[9] Avalos calls to our attention such authors as Richard Dawkins with his 2006 book *The God Delusion*, Sam Harris and his work *The End of Faith* in 2005, and Christopher Hitchens's *God is not great* in 2007.[10] Out of 9/11 came the rise of New Atheism and many books written by atheist authors reached bestseller lists.[11] Of course, he also makes note of the very popular anti-religion movie *Religulous* from 2008 written, produced, and starring Bill Maher who: "focuses on how faith-based claims create conflicts that have the potential to destroy our entire planet."[12] Secular apocalypticism is just one of the many cultural responses to the traumatic events of 9/11.

Occurrences like those of 9/11 always seem to reignite the search for answers to unanswerable questions. While we address these questions in serious terms and methods, we often cannot help ourselves from expressing our pain and insecurities through mediums that involve a more fictional or artistic touch. While books and films such as those mentioned above take a more analytical and scholarly stand, events such as 9/11 are also discussed in artistic and imaginative ways as well. Following the attacks:

> Marvel Comics responded to the tragedy in its hometown with a genuinely heartfelt tale in which the superheroes aimlessly

---

8. Morgan, "Introduction," 1.
9. Avalos, "Explaining Religious Violence," 140.
10. Dawkins, *The God Delusion*; Harris, *The End of Faith*; Hitchens, *God is not great*.
11. Avalos, "Explaining Religious Violence," 140.
12. Ibid., 141.

assembled at Ground Zero. They were compelled to acknowledge the events as if it had occurred in their own simulated universe, but they hadn't been there to prevent it, which negated their entire *raison d'être*. If al-Quaeda could do to Marvel Universe New York what Doctor Doom, Magneto, and Kang the Conqueror had failed to do, surely that meant the Marvel heroes were ineffectual. September 11 was the biggest challenge yet to the relevance of superhero comics.[13]

Marvel's tribute is an interesting mingling of the fictional world with the historical; it somehow makes the unbelievable believable and comforts in an unexplainable way. If a comic book[14] writer can question the relevance of superheroes after an event like 9/11 then a scribe would certainly pose similar questions about God in the aftermath of an event like 70 CE. After the invasion and victory of the Romans in the destruction of the Second Temple, many believers would have been left asking themselves the same questions a lover of superheroes did after the fall of the Towers. In fact, many apocalypses were written during or shortly after a serious crisis. For example, the Book of Daniel was a product of the Maccabean revolt, the Book of Revelation, *4 Ezra*, *2 Baruch*, and *3 Baruch*, four different apocalypses, were all written in the late first or early second century CE and all of them are described as responses to the fall of Jerusalem to the Romans in 70 CE.[15] Apocalyptic thinking was salient in Second Temple Judaism and Early Christianity. Referring to the terms apocalyptic, eschatological, and messianic, Vasily Rudich points out:

> These three terms (as applied to mindset and conduct, or literary products) presume different often interrelated meanings: the term 'visionary' may cover most of these phenomena, although it does not do justice to emotional and spiritual power, or compelling imagery that is sometimes involved; in all cases, however, 'wishful thinking', or what psychologists call 'omnipotence of thought' (particularly characteristic of religious dissent), must have played a major role.[16]

13. Morrison, *Supergods*, 346–347.

14. The main difference between a comic book and a graphic novel is that a graphic novel is an extended comic book; it is also not restricted to the normally low quality production values and limited subject matter of traditional comics. While the term "graphic novel" implies fictional creations, this term, as is understood in the culture, can cover nonfictional subjects as well such as autobiographies, biographies, and histories as well as fiction. See: Tabachnick, *The Quest for Jewish Belief*, 1–6.

15. Aune, *Apocalypticism*, 15.

16. Rudich, *Religious Dissent*, 56.

The destruction of the Second Temple had a traumatic impact on Judean life and culture. The hope for restoration became a common theme in both Jewish and Christian literature. Apocalyptic literature can be seen as the remnants of a difficult time left by communities expressing their grief. The violence found in Revelation can inspire passionate commitment or fierce shock as Christopher A. Frilingos explains:

> That Revelation has inspired marginal groups is a matter of historical record. The book has persuaded Christians of all kinds that the world would end with a whimper *and* a bang, but it has proven especially attractive to antiestablishment movements. The Apocalypse was first venerated by a religious movement that suffered violent persecution under the Roman emperors. Much later, galvanized by Joachim of Fiore's *Exposition on Revelation*, members of the medieval Apostolic Brethren opposed papal power and died at the stake for their insolence. In the modern era, liberation theologians have used the book to protest capitalism and globalization, while "Generation X" will long remember the siege and fiery destruction of the Waco compound of Revelation-interpreter David Koresh.[17]

Revelation preserves some of the Western World's oldest and most violent images of famine, disaster, a final battle, and a great day of cosmic judgement that will, according to the text, destroy this world and give way to a "new heaven and new earth" (Rev 21:1). The poisonous spews of this text have been examined by many academics as Frilingos points out:

> Many scholars, seeking to understand the book in its original context, have concluded that the shrill tone and misanthropic outlook of the Apocalypse reflected the fears of early Christians, a beleaguered minority in an environment hostile to the new religious movement. By promising an imminent reversal of fortunes, the book's visions, like apocalyptic ideology and literature generally, responded to a collective sense of alienation. Indeed, a scholarly consensus has formed around the notion that Revelation rejects the Roman world because it speaks for a community that has cut itself off from this world: Christ and Caesar have nothing in common.[18]

David Aune describes apocalypses as *protest literature*: "That is, they typically represent the perspective of an oppressed minority."[19] The apoca-

17. Frilingos, *Spectacles of Empire*, 2.
18. Ibid., 1.
19. Aune, *Apocalypticism*, 3.

lypses are often explained as being a literature produced under persecution. However, the social situations within which they were written are difficult to reconstruct:

> For much of the twentieth century, it was common for historians to situate Revelation in the context of severe Roman oppression of Christians. This setting offered a plausible explanation of the lust for revenge expressed in the book; otherwise, one scholar [J.A.T. Robinson] observed, Revelation could only be 'the product of perfervid and psychotic imagination.' Some, looking for a specific instance of persecution and finding little evidence of it under Domitian have argued that the Christian heresiologist Irenaeus was wrong to assign the book to Domitian's reign, and have instead pushed it back thirty years, to the days of Nero.[20]

Adela Yarbro Collins describes Revelation as: "not only an artefact from a specific place and time, a historical document; it is also a literary creation, a work of great artistic beauty and power."[21] As such, Yarbro Collins, points to the importance of language and imagery above historical dating:

> Collins introduced the remarkably subtle notion of 'relative deprivation': whether or not the officials of Rome arrested, tortured or killed Christians, John and his readers *felt* oppressed, and this perspective coloured every aspect of life. She argued that Revelation created a 'crisis' out of widespread exasperation with Rome, enhanced rancor, and then resolved it. [. . .] 'Catharsis' was delivered to the audience through Revelation's final visions of judgement and a 'new glorious mode of existence' for the faithful, ameliorating the disquiet evoked elsewhere in the narrative.[22]

When dealing with a text like Revelation it is unavoidable to wonder why an author would want to write such a violent story, most of all because it is not possible to prove that the book was actually written as a response to a specific incident of persecution, but rather: "a translation of all human history into a struggle between the forces of good and the forces of evil. The Apocalypse is literally a 'revelation,' an uncovering of the mundane world that discloses a supernatural actuality—what is really at stake."[23] If the Apocalypse is a response to an assault then it makes it easier to accept the

---

20. Frilingos, *Spectacles of Empire*, 2.
21. Yarbro Collins, *Crisis & Catharsis*, 21.
22. Frilingos, *Spectacles of Empire*, 2.
23. Ibid., 3.

violence it promotes; the apocalypse becomes reprisal rather than instigation. Revelation links Roman authority with an evil of cosmic proportions and audiences were expected to understand this reality. Cruel, bitter, lust for revenge, hostile, and psychotic are all fine ways some describe what is found in the canonized text of a book so many claim to be holy. The idea of 'crisis' or 'persecution' has protected modern scholarship from the obvious: "...namely, the fear that Revelation was indeed the 'product of a perfervid and psychotic imagination.'"[24]

Like the events of 9/11, the fall of the Second Temple altered the course of history and had literary and cultural ramifications. Basing his assertion on the legacy of Michel Foucault, Frilingos writes: "discourses govern the production of truth in a society to determine what will count as knowledge."[25] Using the book of Revelation as a source of truth or knowledge means that there is no reason to avoid the obvious: "the Apocalypse repeatedly positions itself and its audience over against the monstrous Roman Empire."[26] Revelation is proof that the Christian canon sustains at least one text that exhibits violent behavior: "Islam is not the only religion with extremist adherents who have assumed disturbing preference for catastrophic, mass-casualty forms of violence."[27] When empire and religion clash, violence often erupts and the literature produced by such outbursts reflects the emotions felt after a crisis or traumatic event. Revelation can be explained as a reaction to the fall of the Second Temple for which the Jews are seen as the underdogs or the victims of the unforgiving power that was Rome.[28] However, the book of Revelation was written around 95 CE, much later than the fall of the Second Temple and rather than writing to console his fellow Christians of a pressing threat, the author wrote to point out a crisis only he recognized.[29]

The historical milieu of Revelation is very different from our own especially in the ways that people thought about God, the world, and human nature. In a book that debates whether Jesus was apocalyptic or not, Dale Allison rightly says that: "Historians of the Jesus tradition are story-tellers, not scientists. We can do no more than aspire to fashion a narrative that is more persuasive than competing narratives, one that satisfies our aesthetical

24. Ibid., 5.
25. Ibid., 9.
26. Ibid., 13.
27. Morgan, "Introduction," 1.
28. In relation to dating, the fall of the Second Temple did come before the writing of Revelation. However, Revelation is understood as deriving from Jewish Scriptures and building on Jewish traditions as well as a reaction to the attack on the Second Temple.
29. Yarbro Collins, *Crisis & Catharsis*, 54–83.

and historical sensibilities."[30] Depending on how scholars fashion their arguments and tie narratives together readers will either feel satisfied and ultimately agree or disagree. The contents of the book of Revelation can be seen as bizarre and violent; they generally do not fit in with our modern sensibilities. The scenario is always the same after a period of intense conflict and great suffering; God decisively intervenes in history in order to vindicate and reward *his* people and eliminate their oppressors. In other words, God will destroy the entire world, wipe out all his enemies, and save *only* those he deems worth saving: "anyone whose name was not found written in the book of life was thrown into the lake of fire" (Rev 20:15).[31] It is possible to understand Revelation as a book about restoration and that the motive of the text is hope; however, this involves interpretation. Notions of destruction and vengeance are much more obvious and clear, and do not involve much analysis: "the expectation of doom turns to anger, vengeance, and violence, as in many peasant revolts."[32] The expression of resentment for anyone and everyone outside the author's intended audience is obvious in this text: "every eye will see him, even those who pierced him; and on his account all the tribes of the earth will wail" (Rev 1:7).

Comic Books and Apocalypses

What do comic books and apocalypses[33] have in common? For starters they both have a tendency to intermingle history and myth. Discussing God's role in the retaliation against the Romans is, in my opinion, the equivalent of showing Spider-Man helping in the efforts to pick up the pieces of Ground Zero.[34] They both make an attempt to protect fictional characters from the devastating reality check of actual history. Apocalypses defend God's supposed omnipotent strength despite the fact that Rome's very real army destroyed the Second Temple; while post-9/11 comic books demonstrate that legendary superheroes have not abandoned humanity by not having been able to stop the planes from crashing into the towers. Moreover, both comic

30. Allison, "Jesus was an Apocalyptic," 17.
31. All scriptural translations are from the NRSV.
32. Allison, "Jesus was an Apocalyptic," 99.
33. By Apocalypses I am referring to the texts which belong to the genre according to the well-known scholarly definition: "a genre of revelatory literature with a narrative framework, in which a revelation is mediated by an otherworldly being to a human recipient, disclosing a transcendent reality which is both temporal insofar as it envisages eschatological salvation, and spatial insofar as it involves another supernatural world." See Collins, "Towards the Morphology," 14.
34. Straczynski, *The Amazing Spider-Man*.

books (specifically those dealing with the events of 9/11 by means of tribute or in their storylines) and apocalypses can also be regarded as memorials to tragic events in actual history: "In fact, because of their populist and commercial nature, comics act as objects of mass culture and play an important role in the production of collective memory due to their mass appeal."[35] Ancient apocalyptic books function in the same way; they are texts that are popular and part of mass culture that do in fact play a role in the collective memory of a variety of groups even if only as part of canonical books.[36]

The language of victimization used by the authors of these texts plays on the emotions of readers to defend the idea that God will act on their behalf in the near future. Certain comic books do the same; they play on the emotions of readers and defend the idea that no matter how catastrophic or difficult a situation may be America will always rise above. Superhero mythology often addresses the national identity of America and defends the American way of life in the face of real or imaginary danger. John Shelton Lawrence and Robert Jewett built a theory of an American monomyth based on Joseph Campbell's classical monomyth, which describes the archetypal plot for heroic action in traditional mythologies.[37] In their opinion:

> Whereas the classical monomyth seemed to reflect rites of initiation, the American monomyth derives from tales of redemption. It secularizes the Judaeo-Christian dramas of community redemption that have arisen on American soil, combining elements of the selfless servant who impassively gives his life for others and the zealous crusader who destroys evil. The super-saviours in pop culture function as replacements for the Christ figure, whose credibility was eroded by scientific rationalism. But their superhuman abilities reflect hope for divine, redemptive powers that science has never eradicated from the popular mind.[38]

Frank Miller created a graphic novel called *Holy Terror*, in which his created superhero, The Fixer, battles Islamist terrorists after an attack on the fictional Empire City.[39] In his original plan, Miller would have had Batman

---

35. Dony and Linthout, "Comics, Trauma and Cultural Memory(ies)," 180.

36. By this I mean the Hebrew Scriptures and the Christian Scriptures; for example Daniel, which recalls the Maccabean revolt as a memory for the Judaic culture. Revelation also retains the memory of oppression even if it cannot be pin pointed to one specific event.

37. See Campbell, *The Hero*, 30.

38. Lawrence and Jewett, *The Myth of the American Superhero*, 6–7.

39. Miller, *Holy Terror*.

defend Gotham City against a terrorist attack and have the famous character take on al-Qaeda leader Osama Bin Laden, as he noted at a comic book convention in San Francisco:

> It is, not to put too fine a point on it, a piece of propaganda – Batman kicks al-Qa'eda's ass. It just seems silly to chase around the Riddler when you've got al-Qa'eda out there. Superman punched out Hitler. So did Captain America. That's one of the things they're there for. It's an explosion from my gut reaction of what's happening now, a reminder to people who seem to have forgotten who we're up against.[40]

In the end, DC comics would not publish Miller's initial proposal. Miller set out to offend people and reignite the anger and fear that was caused by 9/11. In August 2006, Grant Morrison criticized Miller's idea saying:

> Batman vs. Al Qaeda! It might as well be Bin Laden vs. King Kong! Or how about the sinister Al Qaeda mastermind up against a hungry Hannibal Lecter! For all the good it's likely to do. Cheering on a fictional character as he beats up fictionalized terrorists seems like a decadent indulgence when real terrorists are killing real people in the real world. I'd be so much more impressed if Frank Miller gave up all this graphic novel nonsense, joined the Army and, with a howl of undying hate, rushed headlong onto the front lines with the young soldiers who are actually risking life and limb 'vs.' Al Qaeda.[41]

Holy Terror did indeed anger many people and has been described as appalling, offensive, and vindictive:

> Miller's *Holy Terror* is a screed against Islam, completely uninterested in any nuance or empathy toward 1.2 billion people he conflates with a few murderous conspiracy theorists. It's no accident that it's being released ten years after 9/11. This comic would be unthinkable during the unity that the U.S. felt after the attack. Instead, it's a perfect cultural artifact of this dark period in American life, when the FBI teaches its agents that 'mainstream' Islam is indistinguishable from terrorism and a community center near Ground Zero gets labeled a 'victory mosque'.

---

40. As quoted in Mount, "Holy Propaganda!"
41. See Brady, "Morrison in the Cave."

> Call it the artwork of 9/11 decadence, when all that remains of a horror is a carefully nurtured grievance.[42]

Works like *Holy Terror* encourage Americans to feel like their group has suffered more than their adversaries. Moreover, it contributes to the escalation of conflict by encouraging the biases that promote victimhood and maintains the sense of collective struggle. Miller's personal connection to 9/11 preserves a deep sense of victimization. Revelation, like *Holy Terror*, is in Ackerman's words: "a perfect cultural artifact of this dark period." There is no other judgment being placed here other than the fact that some texts can be dangerous and influence violent behavior. In fact, in my opinion, Revelation is much more dangerous than *Holy Terror* because the biblical text is held by some as truth, whereas the graphic novel is and will always remain fiction. No matter what ugly feelings *Holy Terror* might endorse in its readers, the author does not make any truth claims or any promises. *Holy Terror* is not, and will never be, treated as holy script or presented as evidence of truth. This is the most important difference between graphic novels or comic books and Scripture; one is always treated as fiction, while the other is treated as actuality. Comic books, and more specifically superheroes, are closely intertwined with the American consciousness and play a vital role in popular American mythology:

> Superhero comics emerged in an important point in American history, when the nation was in the process of recovering from the Great Depression and on the eve of World War II. These challenges were great, and superhero comics were about finding strength to overcome great challenges, reflecting themes central to the American Dream. For this reason, superhero comics were (and remain) inextricably linked to notions of American identity and its myths of heroism, social justice, and the potential for transformation... Therefore, they were a product of their time and deeply indebted to propaganda and the popular culture of that period. The superhero was a hybrid of construction of heroism, fantasy, and political idealism that negotiated the tensions that ran throughout American society.[43]

Morrison's exasperations are valid in that *Holy Terror* can be seen as dangerous propaganda. The disappointment on the part of Morrison is mostly due to the fact that for the most part, in superhero mythology, there

---

42. See Ackerman, "Frank Miller's Holy Terror."
43. Murray, *Champions*, 38–39.

is a general consensus as to right and wrong and *Holy Terror* blurs this line, as the course of action of The Fixer is more than questionable.[44]

The ancient Jews lived by the laws of God; biblical texts were precious and those who had the ability to read and explain such texts were accorded prestige and respect. The Hebrew Bible is the product of a scribal culture that presented certain books as Holy and claimed supernatural origins as being from the mouth of God. Through these written texts, God was speaking to human beings. In a time when God was no longer speaking directly to humans, certain texts became treasure boxes filled with hidden secrets and meanings that, while recorded by a scribe, were believed to have been dictated by God.[45] The Jews did not believe that they were living by man-made laws, but by the laws that Moses received through a face-to-face conversation with God. Scribes in Jewish society held the key to God:

> Among the Jews who reverenced every word of that Law, and had no printed Bible with which to check the accuracy of the text read out to them in synagogues, great trust had to be given to the scholar who had copied the text and to the scholar – not, of course, necessarily the same person – who read it aloud.[46]

Ultimately for Rome, although there existed many gods and many superstitions, they did not put their trust in the divine in the same way Jews did wholeheartedly. For example, even in the tales of Daniel which are more open to the idea of Jews being able to prosper under a foreign ruler, Daniel's loyalty to God is not irreconcilable with his service to the king; however, this is only because there is a hope that: "Good Gentile kings will come to acknowledge the God of the Jews. The arrogant will be chastened. Despite the political supremacy of the Gentiles, God's in his heaven and all's well with the world."[47] In short, God is in control of the destinies of all people. But in the second half of Daniel, God is more sinister towards the gentile kingdoms who: "were no longer seen as potential servants of God. Instead they were rebellious monsters that could only be destroyed. The aspiration of the faithful Jews was no longer to rise to high position in the Gentile court but to shine like the host of heaven in the afterlife."[48] The supremacy of the Jewish God was of paramount importance to the Jews and his role in

---

44. For a discussion on good and evil in comic books see: Romagnoli and Pagnucci, "Perceptions of Good."

45. Karel Van Der Toorn discusses some factors that led to the Bible being designated as revelation: Van Der Toorn, "Inventing Revelation."

46. Goodman, *Rome & Jerusalem*, 365.

47. Collins, *The Apocalyptic Imagination*, 98.

48. Ibid., 98–99.

controlling destiny was not restricted to his people or to a particular land, but his power and authority expended to all peoples across the world. The established belief is that all gentile kingdoms will come to an end and the destiny of the wise or chosen ones lie beyond this world in an eternal afterlife. Revelation also drives this point home: "Blessed are those who wash their robes, so they will have the right to the tree of life and may enter the city by the gates. Outside are the dogs and sorcerers and fornicators and murderers and idolaters, and everyone who loves and practices falsehood." (Rev 22:14–15). There is no room for non-believers in apocalyptic works. Apocalypticism is an ideology that stimulates religious fanaticism. At the heart of apocalypticism is the question of why so much evil and destruction has fallen upon Israel, how the wicked will be punished, and how the righteous will be rewarded.[49]

Romans treated their Emperors like gods; in fact they even venerated them as gods. Emperors were people who had: "power that could be understood and thought of as the epiphany of a divine power in the hands of a mortal."[50] The Romans accepted that the gods lived in the world and strove alongside humans. In this way they too participated in Roman affairs and daily life. Roman gods were even consulted on matters in prescribed manners: "despite appearances, the gods to some extent did control the power game, but they did so discreetly and were always represented by other human beings."[51] What this means is that the religious system of Rome was not founded on doctrine authoritatively set in stone: "Their religious system prescribes rituals, not what they should believe. So each individual remained free to understand and think of the gods and the world-system just as he or she pleased."[52] The purpose of Roman religion was not to produce dogmatic revelations about the world: "the only religious belief for Romans consisted in the knowledge that the gods were the benevolent partners of mortals in the management of the world, and that the prescribed rituals represented the rightly expected counterpart to the help offered by the immortals."[53] For the Romans, the number of gods was countless and when they entered new lands, they also understood that they would meet previously unknown deities. It was understood that other deities lived in foreign lands: "If the Romans were active in those lands it seemed to them inevitable that they should enter into relations with these, either setting up a cult for them on

49. See Oegema, *Apocalyptic Interpretation*, 136.
50. Scheid, *An Introduction to Roman Religion*, 165.
51. Ibid., 149.
52. Ibid., 173.
53. Ibid.

the spot, or inviting them to take up residence in Rome."[54] In short, Romans were open to a variety of deities and were known to be flexible enough to work with almost any local mythology. This open approach cannot be extended to the strict monotheism of the Jews and Christians: "Revelation, on the other hand, working with Jewish mythic traditions, did not allow the integration of imperial cults or of other local traditions."[55] John did not encourage his audience to assimilate or adopt the Roman way of life. With the rise of apocalyptic thought, toleration on the part of the Jews for Rome was low at best. It is easy to imagine the Romans as the brutal and unjust persecutors and the Jews as the oppressed minority group. In reality, the Jews, even as a small group, did pose a threat to Roman rule in their obsession with the battle between good and evil. Both Daniel and Revelation stand as proof that Jerusalem was intolerant of Rome, as Rudich explains:

> It stands to reason that the apocalyptic, eschatological, or/and messianic imagery, so far as we know it from the Second Temple Pseudepigrapha, did possess considerable, for some individuals, perhaps, compelling emotional power, rooted further in their engagement with scriptural tradition. This could have not failed to add to the atmosphere of popular anxiety, with its mixture of hopes and fears that seems to have been an undercurrent throughout much of that period, providing a convenient breeding ground for the spread of religious dissent in both its non-violent and violent forms.[56]

It is clear that both Daniel and Revelation deal with fantasy and not real, but potential violence that is in the end completely unrealistic. It also remains that only God, not humans, can initiate the end times. However, it also remains true that the group of people responsible for the creation of such texts were hoping for the complete annihilation of all others but themselves. No matter how fantastical apocalyptic texts are, behind them are communities who did wish for them to be true and ultimately believed that one day God would indeed vindicate his people at the expense of the rest of the world. The violent imagery and divine promises of these works may have served directly or indirectly to arouse anger and hostility towards Rome. The destruction of the Second Temple remains among the major national disasters in the history of the Jewish people and the apocalyptic mindset of that period in no way vindicates Rome from their role. However, it is in our interest to recognize violent or potentially violent forces

---

54. Ibid., 154.
55. Friesen, *Imperial Cults*, 168.
56. Rudich, *Religious Dissent*, 66.

within a society or culture and realize the role they can play in their own self-destruction.

The Towers and the Temple

In his book entitled *Supergods*, acclaimed comic book writer Grant Morrison asserts that since their opening in 1973, the Twin Towers had become a target for imaginary demolitions.[57] Within three years of their completion, King Kong climbed the Towers in a 1976 remake of the 1933 film *King Kong* that had the giant ape originally climb the Empire State Building. After the fall of the Towers, the 2005 filmmakers had King Kong return to the Empire State Building for the iconic scene. Morrison reminisces on the many imagined destructions of the towers where they have been: "smashed by tidal waves, blasted by aliens, shattered by meteor strikes, and pulverized by rogue asteroids."[58] The Twin Towers are not the only buildings to have been creatively destroyed in films. Now that we know the fate of the Towers it is interesting to recall such Hollywood treatments of these buildings. Morrison permits himself to briefly indulge in the idea that the, "terrible fall of the World Trade Center towers on September 11 had the curious inevitability of an answered prayer or the successful result of a black magic ritual."[59] As his discussion persists, Morrison recalls: "creepy clairvoyant comic books published in the weeks and months prior to 9/11, all of them haunted by eerie images of planes and ruined towers."[60] One example, of many shared by Morrison, is *Adventures of Superman* no. 596 by Joe Casey that was published on September 12th, 2001 a day after the attack, but written several months before. The comic portrays a scene showing Lex Luthor's twin Lex Towers in the aftermath of an alien attack: "It mirrored, almost exactly, the photographs on the front pages of the same day's newspapers. So accurately did the pictures match that DC made the book returnable in the event of any inadvertent offense."[61] The cover of the issue has the words: "THIS IS NOT A JOB FOR SUPERMAN" in big yellow letters as if it was eerily suggesting that Superman could not intervene in the actual events of real life 9/11.[62] If that is not coincidental enough, Morrison goes on to describe one of his own works published one month before the September 11 attacks:

57. Morrison, *Supergods*, 346.
58. Ibid.
59. Ibid.
60. Ibid.
61. Ibid.
62. Casey, *The Adventures of Superman*.

My own *New X-Men* no.115 with Frank Quitely, published in August 2001, ended with a scene in which an airliner, fashioned into the shape of a giant fist, was flown through the side of a skyscraper. The following issue, released on September 19, 2001, but written and drawn months before, had X-Men character the Beast in close-up, weeping, with an opening sequence of rescue workers searching through the dusty rubble of fallen buildings for bodies.[63]

Of course, this does not claim that any of these authors had any foresight that inspired their works. The coincidence that such comic books were published prior to the dates of the events of 9/11 is nothing more than just that: a coincidence (no matter how startling or chilling). While these publications remain completely fictional and unintentionally reflective of actual history, none of the authors would claim themselves to be prophets. Matt 24, Mark 13, and Luke 21 all tell the same story of Jesus predicting the fall of the Second Temple.[64] If Jesus actually did prophesize the fall of the Temple then this would speak to his credibility as a Messiah, but given what we now know about these sad coincidental comic books and movies portraying the fall of the Towers, perhaps one could also chalk up the prophecies of the New Testament gospels as "wishful black magic" to borrow the words of Morrison. If it were not for the date stamp on each comic book cover it would be impossible to know which story came before the other. Many publications have tried to date texts within the canon as well as the many non-canonical texts. Some stories from ancient times involving Biblical characters are simply fictional, others incorporate some historical events within the stories. The year 70 CE has been used as a marker in history. Texts that have an accurate description of the fall of the Temple are typically dated after 70 CE and texts with inaccurate descriptions are often dated before 70 CE. But, what if the comic books that were published in the months before 9/11 did not have their date imprinted on the cover? Could the events of 9/11 be used as an anchor in dating such stories? Although their publishing date is so close to the events themselves they were not inspired by the events at all; they are simply a terrible coincidence.

---

63. Morrison, *Supergods*, 346.

64. Concerning Mark 13, Matt 24, and Luke 21, Mark uses the same vocabulary as Dan 12:6–7 and "already presupposes some sort of connection between the tragic events of the 66–70 war and the end of the age. . .This connection did not have to be made by Mark's readers; the frightful events of their own experiences had already raised the question. For them the destruction of the Holy City and its temple was a given or imminent reality." Boring, *Mark*, 355.

New historicism, according to Robert Dale Parker, does not evade history or use it simply for "mere *background* and *context*, with the literature as merely *reflecting* the history."[65] Deconstruction, a popular form of literary criticism, helps us to understand that all things have internal contradictions and make us weary of all encompassing claims. To borrow from Parker again: "By contrast with old historicists, new historicists try to read history and literature together, with each influencing the other, and without a sense of stable facts. For new historicists, history is just as uncertain and complex as literature."[66] New historicists would argue that facts depend on perspective; in other words, facts are a construction and not an essence. Parker gives some good examples in order to illustrate this: one common "fact" that everyone seems to know is that Christopher Columbus discovered America in 1492. As Parker explains:

> In 1492, the name *America* did not even exist, and what Columbus did was no discovery if discovery means being the first person to find something. Untold millions of people knew about "America" before Columbus, and they did not think of it as the "New World" either. By tagging Columbus as the discoverer of America and the New World, we keep ourselves from looking through the perspective that would characterize him as an invader and conqueror, and as a brutally genocidal invader and conqueror.[67]

Stephan Greenblatt coined the term *new historicism* as a way of discussing the relation between history and literature:

> He tries to sort out what he calls 'the circulation of social energy,' the way that literature comes not only from individual authors but also from the cultural controversies of an age, with the controversies provoking the literature and the literature interpreting the controversies, in a continuous cycle of exchange and influence.[68]

Thus, the terms we use to describe Columbus as a discoverer of a new world masks the historical reality of the brutality of his voyage. Somehow, the initiation of America is no longer an event that deserves celebration. As John J. Collins explains:

---

65. As quoted by Parker, *How to Interpret Literature*, 259.
66. Ibid., 260.
67. Ibid., 262.
68. Ibid., 264.

The visions of Daniel are not, of course mere reflections of the historical crisis. They are highly imaginative constructions of it, shaped as much by mythic paradigms as by the actual events...This imaginative construction enables the persecuted Jews to cope with the crisis of persecution, first by bringing its enormity to expression so that it can be clearly recognized, second by providing assurance that the forces of evil will inevitably be overcome by a higher power, and ultimately by providing a framework for action since it furnishes an explanation of the world that supports those who have to lay down their lives if they remain faithful to their religion. It provides a basis for nonviolent resistance to Hellenistic rule, even in the thrones of the Maccabean revolt.[69]

The images found in *Heroes* are violent images full of pain and agony. The opening page by Joe Quesada reads: "What happened on September 11th, 2001 was not God's will. God's will was in the courage of every man, woman and child who stood up and came to the aid of their fellow humans. God's will was in the strength that was shown in the face of great tragedy and the desire displayed to rebuild, to move on and to do so with love."[70] Of course, these words are printed above a sad and broken looking Hulk (known for his immense strength, endurance, durability, and regeneration) who is picking up a fallen fireman's helmet. It is a powerful image along with powerful words. For anyone affected by the attacks on the Twin Towers, this tribute combines what Collins describes as highly imaginative constructions of historical crisis with mythic paradigms; it has the same effect of coping mechanism and proving assurance. The problem is that by page 51 of the same volume, Stan Lee's words inspire less love than Quesada's:

A day there was of monumental villainy. A day when a great nation lost its innocence and naked evil stood revealed before a stunned and shattered world. A day there was when a serpent struck a sleeping giant, a giant who will sleep no more. Soon shall the serpent know the wrath of the mighty, the vengeance of the just. A day there was when Liberty lost her heart – and found the strength within her soul.[71]

In this scene there is a sentiment of anger and desire to inflict violence and have vengeance. This is the problem when we describe apocalypses as crisis literature. The problem is that although this literature may comfort

---

69. Collins, *The Apocalyptic Imagination*, 114.
70. Quesada, *Heroes*, 1.
71. Ibid., 51.

and provide reassurance it can simultaneously call believers to action. In fact, there is a distinction to be made between non-violence and deferred violence. In *The Bad Jesus: The Ethics of New Testament Ethics*, Hector Avalos compares deferred violence to non-violence and explains that the putting aside of violence for a future time gives the false impression of non-violence: "Christian pacifists often automatically count an appeal against violence by Jesus without accounting for the fact that Jesus means to delay, rather than absolutely refuse, the use of violence."[72] Apocalyptic literature is the literature of desperate people who turn to it when they feel like their cause is lost:

> The theory is that the apocalyptic hope for the future is born out of abysmal despair. The vision of a new world is compensation for the miserable circumstances of the present. As soon as one asks whether this theoretical framework fits Revelation, one gets into difficulties. . .Sometimes millenarian mentality arises because traditional expectations can no longer be met. . .From this point of view, the book of Revelation is not simply a product of a certain social situation, not even a simple response to circumstances. At root is a particular religious view of reality, inherited in large part, which is the framework within which John interpreted his environment. The book of Revelation is thus a product of the interaction between a kind of pre-understanding and the socio-historical situation in which John lived.[73]

What this means is that apocalyptic literature encourages people to fight or to give up their lives for the sake of a religious belief and therein lays the reason why books like Daniel and Revelation need to be regarded as violent texts that no longer fit in with our current secular and humanist worldview. As Hector Avalos warns, scholars of religion should not endorse views of religion that have the potential to be harmful. In his opinion: "establishing any link between religion and violence is in the self-interest of humanity itself. Whether we are secular or religious, the goal should be the promotion of a harmonious human existence."[74] The apocalypses show just how dangerous both Judaism and Christianity can be. Of course, apocalypses and works like *Holy Terror* may help console or serve to purge emotional tension, but they also serve to keep the memory of the event (and the wounds of such events) so that even as time goes forward and we are one reminder away from being pulled back into that moment of loss. These

---

72. Avalos, *The Bad Jesus*, 101.
73. Yarbro Collins, *Crisis & Catharsis*, 105–106.
74. Avalos, "Explaining Religious Violence," 145.

types of documents can sometimes serve to perpetuate feelings of hate and violence for generations who were not part of the actual tragedy because they can experience the emotions as if they were there when they read these texts. Yarbo Collins reminds us that the book of Revelation:

> Highlighted and emphasized the suffering of Christians at the hands of Rome and painted a picture of the empire which put this trait of persecutor at the very center. In this way [John] apparently hoped to reinforce whatever hostility to Rome his readers might already have had and to awaken an anti-Roman attitude in those who were neutral or even open to Roman culture.[75]

Should these tragedies be forgotten? No, but we should be careful with how we use this type of literature and realize that it can serve as propaganda for hate as much as it might console us. In light of the historical situation, Revelation can be understood as a response to the experience of trauma:

> ...both individual and collective, personal and communal...The name Babylon is used to describe Rome as the second destroyer or the temple and Jerusalem. The frequent and intense use of this symbol suggests that the destruction of Jerusalem was a traumatic event; at least for John himself. . .it is likely that its destruction meant the loss of his spiritual and symbolic centre. In Revelation, language about a heavenly temple and a New Jerusalem seems to compensate for the loss of the earthly temple and city as a symbolic centre.[76]

The fall of the Temple inspired much literature. New historicism, or simply historicism, works with the general principal that literature and history shape each other as opposed to the habit of seeing literature as a passive reflector of history. The value of literature is in its capacity to both reflect and rethink the world: "New historicism has tried to craft a model for criticism that takes that combination of passive reflection and active thinking into account, both in literary art and in the art of criticism."[77] The Bible is made up of creative stories that mingle history with fiction in order to get a particular message across. As we have seen with comic books, there is a lot to say about these almost medicinal expressions of hope, loss, and anger:

> Children who are exposed to superhero characters learn that Superman always wins, Wonder Woman protects people, and

---

75. Yarbro Collins, *Crisis & Catharsis*, 111.
76. Ibid., 99.
77. Parker, *How to Interpret Literature*, 264.

the friendly neighborhood Spider-Man makes sure everyone is aware of his quest to defend the innocent. It's comforting to grow up with stories that share positive messages like this. As we grow older and we mature (again, hopefully), our lens though which we experience the world begins to get a bit grimy, and we start to question the role of the superhero and heroes in general. The realization that superheroes aren't real, various life experiences, changing interests, puberty, and many other natural progressions of life lead to challenging these representatives of both culture and our childhood.[78]

Most people understand that superhero mythology is just a mythology and no matter how adoring a fan might be, no one in their right mind would believe that Superman could have come flying through the sky to stop the airplanes from hitting the Twin Towers. In fact, no die-hard fan in his or her right mind would lay their life on the line in order to remain faithful to any superhero. The dangers are not in the literature or the art we create, but in the importance and authority we ascribe them.

In discussions of the events of the year 70 CE, the Romans are often vilified, while the Jews are often victimized:

> The picturesque ruins of the imperial city have both fascinated and repelled, stimulating admiration for brilliant achievements by past generations and rumination on the fallibility of human desire for glory...In contrast, Jerusalem has been idealized as a holy place of revelations, miracles and spiritual intensity."[79]

The more I explore apocalyptic thinking and its anti-empire language the more I see that, if Rome understood this mentality to be the basis of many Jewish groups at the time, it could then have been the leading reason behind the decision to tear down the Second Temple. This does not justify the actions of the Romans, but it does call attention to the question of why humans are still allowing religious ideology to move them to violent actions such as the attack on the Twin Towers. 9/11 and 70 CE have something more in common than just leaving behind works of art that have memorialized and glorified the victims of both events. The scars that have been left behind in the art and literature we preserve is built on the idea of victims:

> War finds its meaning in death. The cause is built on the backs of victims, portrayed as innocent. Indeed, most conflicts are ignited with martyrs, whether real or created. The death of an

---

78. Romagnoli and Pagnucci, "Perceptions of Good," 116.
79. Goodman, *Rome & Jerusalem*, 33.

innocent one, who is perceived as emblematic of the nation or the group under attack, becomes the initial rallying point for war. The dead become the standard-bearers of the cause and all the causes feed of a steady supply of corpses.[80]

Narratives are powerful tools: "The simple point is that literature belongs to the world man constructs, not to the world he sees; to his home, not his environment. Literature's world is a concrete human world of immediate experience."[81] The world of literature combines the real with the imaginative and it creates a sort of bandage in order to help communities get through difficult times:

> In the imagination anything goes that can be imagined and the limit of the imagination is a totally human world. . .Religion presents us with visions of eternal and infinite heavens or paradises. . .they indicate what the limits of the imagination are. They indicate too that in the human world the imagination has no limits.[82]

It is important to highlight that what is most dangerous is not the texts themselves, but the devotion that is imparted on constructed narratives:

> While it may be perfectly reasonable to dismiss fundamentalist readings of history as transparent manipulations of events and data, as mere projections of religious fanaticism and millenarian enthusiasm, it is important to underscore the fundamentalists' devotion to the narratives they have constructed, and their attention to the details they have embedded in the narrative to reinforce its eschatological themes. More than the general public, activist fundamentalists are engrossed in the events of history and spend significant time and resources indoctrinating recruits and educating the devout in its moral and political lessons.[83]

Comic books are not made of the same cloth as apocalypses because they are understood to be fictional; regardless of the real or historical topics addressed. The comic books produced as tributes to the victims of 9/11 are testimonies of the actual event; they provide evidence to both the event itself and the emotions felt by the collective group immediately following the event. By using fictional characters to lament actual people who have by and large remained faceless and nameless, the collective group feels reassured

---

80. Hedges, *War is a Force*, 121.
81. Frye, *The Educated Imagination*, 12.
82. Ibid., 13.
83. Appleby, "History in the Fundamentalist Imagination," 172.

that they can still remember all those lost. Most of all are the feelings of loss and tragedy experienced that particular day as the real ramifications come to light over time. It is difficult to come to terms with how one day can change the course of history, but these reminders help us realize the enormousness of actions, and how as a group we can go back to living our ordinary lives when everything still feels abnormal. For many people facts do not fill the void created by traumatic events and so they slip into their imaginations. Sometime in 1987, Will Eisner reflected on the radiation of human interaction absorbed by buildings. His words are eerily evocative when applied to the Twin Towers. However, when we realize that Eisner's intention was to create a work of humor the association no longer feels appropriate; this is how we need to feel about applying biblical texts to present day situations.

Bibliography

Ackerman, Spencer. "Frank Miller's Holy Terror is Fodder for Anti-Islam Set." *Wired.* September 28, 2011. http://www.wired.com/2011/09/holy-terror-frank-miller/.

Allison, Dale. "Jesus was an Apocalyptic Prophet." in *The Apocalyptic Jesus: A Debate.* Edited by Robert J. Miller. Santa Rosa: Polebridge, 2001.

Anson, Jay. *The Amityville Horror*. Englewood Cliffs, New Jersey: Prentice-Hall, 1977.

Appleby, R. Scott. "History in the Fundamentalist Imagination." Pages 157–174 in *History and September 11th*. Edited by Johanna Meyerowitz. Philadelphia: Temple University Press, 2003.

Aune, David E. *Apocalypticism, Prophecy, and Magic in Early Christianity*. Grand Rapids: Baker Academic, 2006.

Avalos, Hector. *The Bad Jesus: The Ethics of New Testament Ethics*. Sheffield: Sheffield Phoenix, 2015.

———. "Explaining Religious Violence: Retrospects and Prospects." Pages 137–146 in *The Blackwell Companion to Religion and Violence*. Edited by Andrew R. Murphy. Oxford: Wiley-Blackwell, 2011.

Brady, Matt. "Morrison in the Cave: Grant Morrison Talks Batman." *Newsarama.* August 23, 2006. Archived at http://web.archive.org/web/20060830185703/http://www.newsarama.com/dcnew/Batman/Morrison/Morrison_Batman.html.

Boring, M. Eugene. *Mark: A Commentary*. Louisville: Westminster John Knox, 2006.

Campbell, Joseph. *The Hero With a Thousand Faces*. New York: Meridian, 1956.

Casey, Joe. *The Adventures of Superman.* vol. 596. New York: DC Comics, November 2001.

Collins, John J. *The Apocalyptic Imagination: An Introduction to Jewish Apocalyptic Literature*. Grand Rapids: Eerdmans, 1984.

———. "Towards the Morphology of a Genre." *Semeia* 14 (1979) 1–19.

Dawkins, Richard. *The God Delusion*. Boston: Mariner Books, 2008.

Dony, Christophe and Caroline van Linthout. "Comics, Trauma and Cultural Memory(ies) of 9/11." Pages 178–187 in *The Rise and Reason of Comics and Graphic Literature: Critical Essays on the Form*. Edited by Joyce Goggin and Dan Hassler-Forest. Jefferson: McFarland & Company, 2010.

Eisner, Will. *The Building*. New York: Kitchen Sink Press, 1987.

Friesen, Steven J. *Imperial Cults and the Apocalypse of John: Reading Revelation in the Ruins*. New York: Oxford University Press, 2001.

Frilingos, Christopher A. *Spectacles of Empire: Monsters, Martyrs, and the Book of Revelation*. Philadelphia: University of Pennsylvania Press, 2004.

Frye, Northrop. *The Educated Imagination*. CBC Massey Lectures Series. Toronto: House of Anansi, 2002.

Goodman, Martin. *Rome & Jerusalem: The Clash of Ancient Civilizations*. New York: Penguin Books, 2008.

Harris, Sam. *The End of Faith: Religion, Terror, and the Future of Reason*. New York: W.W. Norton, 2005.

Hedges, Chris. *War is a Force that gives us Meaning*. New York: Public Affairs, 2002.

Hitchens, Christopher. *God is not great: How Religion Poisons Everything*. Toronto: McClelland & Stewart, 2007.

King, Stephen. *The Shining*. Garden City, New York: Doubleday, 1977.

Lawrence, John Shelton and Robert Jewett. *The Myth of the American Superhero*. Grand Rapids: Eerdmans, 2002.

Lehane, Dennis. *Shutter Island*. New York: HarperCollins, 2003.

Miller, Frank. *Holy Terror*. Burbank: Legendary Comics. September 2011.

Morgan, Matthew J. "Introduction." Pages 1–4 in *The Impact of 9/11 on Religion and Philosophy: The Day That Changed Everything?* Edited by Matthew J. Morgan. New York: Palgrave Macmillan, 2009.

Morrison, Grant. *Supergods: What Masked Vigilantes, Miraculous Mutants and A Sun God from Smallville can teach us about Being Human*. New York: Spiegel & Grau, 2012.

Mount, Harry. "Holy Propaganda! Batman is Tackling Osama bin Laden." *The Telegraph*. February 15, 2006. http://www.telegraph.co.uk/news/worldnews/northamerica/usa/1510556/Holy-propaganda-Batman-is-tackling-Osama-bin-Laden.html.

Murray, Christopher. *Champions of the Oppressed? Superhero Comics, Popular Culture, and Propaganda in America During World War II*. Cresskill: Hampton, 2011.

Oegema, Gerbern S. *Apocalyptic Interpretation of the Bible: Apocalypticism and Biblical Interpretation in Early Judaism, the Apostle Paul, the Historical Jesus, and their Reception History*. New York: T&T Clark, 2012.

Parker, Robert Dale. *How to Interpret Literature: Critical Theory for Literary and Cultural Studies*. New York: Oxford University Press, 2015.

Quesada, Joe. *Heroes: The World's Greatest Super Hero Creators Honor the World's Greatest Heroes*. Vol. 1:1. Edited by Joe Quesada. New York: Marvel Publishing Group, December 2001.

Romagnoli, Alex S. and Gian S. Pagnucci. "Perceptions of Good in Evil." Pages 7–11 in *Enter the Superheroes: American Values, Culture and the Canon of Superhero Literature*. Toronto: Scarecrow, 2013.

Rudich, Vasily. *Religious Dissent in the Roman Empire: Violence in Judaea at the Time of Nero*. New York: Routledge, 2015.

Scheid, John. *An Introduction to Roman Religion*. Translated by Janet Lloyd. Bloomington: Indiana University Press, 2003.

Straczynski, J. Michael. *The Amazing Spider-Man*. vol. 2:36. October 2001.

Tabachnick, Stephen E. *The Quest for Jewish Belief and Identity in the Graphic Novel*. Tuscaloosa: University of Alabama Press, 2014.

Van Der Toorn, Karel. "Inventing Revelation: The Scribal Construct of Holy Writ." Pages 205–232 in *Scribal Culture and the Making of the Hebrew Bible*. Massachusetts: Harvard University Press, 2007.

Yarbro Collins, Adela. *Crisis & Catharsis: The Power of the Apocalypse*. Philadelphia: Westminster, 1984.

3

The Common Good Gone Bad[1]

Costa Babalis

THE UNIVERSAL NOTION OF the common good can be understood as a given moral way of living that satisfies the needs of a group and, to a larger extent, the needs of an individual within the context of a group. In such a case the common good is directly connected to the wants and desires of a collective group. A group, therefore, identifies what it lacks—for example a resource such as food or land—and initiates strategies in order to acquire such resources. Conversely, a competing group has many of the same needs and requirements since such resources, at the basic level, are a matter of survival. If the sharing of resources between groups becomes unattainable through negotiation or other peaceful means, then the threat of violent intervention can take place and it becomes in the interest of each group to defend or acquire its own necessities. In this sense, the morality of survival is, to some degree, justifiable. That being said, the "more tragic source of violence," as Hector Avalos describes in *Fighting Words*, is the factually unverifiable involvement of religious violence based on "the existence of, and a relationship with, supernatural forces and/or beings."[2] As such, the common good can be seen as an arbitrary term that qualifies common or individual needs; it is, more precisely, a rhetorical-political term than one with ethical considerations.[3] Yet, as we will see, oftentimes the term is employed by religious authorities as a moral basis in order to sway and convince those who will listen. In this light, we can conceive of a feasible argument that proposes that violence expedited for the appropriation of goods and materials in order to

---

1. This essay is a slightly expanded version of a paper planned for, but not presented at, the "Religion, Violence, and the Ethics of Biblical and Religious Studies" conference held at Concordia University (Montreal, Quebec, Canada) on June 16th, 2015.

2. Avalos, *Fighting Words*, 103.

3. Smith, "Aristotle on the Conditions," 625.

fulfill a group's needs is more ethically reasonable than inflicting violence *per* religious and salvific ends. Inflicting violence on religious grounds, because of the unverifiable nature of religious belief itself, exploits and disguises religious imperialism with that of the human instinct for survival. Now, of course, some may interpret this statement as comparing two different components, the macro with the micro. Such is not the case. What I attempt to do in the following short essay is to demonstrate that religions increase their propensity to inflict violence when they exploit the ambiguity between the physical and spiritual worlds. The tendency is to conflate one's measure of well being with the extension of religious hegemony. How many times have religious authorities invoked the common good, which in itself suggests the well being of the individual, the community, and ultimately humanity, only to persecute and obliterate their opponents?

Thus, the following essay explores two important issues: 1) the appropriation of the notion of the common good and its rhetorical use in light of competing interests and; 2) the emphasis that rather than servicing universal ethical considerations, the common good can often turn into political and religious hegemony.

Competing Notions of the Common Good

The common good invokes in many who come across it a sense of communal benefit. It suggests a sense of equality; a preference to compel each and every individual to be responsible for one another—values which are noble in their own regard. Such ideals are typically seen as common towards the betterment of humanity. The "good," as a noun, compels one to understand its meaning as a hermeneutical tool in its function in human affairs and relationships. Therefore, what does the "good" mean in concrete terms and what, more precisely, is implied by "common" when preceded by the definite article? The implication here is that there is but one common and universal "good" that transcends the distinctive and applies to the whole. Contrast this with Thomas W. Smith's idea that "the common good is always someone's bad"[4] and we find ourselves at a separation of ways where there are potentially as many perspectives aligned with the common good as there are individuals, groups, or communities—neither of which can lay claim to that which is "common" or "good" or "the" only one, except to that which they judge beneficial to themselves.[5] Interesting as this is, none of the words

---

4. Ibid.
5. Ibid.

arranged together offer a phrase that has universal cohesiveness incumbent on the whole of humanity.

Many times throughout history we have seen what is stated above in the carnage of religious wars. Some examples can be used to illustrate. We begin with the Crusades (1095–1291 CE)[6] initiated by the popes, kings, and princes of Christendom who incited the masses to march off against the Muslims in order to free the Holy Land in the name of Christ with the idea that *"Deus lo vult"*—God wills it,[7] and with the battle cry of *"Deus adjuva"*— God assist us.[8] In these two phrases we can extrapolate that the idea of the common good is embedded—if not explicitly then implicitly—by conveying the notion that God's sanction is recognizably demonstrated by the idea of his will as conveyed in 1095 by Pope Urban II at the Council of Clermont prior to the First Crusade (1096–1099 CE):

> They have killed and captured many, and have destroyed the churches and devastated the empire. If you permit them to continue thus for awhile with impurity, the faithful of God will be much more widely attacked by them. On this account I, or rather the Lord, beseech you as Christ's heralds to publish this everywhere and to persuade all people of whatever rank, foot-soldiers and knights, poor and rich, to carry aid promptly to those Christians and to destroy that vile race from the lands of our friends. I say this to those who are present, it meant also for those who are absent. Moreover, Christ commands it.
>
> All who die by the way, whether by land or by sea, or in battle against the pagans, shall have immediate remission of sins. This I grant them through the power of God with which I am invested. O what a disgrace if such a despised and base race, which worships demons, should conquer a people which has the faith of omnipotent God and is made glorious with the name of Christ! With what reproaches will the Lord overwhelm us if you do not aid those who, with us, profess the Christian religion!"[9]

The Muslim crime, according to Christians at the time, was against God for occupying the Holy Land and attacking the church and the faithful. Pope Urban II's call was most likely understood by the Crusaders as a message promoting the common good that would benefit themselves and their Christian brethren. One would be hard pressed to interpret the Pope's

6. For more on the history of the Crusades, see Tyerman, *God's War*.
7. Gonzalez, *Story of Christianity*, 293.
8. Mackay, *Memoires*, 220.
9. Thatcher and McNeal, *Source Book*, 516–517; see also Avalos, *Fighting Words*, 181–186.

speech otherwise given the offered reward for the remission of previous sins that persisted with succeeding popes until the final Christian defeat led by Prince Edward in 1272 CE.

Unfortunately, the Crusades were not the first, nor the last, of religiously sanctioned wars fought with a purposeful eye towards perpetuating one's biased religious adherence to the common good. There were many others of which I mention but two: the French Wars of Religion lasting between 1562–1598 CE—which saw the massacre of the Huguenots by the Roman Catholic Guise family—and the Thirty Years War (1618–1648 CE) when Ferdinand II, the Holy-Roman Emperor, tried to enforce Roman Catholic absolutism on his domains. Both of these historical cases are significant given the religious authorities under which they were waged. In the case of the former, Catholic victors were celebrated by the sitting Pope Gregory XIII.[10] In the latter, Catholic hegemony was beaten off by the northern Protestant states. Protestant against Catholic was the order of the day as the two sides fought indecisive skirmishes that appealed to their respective sectarian dogma. Either Christian faction, of which both camps claimed superior religious insight, nevertheless, compelled them to arms against the other under a political guise that was fostered by the need for religious hegemony.[11]

Independent of political aims the battles and loss of life were fought under the standards of competing religious factions that went forth with ecclesiastical fervor for domination. The cause of the common good, as it were, was to establish under what dogma people were to be governed. In the final tally, neither side gained much more than when the war began and ended with the signing of the Peace of Westphalia in 1648 CE. What may have begun with the righteous cause of the ruling factions to secure the common good for all deteriorated into something not so good that was endured by all sides.

Referring to the First World War (1914–1918 CE), George Bernard Shaw's eloquent prose, even if written for the Second World War, would have been just as significant:

> Thanks to the machine gun. . .he fought with the strength of a thousand; but the idolized Bible was still. . .full of the spirit of the campaigns of Joshua, holding up our sword as the sword of the Lord and Gideon, and hounding us on to the slaughter of those modern Amelekites and Canaanites, the Germans, as

---

10. See Avalos, *Fighting Words*, 337–342; Avalos, "Response to Professor Paul Allen."

11. For more on the Thirty Years War, see Asbach and Schröder, *Ashgate Research Companion*.

idolaters, and children of the devil. Though the formula (King and Country) was different, the spirit was the same: it was the old imaginary conflict of Jehovah against Baal; only, as the Germans were also fighting for King and Country, and were quite convinced as we that Jehovah, the Lord strong and mighty...was their God, and that ours was his enemy...the wounds to civilization were so serious...because they are being kept open by the Old Testament spirit and methods of superstition.[12]

Here, we find an interesting take on the idea of the common good; one that reflect Avalos's own perspective. Like Shaw, Avalos rightly expresses the futility of basing the idea of the "good" on an argument: "...it is not ethical or moral to bring good based on myth or premises that cannot be verified."[13]

The Common Good and Religious Ethics

In most historical sequences, political powers—and let us note that religious institutions are themselves political—adopt the concept of the common good to fulfill their mandate to a particular deity in service of the well-being of humanity. This, as stated above, is a very noble and inspiring cause. It is, however, quite impossible to achieve given the competing interests that those individuals, groups, and communities require. It is all very nice to accept these notions of community that transcend needs, but it is quite another to actually fulfill them especially when god or gods are more often than not quite capricious, and just as Shaw would say "all written words are equally open to inspiration from the eternal fount and equally subject to error from the mortal imperfection of their authors."[14] As such, it is an anathema to humanity, whereby inhuman cruelties, as perceived to be sanctioned by Scripture, are perpetrated on fellow human beings. In such cases, a cursory overview demonstrates that many religious enterprises embrace a particularly narrow view of salvation.

A few examples, I believe are in order such as Christendom's failure to abide by the second commandment's injunction against graven images (Exod 20:4–6; Deut 5:8–10), which are an abomination to the sensibilities of a Muslim adherer and justification for murder for a fundamentalist Jihadist. The world was exposed to such atrocities in newsreels and articles reporting on ISIS fighters destroying ancient religious sites and artifacts and

---

12. Shaw, *Adventures of the Black Girl*, 64.
13. Avalos, *Fighting Words*, 368.
14. Shaw, *Adventures of the Black Girl*, 65.

killing those charged with their conservation.[15] Neuroscientist Sam Harris provides a vigorous list of episodes and personalities from the 9/11 hijackers to Justice Scalia's opinion on Christian morality where the former were not "cowards," but rather "men of faith—perfect faith, as it turns out—and this, it must finally be acknowledged, is a terrible thing to be."[16] Justice Scalia subsequently trusted the edicts of his faith when upholding the death penalty (even when the defendant was deemed intellectually disabled) and laws against sodomy (used against homosexuals) basing his judgments on Leviticus (Lev 18:22, 20:13).[17] In between these two are legislators that honestly believe that they are doing God's work by furthering what they consider Christian ethics and retribution, such as former Republican House Majority Leader, Tom DeLay (in office from 2003–2005) who "attributed the shootings at Columbine High School in Colorado to the fact that our schools teach the Theory of Evolution."[18]

In the examples above, the offended party or parties are all but outraged at the compulsion placed on them to change, accept, or conform to a religious dictate. As the Jihadist finds sanction for his duty to destroy and kill what he understands to be contrary to the Qur'an[19] and Hadiths' seemingly hostile stance in the production of images or idols, so the Christian interpretations of Scripture, which sanction violence and murder against homosexuality and abortion, are either ignored or reinterpreted. Extremists perform radical actions for the common good they wish to religiously enforce when deemed necessary.[20]

Extremists cannot service the common good for the simple reason that their premise is based (at least overtly) on the existence of a supernatural being that they define as "good." This divine entity must, in turn, act in the interest of humanity's common good, as perceived by the extremist group. At the same time, it seems that this supernatural being behaves as contrary to the common good and its divine law is, in many instances, contradictory. Once again, as Hector Avalos succinctly points out: ". . .it is not ethical or

---

15. Shaheen and Black, "Beheaded Syrian Scholar."

16. Harris, *The End of Faith*, 67.

17. Ibid., 156; 158.

18. Ibid., 156.

19. Sajoo, *Companion to Muslim Ethics*: "The Holy Quran does not provide explicit guidance on representational art. But it does mention the use of idols in worship in this verse (6:74) about the prophet Ibrahim (Abraham): And when Ibrahim said to his father, Azar: 'Do you take idols [*asnam*] for gods? Surely I see you and your people in manifest error.'"

20. Hoffman, *Inside Terrorism*, 116. See also: Associated Press in New York, "Islamic State."

moral to bring good based on myth or premises that cannot be verified."[21] This phrase is significant in light of the violence and misappropriation of the common good that extremists take it upon themselves to interpret according to their own self-interest and that of their own religious dogma that is contrary to the common good.

In conclusion, this short essay focused on the incompatibility of the state and religion whereby the common good cannot be equally applied. Religious edicts and questionable interpretations of Scripture fundamentally oppose the good championed as being held in common. In the end, it comes down to the political realm, as Smith remarks concerning Aristotle who envisioned the common good to be most applicable.[22] Aristotle did not base his arguments concerning the common good on aspects of religion likely because he considered justice to be the cornerstone of ideology. What thwarts the common good is indeed injustice and that can be, as we have seen, one of the dominant features of religion when juxtaposed with other competing religious ideologies. Smith's opinion is the most relevant when considering the common good in that "perhaps it is better to begin thinking about the common good by exploring the injustice that stand in its way."[23] Unfortunately, this injustice can also sometimes be perpetrated by religions.

---

21. Avalos, *Fighting Words*, 368.
22. Smith, "Aristotle on the Conditions."
23. Ibid., 626.

Bibliography

Asbach, Olaf, and Peter Schröder. *The Ashgate Research Companion to the Thirty Years' War*. Surrey; Burlington: Ashgate, 2014.

Associated Press in New York. "Islamic State has killed at least 30 People for Sodomy, UN Told." *The Guardian*. August 25, 2015. https://www.theguardian.com/world/2015/aug/25/islamic-state-has-killed-at-least-30-people-for-sodomy-un-told.

Avalos, Hector. *Fighting Words: The Origins of Religious Violence*. Amherst, New York: Prometheus Books, 2005.

———. "A Response to Professor Paul Allen: The Supposed Myth of Religious Violence and Religionism in Secular Academia." *Debunking Christianity*. June 29, 2015. http://debunkingchristianity.blogspot.ca/2015/06/a-response-to-professor-paul-allen.html.

Gonzalez, Justo L. *The Story of Christianity, Volume 1: The Early Church to the Dawn of the Reformation*. 2nd Edition. New York: HarperColllins, 2010.

Harris, Sam. *The End of Faith: Religion, Terror, and the Future of Reason*. New York: W.W. Norton, 2005.

Hoffman, Bruce. *Inside Terrorism*. 2nd Edition. New York: Columbia University Press, 2006.

Mackay, Charles. *Memoirs of Extraordinary Popular Delusions and the Madness of Crowds*. London; New York: Routledge and Sons, 1852.

Sajoo, Amyn B. *A Companion to Muslim Ethics*. London: I.B. Tauris, 2010.

Shaheen, Kareem, and Ian Black. "Beheaded Syrian Scholar Refused to Lead Isis to Hidden Palmyra Antiquities." *The Guardian*. August 19, 2015. https://www.theguardian.com/world/2015/aug/18/isis-beheads-archaeologist-syria.

Shaw, George Bernard. *The Adventures of the Black Girl in her Search for God*. New York: Dodd, Mead, 1933.

Smith, Thomas W. "Aristotle on the Conditions for and Limits of the Common Good." *The American Political Science Review* 93:3 (1999) 625–636.

Thatcher, Oliver J., and Edgar Holmes McNeal, eds. *A Source Book for Medieval History: Selected Documents Illustrating the History of Europe in the Middle Age*. New York: Charles Scribner's Sons, 1905.

Tyerman, Christopher. *God's War: A New History of the Crusades*. Cambridge: Harvard University Press, 2006.

4

Genocide and Religion in Rwanda in the 1990s

"*What Weapons Shall We Use to Conquer the Cockroaches Once and For All?*"[1]

Spyridon Loumakis

Euphrasie Kamatamu was a notorious female *génocidaire*[2] and councilor of the sector of Muhima in the commune of Nyarugenge in Kigali, capital of Rwanda. She was described by Tutsi witnesses as regularly attending all the morning masses at the St. Famille Church in Kigali, carrying her rosary, often praying, and presiding over the prayer group Légion Marie in Muhima, before entering into politics in the early 1990s.[3] According to London–based NGO "African Rights"[4] she then became a member of *MRND*[5] and her hus-

---

1. This phrase is adopted from the pro-Hutu racist Rwandan magazine *Kangura*; see Chrétien et al., *Les medias*, 114.

2. This is the most commonly used term in both French and English scholarship in order to describe those who actively participated in the 1994 Rwanda genocide.

3. African Rights, *Rwanda, not so Innocent*, 140, 142. The so-called International Human Rights Fact-Finding has been critiqued the last past decades. For this critique, see Alston and Knuckey, *Transformation*. It offers articles in relation to the existence or nonexistence of facts, the impact of the fact-finding process upon the facts themselves and the witnesses, the reproduction of hierarchies in the fact-finding process, the gender politics within this process, the implications of trauma on testimonial evidence, and the dangers of producing a "single story." The works used in this essay that have been produced either by the London–based NGO "African Rights" or the New York–based NGO "Human Rights Watch" are products of careful field research, sometimes under the supervision of reliable, properly educated, and experienced scholars, such as Alison Des Forges or Timothy Longman.

4. Ibid., 134.

5. *MRND* stands for the *Mouvement républicain national pour le développement*

band became a member of the extremist party *CDR*.⁶ She started recruiting for the violent, militant groups of *interahamwe*.⁷ It has been reported by witnesses that during the genocide, her house became the principal meeting place for the killers, while weapons and ammunitions were kept there. All of her children, according to similar sources, participated actively in the genocide and one of her sons manned a bloody roadblock next to their house. Euphrasie Kamatamu had a list of Tutsi to be killed and regularly checked the roadblocks since she was personally responsible for hunting down specific targets from the list of Tutsi and handing them over to be killed. Despite this, eyewitnesses testified having seen her regularly attending mass and wearing her rosary throughout the genocide.⁸ A Hutu witness, named Bosco Harerimana, interviewed in Kigali on August 4, 1995, confirmed: "Her whole house was full of assassins. But it didn't stop her from wearing her long rosary."⁹ Another Hutu witness, Ali Rigamba, interviewed on August 14, 1995, remarked on the contradiction of her actions: "I clearly remember how, during the genocide, Euphrasie always carried her rosary around, despite the fact that her hands and heart were stained with blood."¹⁰

Christopher C. Taylor—one of the few who lived in Rwanda and experienced the events during the first couple of days of the genocide—conducted one of the earliest researches on the events during the time when the genocide was taking place. In his book, *Sacrifice as Terror*, he argues that understanding the Rwandan genocide undeniably requires one to comprehend the historical and political preconditions of the event; however, what is also needed, according to Taylor, is an analysis of the social and cultural

---

et la démocratie founded by general Juvénal Habyarimana who ruled Rwanda from his coup d'état in July 1973 until his assassination on April 6, 1994 when his flight from Arusha, Tanzania to Kigali, Rwanda was shot down near the airport of Kigali, urging into action the hardliners of the radical anti-Tutsi faction of his party.

6. *CDR* stands for the *Coalition pour la défense de la République*, the far-right Hutu Power political party, founded in 1992 and allied with the ruling *MRND*. Several important members of the *CDR* were convicted by the *International Criminal Tribunal for Rwanda* for genocide, and other crimes against humanity. The *CDR* had created its own militia, the *Impuzamugambi* ("Those who have the same goal"), which took part in the killings.

7. *Interahamwe* means "those who attack together" and consisted of young Hutu extremist militias, created in the 1990s by members of the Habyarimana regime. The *interahamwe* led citizens to kill Tutsi during the genocide, along with the Rwandan army and the gendarmerie. They were notorious for their cruelty; killing their victims with machetes, clubs with nails, and grenades.

8. African Rights, *Rwanda, not so Innocent*, 134–143.

9. Ibid., 142.

10. Ibid., 138.

factors.[11] That being said neither Taylor nor many of the other scholars have tried to understand the Rwandan genocide with an analysis of the *religious factors*, except for some brief mentions concerning the Church.[12] Of course, extensive work has already been done on the complicity of the churches and priests in the Rwandan genocide with remarkable results, both from foundational fieldwork,[13] and also from more elaborate modern research with an overwhelming emphasis on the colonial and postcolonial period of Rwandan history leading to the turbulent years between 1990–1994 which is further explored below. The problem is that religion, in this case Christianity, is neither exclusively the Church as an institution, nor predominately its priesthood or the teachings that come from Christians' sacred texts. These are significant factors to consider, arguably, but the life of Euphrasie Kamatamu, already mentioned at the outset of this essay, is quite telling of how deeply connected religion and violence was in the 1994 Rwanda genocide; deeper than scholars have realized.

The present work seeks to establish the connection between the violent events of the 1994 Rwanda genocide and the Christian religion as experienced and lived by the people of this country, influencing each other, both top-down and bottom-up, in the everyday interactions and everyday aspects of their lives; from high politics and decision making to bloody roadblocks in a small village in the countryside. I offer examples of violence and religion beyond the sphere of the Church, mainly from three sources: 1) eyewitness accounts from everyday Rwandans who either participated in or became victims of the 1994 genocide;[14] 2) evidence from the discourse

---

11. Taylor, *Sacrifice as Terror*, 29.

12. What lies behind this attitude of scholars can be summarized by the following view within modern scholarship, which is far from being just an isolated voice: "While religious beliefs alone do not account for war, the processes through which religious organizations are formed, become involved in politics, and relate to particular conflict parties should form a central part of conflict analysis," Williams, *War and Conflict*, 129. That institutionalized religion takes the biggest share in discussions about religion and the genocide in Rwanda can be seen in Timothy Longman's contribution to a volume edited by prominent scholar Niels Kastfelt in 2005, which was limited to the role of the Church during the genocide, although the volume was dedicated to the *Religion and African Civil Wars*. See Longman, "Churches and Social Upheaval."

13. See Omaar and de Waal, *Who Is Killing*, 16–21; Omaar and de Waal, *Death, Despair and Defiance*, 862–930; Des Forges et al., *Aucun témoin ne doit survivre*, 290–293.

14. Some of the most remarkable collections of witnesses (apart from those used in the present article) are the following: Malagardis and Sanner, *Rwanda, le jour d'après*; Bührer, *Rwanda: Mémoire*; Berry and Berry, *Genocide in Rwanda*; Lumurerwa, *Comme la langue entre les dents*; Janzen and Janzen, *Do I Still*; Kabagema, *Carnage d'une nation*; Kehrer, *Rwanda: Part de dieu part du diable*; Karemano, *Au-delà des barrières*; Mujawayo and Belhaddad, *Survivantes*; Hatzfeld, *Life Laid Bare*; Straus, *Intimate Enemy*; de

of opinion and decision makers in the media and in public speeches during the genocide (April 7, 1994–mid July 1994); and 3) judicial records of the *International Criminal Tribunal for Rwanda* (henceforth *ICTR*).[15] Reli-

---

Brouwer and Ka Hon Chu, *The Men Who Killed Me*; Burnet, *Genocide Lives in us*. The use of personal narratives in history, integrated in a historical work that synthesises traditional sources and this "alternative" material is crucial in order to understand a complicated phenomenon such as genocide. Personal narratives help us to present marginalized voices (i.e. that of raped women or genocide perpetrators in jail), to provide subjective counter-narratives (i.e. that religion does matter for common people during genocide), and to work from a research base that is more inclusive. See Maynes, Pierce, and Laslett, *Telling Stories*. For various ethical issues that are raised, mostly by Rwandans, in the use of their testimonies by third parties see Taylor, Sollange, and Rwigema, "The Ethics of Learning." For the fundamental historiographical and methodological issues raised by the production and use of such personal accounts in history see Grele, "Oral History as Evidence." The truth is that for studying war crimes and traumatic experiences, such as rape and genocide, oral histories are quintessential.

15. The *ICTR* was established with the UN Resolution 955 in 1994. On January 9, 1997, the first trial started (Prosecutor v. Jean–Paul Akayesu) which sentenced the accused to life imprisonment. Since its creation, 83 suspects were tracked down and arrested, the majority of which were found guilty and sentenced to imprisonment (ranging from life sentences to serving some years in prison). The first to plead guilty was the Prime Minister of the Interim Government during the 1994 genocide Jean Kambanda. On May 9, 1998, before the Tribunal, he became the first head of state to ever do so in the history of international criminal law. By May 23, 2006, the *ICTR* managed to recognise the 1994 Rwanda genocide as an *established fact beyond dispute*. On June 24, 2011, the first woman in the history of the UN's International Criminal Courts (Pauline Nyiramasuhuko) was convicted for acts of genocide. On December 20, 2012, the *ICTR* delivered its last judgement, but as of April 2014 three more suspects are still at large, to be tried by the *ICTR*. For more information see the website of the United Nations Mechanism for International Criminal Tribunals at: http://unictr.unmict.org/. The site also offers online access to its rich Juridical Records and Archives Database. This paper brings forth a few preliminary results of a much broader and thorough research (currently in preparation) on the role of religion in the 1994 Rwandan Genocide, conducted through the study of over 2,000 documents, which amounts to tens of thousands of pages (Acts of Examination-In-Chief and of Cross-Examination, Judgements, Appeals, Exhibits, and Experts's Reports). The scientific community has raised specific worries with regards to the work of the Tribunal and to its agenda behind some of the trials. See Strizek, *Der Internationale Strafgerichtshof für Ruanda*; Moghalu, *Rwanda's Genocide*; Essoungou, *Justice à Arusha*; Clark and Kaufman, *After Genocide*; Jones, *The Courts of Genocide*. For very interesting points on how unsuccessfully the *ICTR* tried to write history, failing to understand basic concepts of Rwandan society, see Wilson, *Writing History*, 43–48, 172–173, 178, 180–181. See also Combs, *Fact-Finding without Facts*, 106–118, 120–121, 125–126, 149–163, 176, 179–180, 186, 191–192, 254–259, 264–265. Combs provides extensive documentation from the *ICTR* on educational deficiencies and cultural divergences of witnesses, translation errors from Kinyarwanda to French and English, inconsistencies in testimonies (sometimes about core features of the events), difficulties of recollecting precise details several years after the occurrence of the events, high rates of discrepancies in all of the cases, contradictions among witnesses, imprecise or nonresponsive testimonies, accusations against proper investigation,

gious violence goes beyond the Church or the Bible, penetrating deep into the Rwandan society. It makes horrible actions—such as those committed during genocide—justifiable and acceptable. Finally, this approach poses important questions about the nature of religious violence in relation to Hector Avalos's scarce resource theory.

It needs to be understood that Rwandan Christianity is *not only* the Church itself as a place of worship and a meeting place for worshippers, or Sunday as the day of the Lord for praying and chanting, or the priests who communicated through their sermons with the laymen, or sometimes various visionaries and charismatic persons whose dreams and visions gave them a privileged access to apparitions of the Virgin Mary (as will be further explored below). Similarly, it does not deal exclusively with canons, synodical acts, ecumenical councils, Church Fathers, the creed or the Bible as written word. We need to examine things more carefully and thoroughly in order to realize how penetrating religion is in the Rwandan society, even during times of havoc and massacres. What role did religion play in the minds of those committing such atrocities or in those treated like animals that were brutally beaten to death, slaughtered without discrimination of sex and age, and butchered with machetes and knives? How did people equate these events to God's will?

The Church of Rwanda and the 1994 Genocide

Since the predominant aspect in studying religion in Rwanda is the established institution of the Church, we begin with a brief overview of the major and important contributions on this topic. The history of the Church in Rwanda has often been the subject of excellent studies. Therefore, what follows are the most influential works that help to paint a picture of the role of the Church during the violent political history of Rwanda up until the eve of the most notoriously violent phase of its history, the 1994 Rwandan genocide.

Ian Linden's *Church and Revolution in Rwanda* (1977) is beyond doubt an excellent work on the Rwandan Church during the colonial and early post-colonial period.[16] Although without the hindsight of the 1994 geno-

---

many incidences of perjury, and so forth. Yet, most of this critique comes from a legal point-of-view. For historians, the matter is not about history *in* the ICTR, but history *from* the judicial records of ICTR. It is a rich and useful source, which cannot be overlooked, but admittedly had advantages and pitfalls much like any other major source in history.

16. Linden, *Church and Revolution*.

cide, Linden pictures the Rwandan Church as closely interacting with the political elite under the specific historical conditions in the region. Linden describes the missionary activity in the early colonial period as initially failing to Christianize the ruling elite and, until the mid-1920s, flourishing largely in the countryside and around isolated mission stations only to change under the Belgians when the region turns to Catholicism, creating a triumphant Tutsi-dominated Church.[17]

The formation of political parties in 1959 and the polarized climate during that year is, for Linden, a decisive point leading to the alliance between the Rwandan Church and the movement towards the self-awareness of those portions of the population that identified themselves as "Hutu." Church leadership was forced to choose sides.[18] On the one hand, the *Association pour la promotion sociale de la masse* (henceforth *APROSOMA*) was founded in November 1957 and soon became a political party (15 February, 1959). It was co-founded by an ex-seminarian, Joseph Gitera, often described as a radical Christian, and even sometimes as fanatical, who was the first to see politics as a Christian crusade and clashed with the largely Tutsi dominated Catholic clergy.[19] In one of his letters, Gitera even threatened to castrate all Tutsi, without having any problem invoking the Holy Trinity in the same writing.[20] At the same time, the Flemish-speaking Belgian missionaries sympathized with those Hutus who were portraying themselves as *oppressed*, and the newly arrived European priests who represented a "social Catholicism" aligned with the *APROSOMA* movement because its Hutu counter–elite was promising to bring social and political changes. On the other hand, the conservative Tutsi court elite saw this alliance as colonial and anti-national.[21] The court elite allied with northern Tutsi chiefs in November 1959 in order to create the political party *Union Nationale Rwandaise* (henceforth *UNAR*), which quickly demonstrated its anti-clerical, anti-missionary, and anti-Catholic sentiments. The French-speaking Belgian colonial administration of the entire region was also distancing

17. Ibid., 2–4.

18. Ibid., 6–8, 260.

19. Ibid., 251–252. Both *APROSOMA* and its journal *La voix du menu peuple* (*Ijwi rya rubanda rugufi*) were using radical anti-Tutsi rhetoric, which led to the pogroms of Tutsi in 1959 and in 1963–1964. The journal was calling young Hutu to free themselves from Tutsi slavery and saw the killing of Tutsi as a rightful act of vengeance. Joseph Habyarimana, the other co-founder of *APROSOMA*—who was sometimes invoking the "good God,"—was also responsible for the publication of the aggressive and heinous Ten Commandments. For more details see Semujanga et al., *Le Manifeste des Bahutu*, 43–61, 88–90.

20. Linden, *Church and Revolution*, 256.

21. Ibid., 254, 256.

itself from the Flemish-speaking Belgian missionaries and strengthening its relations with the Tutsi monarchy. It comes as no surprise that it also perceived the official institutional Church as pro-Hutu. Therefore, monarchists were seen tearing the rosaries of Christians and so on.[22] Amidst all of this, in 1959 the radical anti-Tutsi party *Parti pour l'émancipation hutu* (henceforth *PARMEHUTU*) was created by Grégoire Kayibanda.[23] Educated Hutu who were closely aligned with the Church shared the ideas of Kayibanda. He succeeded in his remarkable rise to power—a landslide victory in the July 1960 elections—precisely as a result of support from the White Fathers,[24] the Catholic Church, as well as an anti-Tutsi-oligarchy peasant population craving for reforms.[25] As Linden concludes:

> Whatever its intentions, the Church had presided over a dramatic transfer of power from the Tutsi noble linages to the counter-elite of teachers and ex-seminarians.[26]

Timothy Longman has undoubtedly contributed to our level of knowledge on the church of Rwanda. In his book, *Christianity and Genocide in Rwanda*, he argues that the various churches (predominantly Catholic, Anglican, and Adventist) actively shaped the ethnic and political realities during the post-colonial period that made the 1994 genocide possible. The churches even acted to legitimize the authoritarian regime of Juvénal Habyarimana[27] and encouraged the people of Rwanda to obey political authorities. What is important is that for Longman, an experienced field researcher for the New York-based NGO "Human Rights Watch" (field work

22. Ibid., 260–266.

23. Grégoire Kayibanda would be the future first President of the independent Republic of Rwanda. He was formerly a student at the Nyakibanda seminary and responsible for the so-called *Bahutu Manifesto* aimed at emancipating Hutu consciousness.

24. The so-called "White Fathers," also known as *Société des Missionnaires d'Afrique/Pères Blancs*, were founded by the archbishop of Alger, Algeria, Charles Lavigerie, who by 1868 has started missionary activity in West Africa, and in 1878 in Central Africa. In the 1890s, White Father Jean-Joseph Hirth started the Christianization of what is today Rwanda, while at that point was still a German colony. For more information, see Strizek, *Geschenkte Kolonien*, 119–123. For a more detailed account, see Shorter, *Les Pères Blancs*; Nolan, *Les Pères Blancs*. In the 1960s, the White Fathers were credited with the oldest Christian presence in the region and their influence in Rwandan society was significant. For their activities in the early post-colonial period, see Linden, *Church and Revolution*.

25. Linden, *Church and Revolution*, 266–271.

26. Ibid., 271.

27. Habyarimana established a Hutu-dominated regime, which had seized power in 1973 from the *PARMEHUTU* government, established the Second Republic of Rwanda, and remained in power until the 1994 genocide.

in 1992–1993 and 1995–1996 from three Catholic and three Protestant parishes, as well as interviews and archival work), the churches in Rwanda made ethnic prejudices seem consistent with Christian teachings. They were too closely associated with the state in order to express any official, public anti-government opinion, or criticism. At the same time, the 1994 genocide, and all those committed before, served the interests of the church hierarchy, never clearly condemning in public the government-led Hutu violence since its beginnings. The first public declaration about the violence did not come out earlier than the May 13, 1994, by Catholic and Protestant church leaders, in which they implied that the *Rwanda Patriotic Front* (henceforth *RPF*),[28] whose advance had led them at a refuge in Kabgayi,[29] and the government are equally responsible for the violent events; careful never to label these events as (at that time a full-blown) "genocide." After all, the political power has proven a very good ally for their interests in curtailing reform movements within the Church in the region. Heightening ethnic tensions undermined any democratic reform movement.[30]

28. The *Rwanda Patriotic Front* was the main army of Tutsi while living in exile in Uganda and fighting the government army in Rwanda, especially since 1990 with constant intrusions into the Rwandan soil. In the days following Habyarimana's death, RPF advanced as far as the capital of Rwanda, Kigali, and captured the densely Hutu-populated northern provinces of Rwanda, while the genocide was taking place in the rest of the country.

29. Kabgayi is 40 km southwest of the capital Kigali, in the southern province of Gitarama. At that moment, it was the center for the Catholic Church in Rwanda, with the oldest cathedral in the country. It also became a notorious theatre of mass killings during the 1994 genocide. While this was taking place one wonders exactly what was the assistant bishop of Kigali, Jonathan Ruhumuliza, trying to convey with a letter he wrote one day before, on May 12, 1994, referring (a) to the (exclusively Hutu-run) government which was trying to bring peace in the country against the rebels (of exclusively Tutsi stock) who were destroying everything; and (b) to the churches trying their best with the belief that "God will help his people." (For the full quotation, see Longman, *Christianity and* Genocide, 191). It is not difficult to argue that for high-church dignitaries, the God (of the Hutu) was expecting to help the (Hutu) people. Indeed, a few weeks later in a press conference in Nairobi, high-church dignitaries were attempting to explain events in Rwanda as a result of all the mistakes the RPF had committed, aligning themselves to the genocidal government. See Longman, *Christianity and* Genocide, 192.

30. Longman, "Church Politics and the Genocide"; Longman, *Christianity and Genocide*; Longman and Rutagengwa, "Religion, Memory, and Violence." For the Church's silence during the genocide see also experienced Canadian journalist Hugh McCullum's report: McCullum, *The Angels*, 65, 68, 73, 75, 79–82. Not far from this reading of Rwandan Church history are the following important works: Theunis, "Le rôle de l'église catholique;" Hoyweghen, "The Disintegration of the Catholic Church;" Bizimana, *L'Église et le génocide*; Ugirashebuja, "The Church and the Genocide;" Bjørnlund et al., "Christian Churches."

For the May 13 declaration of Rwandan bishops, the NGO "African Rights" stated

Through his long and thorough research, Timothy Longman comes to a very interesting conclusion with respect to the role of the Church in Rwanda during the 1994 genocide:

> The fact that people could desecrate church buildings and kill even at the foot of the altar or in the sacristy is not evidence of a lack of respect for Christianity or a shallowness of Christian faith. Instead it reveals the nature of Christianity in Rwanda as a politicized, conservative, discriminatory faith.[31]

The Rwandan people could hear the conspicuously anti-Tutsi message of prominent church leaders in the period leading up to the genocide and could see priests and pastors gathering the Tutsi in order to organize their killings on church property along with organizing patrols and barriers. All of these actions could not but assure them that their own participation was morally acceptable. "Death squads" were easily seen as "civil self-defense" by the sanction of the Church.[32]

Finally, the most recent contribution to this topic comes from James Jay Carney who, in his work *Rwanda before the Genocide*, shifts his emphasis away from a top-down evangelization of Rwanda towards "early Catholic missions that supported a counter-cultural, pan-ethnic community of poor peasants and counter-elites."[33] For Carney, the colonial and early post-colonial period (the 1950s and 1960s) represent the triumph of the "church from below." However, what started as an alliance between Hutu leaders and

---

that: "[N]o-one who reads it in the light of the massacres and desecration of churches, and the murder of priests and nuns, can avoid being struck by its conspicuous failure to call evil by its name, the deliberate confusion of the war and the genocide, and the reluctance to confront those who were propagating crimes against humanity." Omaar and de Waal, *Death, Despair and Defiance*, 896–897.

The bishops decided to describe the massacres as "tragic events" and not as "genocide," at a time when they were forced to accompany the interim government from RPF-besieged Kigali to Gitarama, which was safer for the Hutu, but a notorious killing place for Tutsi; see Carney, *Rwanda before the Genocide*, 198. On June 20, 1994, in a common statement by Catholic and Protestant church leaders, RPF was again accused as being responsible for "this dramatic situation" with no mention about the responsibilities of the interim government. But, these were not the first instances since in March 1991, during their Easter message, the Catholic bishops preached love for the enemy, but failed to mention the Tutsi massacre at Ruhengeri only a month before; see Carney, *Rwanda before the Genocide*, 317, n.111). Similarly, during Lent 1992, the bishops' annual statement spoke about Hutu and Tutsi fighting each other and communities having turned against each other, but failing to name or condemn the Tutsi massacre in Bugesera shortly before; see Carney, *Rwanda before the Genocide*, 197.

31. Longman, *Christianity and Genocide*, 197.
32. Ibid., 297.
33. Carney, *Rwanda before the Genocide*, 2.

missionaries towards the liberation of the poor masses and the establishment of a more egalitarian Rwandan society based on demands for social justice, democracy, and economic equality, very soon turned into another aspect of the Hutu-Tutsi dynamic, as "a mission to empower Hutu masses over and against perceived Tutsi oligarchy."[34]

Carney also sees the growing missionary support for Hutu parties in the late colonial period, less as a result of ethnicism, and more as the Church's perceived institutional self-interest.[35] The Church's fear was that the Tutsi-dominated *UNAR* was perceived as an anti-colonial, anti-Catholic, and anti-clergy nationalist (with alleged communist affiliations) party. However, out of this era and because of this fear, the ideology and the rhetoric that would ultimately culminate with the 1994 genocide was established.[36]

The above-mentioned works are based on the words and deeds of the Rwandan bishops, clergy, and lay elites working in the Catholic media, as well as on intra-clerical relations between European missionaries and African priests, and their relation with the ruling political elite. This, however, does not offer the entire picture of Christianity in the region. The religious phenomenon of Christianity in Rwanda stretches beyond its clergy and bishops.

The God of Hutus and the God of Tutsis

We begin with a source that does *not* come from the days during the genocide, but is nevertheless one of the most well known and often cited in the majority of works on the 1994 Rwanda genocide. Léon Mugesera, who at that moment was vice-president of the *MRND* and close friend and advisor of President Habyarimana,[37] made a call to the Hutu people to crush their enemies, to cut their throats, and to eliminate what he called the "vermin," the "snake," the "hyena," and the "cockroach." The reason for doing so was

---

34. Ibid., 3.

35. Ibid. A few years ago, Bjørnlund et al. concluded that the Church of Rwanda:
". . .as an institution. . .did not have a clearly defined agenda, mentality, or policy, genocidal or otherwise-other than perhaps becoming (and staying) powerful, and Christianizing the country. . .[I]t remained generally uncontested among Church clergy-from the beginning of colonization to the genocide–that the Church should become and remain powerful, just as the country should become and remain Christian." Bjørnlund et al., "Christian Churches," 159.

36. Carney, *Rwanda before the Genocide*, 4–5. The influence from Linden, *Church and Revolution* is more than obvious.

37. Gourevitch, *We Wish to Inform*, 96; Des Forges et al., *Aucun témoin ne doit survivre*, 103–106.

evident: "[I]f someone is going to die it is because he already has the disease in him!"[38] This call was made during his notorious speech at Kabaya in western Rwanda, on November 22, 1992, at a *MRND* meeting, in front of a crowd drunken with beer, while listening to music, and dancing:

> I am telling you the Gospel has changed in our Movement: if they slap you on one cheek, you will slap them twice on one cheek so that they will crash to the ground and will be gone for good![39]

Mugesera is indeed paraphrasing biblical passages and is beyond doubt applying a unique interpretation of them. He also declared that day, again by heavily paraphrasing the Bible:

> I tell you sincerely as is written in the Scriptures: "If you allow a snake which has come to bite you to hang on to you, then you will be finished."[40]

That was the justification for Mugesera to claim in subsequent statements that the Hutu needed to work for themselves and exterminate "those bastards." The irony in his speech is that a few months before, in March 1992, the Bugesera massacre of Tutsi by soldiers and *interahamwe* had taken place. He even recalled, in front of his audience, having asked a member of the Liberal Party:[41]

> Do you not listen to the news; do you not know how to read? I then told him that he belonged in Ethiopia and that we would

---

38. The English translation was provided to the International Criminal Tribunal for Rwanda in the case of Prosecutor v. Akayesu as Prosecutor's Exhibit 74 (received by the ICTR Criminal Registry on May 11, 1998).

39. Prosecutor v. Akayesu, *Trial Chamber I - Prosecutor's Exhibit 74*, ICTR-96-4-T, 11 May 1998.

40. Ibid. Does Mugesera have in his mind Num. 21:4-9? It is hard to tell since the serpent appears very often in biblical narratives, mostly to symbolize the enemy, evil, Satan's work, or even God's punishment with sometimes apotropaic function. Mugesera's Christian audience was very likely aware of the serpent's clearly negative connotation.

41. *PL* or *Parti liberal*, like other democratic and republican parties, was formed in July 1991 and constituted the official opposition to Habyarimana's monocracy as the result of his party's agreement to separate itself from the state and establish a multi-party democracy. This was done due to the pressure from Western aid donors, together with the abolition of the identity cards. However, the identity cards were not really abolished and nor was the political polyphony ever really tolerated or accepted. This new political situation had, however, a concrete result towards galvanizing an even stronger and more aggressive sense of Hutuness and the feeling of threatening by the Tutsi.

send him there via the Nyabarongo [River] so that he would get there quickly.[42]

Why is this speech important? According to New York-based NGO "Human Rights Watch," his sentiments were frequently repeated on *Radio-Télévision libre des Mille Collines* (henceforth *RTLM*). His speech was tape-recorded and broadcast on national radio. Cassettes of his speech were copied and circulated in the capital Kigali.[43]

Mugesera was not the only one using this kind of language. On April 14, 1994, Dr. Théodore Sindikubwabo, Interim President of the Republic of Rwanda[44] and head of the Hutu-majority party *MRND*—serving as President during almost the entire period of the genocide—delivered a speech that was also broadcast from the national radio. He incited people to "identify and denounce any person with ill intent who wishes to make us plunge back into the abyss, and furthermore" to "provide information to the soldiers and other security forces," and to "continue to carry out night patrols."[45] He promised that gunshots would be replaced by cries of joy at the end and that Rwandans would be happy to have contributed to "the building of Rwanda." He concluded by stating, "God will assist us."[46] Nowhere in his speech did he denounce the mass killings that were taking place by his supporters during his presidency across the country. Does this mean that Sindikubwabo believed that God's assistance would come to Rwandans along the roadblocks, the night patrols, and the denouncing of people to the soldiers and "other security forces"? A few days later, he gave another public speech, which was broadcast on the radio asking people to locate the "killers," "wrongdoers"

---

42. Prosecutor v. Akayesu, *Trial Chamber I - Prosecutor's Exhibit 74*, ICTR-96-4-T, 11 May 1998.

43. Des Forges et al., *Aucun témoin ne doit survivre*, 106; Mitchell, "Cultivating Violence," 80. On *RTLM* see further below.

44. During the genocide, Rwanda was governed by an amorphous not officially recognized interim government-in-exile composed of the Rwandan Armed Forces, extremist militias, and militant members of the former government. That is why this genocide is often seen as an instance of state-sponsored mass murder driven by ideology in a context of revolution and war. For this turbulent period of Rwandan history the bibliography is vast, but the foundational works in chronological order are the following: Braeckman, *Rwanda: Histoire d'un génocide*; Reyntjens, *L'Afrique des grands lacs en crise*; Prunier, *Rwanda Crisis*; Guichaoua, *Les crises politiques*; Braeckman, *Terreur Africaine*; Des Forges et al., *Aucun témoin ne doit survivre*; Semujanga, *Récits fondateurs*; Guichaoua and Dégni-Ségui, *Rwanda, de la guerre au génocide*.

45. Prosecutor v. Bizimungu, Mugenzi, Bicamumpaka and Mugiraneza, *Trial Chamber II - Continued Trial*, ICTR-99-50-T, 22 October 2007, 67.

46. Ibid. See also Des Forges et al., *Aucun témoin ne doit survivre*, 291.

and "criminals...so that they can be given exemplary punishment."[47] His speech ended with the following commands to his people: "Be brave always, we must not allow evil to triumph over good. Stay united always, and pray to God, who will hear our prayers."[48] While his vocabulary of hate is masked behind general terms, God is nevertheless called upon to hear the prayers of a man who, according to an overwhelming number of witnesses, is reported to have visited various prefectures (Butare, Kibuye, etc.) in April and May 1994 in order to congratulate the people for their "work" during which some of the bloodiest episodes in the Rwandan genocide were recorded. So, what exactly do these "prayers" contain? As it was also the case with Euphrasie Kamatamu, already mentioned at the outset of this essay, prayers in real life can be very well combined with actions of the outmost cruelty. Does this also mean that the "good" which is to triumph over the "evil," is represented by the *génocidaires* who were "working" hard during this battle between good and evil? If the answer is yes, then this "battle" is a nice way to mask "genocide."

According to protected witness KK in the trial of Prosecutor v. Jean-Paul Akayesu,[49] the *interahamwe* addressed Tutsi fugitives at the *bureau communal* of Taba, in front of the mayor, announcing that they had uncovered an alleged Tutsi plan to kill the Hutu. However, it is also reported that these *interahamwe* stated that they were going to put the Tutsi where the Tutsi had planned to put the Hutu, since their (*interahamwe*'s) God was never far.[50] The *interahamwe*, who were the bloodiest killers during the 1994 genocide, had their God by their side in trying to avenge a crime the Tutsi were allegedly about to commit. God was aiding the Hutu in the mind of *interahamwe* for their perceived act of self-defense. Protected witness KAB, in the case Prosecutor v. Dominque Ntawukulilyayo,[51] testified that, in a

---

47. Excerpts taken from his speech recorded on cassette AV/919 dated 17 April 1994, and submitted as Exhibit D357(b) in the case Prosecutor v. Nyiramasuhuko et al. (Case no. ICTR-98-42-T, 28 September 2005).

48. Prosecutor v. Nyiramasuhuko et al., *Trial Chamber II - Exhibit D357(b)*, ICTR-98-42-T, 28 September 2005.

49. The accused was the mayor of Taba during the genocide. The *ICTR* sentenced him to life imprisonment affirmed on appeal. This information and similar ones on the fate of the accused persons named in this paper is taken from the official site of the ICTR.

50. Prosecutor v. Akayesu, *Trial Chamber I - Judgement*, ICTR-96-4-T, 2 September 1998, par. 285.

51. The accused was the sub-prefect in Gisagara, a sub-prefecture in Butare district during the genocide in 1994. The *ICTR* sentenced him to 20 years of imprisonment, a sentence affirmed on appeal. He was convicted of being responsible for the death of around 25,000 Tutsi refugees.

gathering he had attended in the trading center of Gikera, south Rwanda, in late May 1994, the president of the Court of First Instance in Butare, named Ruzindaza, held the Bible and said that those who were fighting the enemy with success would be rewarded by God.[52] Similarly, in the case Prosecutor v. Tharcisse Muvunyi[53] the protected witness CCP remembers that the same Ruzindaza prayed asking that God should teach his Hutu audience to kill because the Tutsi grow up knowing how to kill and urged the Hutu people to leave behind no traces seemingly quoting the Bible: "God's words say that everything will be unearthed [Luke 8:17?]."[54] Ruzindaza made no mention of the horrible, mass, and indiscriminate killings; therefore, there was no obstacle in quoting from the Bible, and mentioning God's reward for those Hutu killing their perceived enemy, the Tutsi.

Justin Mugenzi, who was Minister of Trade and Industry in the Interim Government in Rwanda until July 1994 and who was recently acquitted by the *ICTR* on appeal, was accused by a witness in front of the tribunal for intentionally using quotations from the Bible in his speeches in order that his messages could be more easily understood by the Christian Rwandans.[55] During his trial, the prosecutor read passages from his speech from a few months before the official beginning of the 1994 Rwanda genocide, on January 16, 1994 in Kibuye, where Mugenzi attacked his political opposition; political parties which had joined a coalition with the *RPF*. In his cross-examination before the tribunal, Justin Mugenzi was asked about that speech, where he was recorded as having asked to observe one minute of silence in memory of the assassinated president Habyarimana "in order to entrust him to God,"[56] while he also attacked the Liberal Party with the following words:

---

52. Prosecutor v. Ntawukulilyayo, *Trial Chamber III - Judgement and Sentence*, ICTR-05–82-T, 3 August 2010, par. 338.

53. The accused was the commander of the *École des sous-officiers* (henceforth *ESO*) in Butare during the genocide, who was sentenced to 15 years imprisonment, a sentence affirmed on appeal. The Prosecution alleged that Tharcisse Muvunyi, in the company of other local authority figures, went to various communes all over Butare prefecture to incite the local population to perpetrate massacres against the Tutsi. Muvunyi was accused of having participated directly in the provision of weapons, such as grenades, to the militiamen and ordered all the *ESO* officer corps to carry out massacres.

54. Prosecutor v. Muvunyi, *Trial Chamber II - Prosecutor's Closing Brief*, ICTR-2000–55A-T, 15 June 2006, par. 1094, 1252; Prosecutor v. Muvunyi, *Trial Chamber II - Final Brief*, ICTR-2000–55A-T, 15 June 2006, 67.

55. Prosecutor v. Bizimungu, Mugenzi, Bicamumpaka and Mugiraneza, *Trial Chamber II - Continued Trial*, ICTR-99–50-T, 19 April 2006, 35–36.

56. Prosecutor v. Bizimungu, Mugenzi, Bicamumpaka and Mugiraneza, *Trial Chamber II - Continued Trial*, ICTR-99–50-T, 22 November 2005, 16–17.

Let it be understood once again; let it be clearly understood as it is said in the Bible, 'Woe betide them, woe unto them, woe unto them.' Woe unto who? Woe unto them, woe unto them, those who dare to ignore the interests of the people, to ignore the interests of which Rwandans have fought so hard for and they want to reduce that to nothingness, in order to please the *Inkotanyi*.[57] Woe unto them.[58]

During the cross-examination by the prosecutor, Mugenzi admitted, "I used the Bible citation which in our context, the Bible was well known to Rwandans."[59] Under the pressure of the prosecutor he further explained, ". . .it was a way of expressing my unhappiness with the behavior of certain leaders, who instead of thinking of the interests of the population were thinking rather to please the *Inkotanyi*, this is clear."[60] In addition, when the prosecutor asked Mugenzi to provide an example of how that expression was used in the Bible, Mugenzi's reply was the following:

> I remember there is[sic] a series of citations where the prophet Isaiah gives warning to the Israeli people, telling them those who were mismanaging the. . .their duties, different people, telling them that if they don't come back to God, they will face problems. They will face misfortunes.[61]

Even in a case where the accused was acquitted, the cross-examination process revealed that Mugenzi tried to entice his audience to have a negative disposition towards *Inkotanyi* sympathizers in general and all those

---

57. *Inkotanyi* means "invisible" and refers to the Tutsi soldiers who were living in exile in Uganda and formed the army, which opposed the Habyarimana regime, later to be called the *RPF*. This term also describes the accomplices and the sympathizers of *RPF*. It ended up including all Tutsi and those opposed to Habyarimana regime. To understand the negative connotation of this pre-colonial warrior term, we should keep in mind that during the major period of anti–Tutsi polemic (1990–1994) that led to the genocide of 1994, the *RPF* had conducted two major attacks deep into Rwandan soil: one in October 1990 and one in February 1993. *RPF* troops were even installed in Kigali before the end of 1993 out of international pressure towards Habyarimana's regime for a transitional government of power sharing with *RPF*, and they were still there when the airplane of president Habyarimana was shot down. At the same time the political party of Habyarimana was arming and training its youth wing, the *interahamwe* who were growing stronger, with the result of increased number of political assassinations in Rwanda from both camps (the Hutu extremist camp and the opposition camp).

58. Prosecutor v. Bizimungu, Mugenzi, Bicamumpaka and Mugiraneza, *Trial Chamber II - Continued Trial*, ICTR-99-50-T, 22 November 2005, 72.

59. Ibid., 74.

60. Ibid.

61. Ibid., 76.

persons named in his speech, threatened with biblical misfortunes. Indeed, Ndasingwa, Nzamurambaho, and Ngurinzira (all mentioned in his speech) were assassinated on April 7, 1994. They faced the single most important accusation, namely that they were supporters of the *Inkotanyi* or that they themselves were *Inkotanyi*. A vast number of victims during the genocide were also facing the same accusation by all those hunting them down, tracking them, and massacring them in large numbers with the cruelest way. Therefore, on the one hand we have the supporters of Habyarimana, who were entrusted to God through their prayers, showing divine favor to their cause, and on the other hand the *Inkotanyi* and their supporters upon whom biblical woes were about to befall, citing the Bible because "the Bible was well known to Rwandans."

Within this context, *Kangura*, the leading newspaper for disseminating racist hatred against the Tutsis, published in December 1990 the notorious "Hutu Ten Commandments."[62] These Commandments—obviously named after the Ten Commandments from the Bible (Exod 20:1–17; Deut 5:4–21)—were rules on what a Hutu must do, and defined a Hutu traitor. For example, the Hutu must stand firm and vigilant against their common enemy, the Tutsi, and they must spread the Hutu ideology wherever they go. Similarly, any Hutu is a traitor when he acquires a Tutsi wife or concubine, a secretary or a protégée, forms a business alliance with a Tutsi, invests his own funds or public funds in a Tutsi enterprise, borrows money from or loans money to a Tusti, or grants favors to Tutsis. Furthermore, the "Hutu Ten Commandments" dictate that strategic positions such as politics, administration, economics, the military, and security must be restricted to the Hutu, the educational system (pupils, scholars, and teachers) must be dominated by the Hutu in majority, and the Rwandan army must be exclusively Hutu. The biblical Ten Commandments contain the ethical obligations of ancient Israelites within their own peculiar worldview. Similarly, the "Hutu Ten Commandments" are the Hutu version of the ethical obligation of Hutu Rwandans within their own worldview, divided between Hutus and Tutsis. But, the use of the title "Ten Commandments" is not coincidental. The Hutu authors of these commandments were presenting their own biblical version of a legal code for an ordered and exclusively Hutu society.

We can better understand the "Hutu Ten Commandments" by looking at the first version, as they appeared on September 27, 1959 in Ngoma, in southeastern Rwanda, at a meeting of the *APROSOMA*. Some of these were simpler and more straightforward, reminiscent of the biblical Ten

---

62. They were originally published in French on *Kangura* newspaper issue no. 6. For an English translation see McCullum, *The Angels*, appendix 2; Des Forges et al., *Aucun témoin ne doit survivre*, 89.

Commandments, but purposefully modified to target the Tutsi. They are as follows: "Do not trust anyone, but count only on God and on yourself;" "Never trust or count on a Tutsi;" "Never commit adultery with Tutsi women or girls;" "Never tell lie like a Tutsi;" and "Do not steal like a Tutsi." However, their message was not less gruesome: "his [e.g. Tutsi's] greed is the scourge which exterminate us," or "If you were avenging the evil he did to you, no Tutsi would survive in Rwanda."[63]

It comes as no surprise that the "The Hutu Ten Commandments" were published in a newspaper which served as an important political tool in a country where a large portion of the population was literate and where newspapers were circulated widely.[64] In January 1992, *Kangura* also published a prayer where the concept of unity between the three ethnic groups of Rwanda (i.e. the Hutu, Tutsi, and Twa populations) was contested. In the prayer, the supposed unity was referred to as a detested unity, which cannot be applied on earth, unlike the Holy Trinity in the heavens.[65] This is an example similar to the speech of Mugesera at the end of the same year, as mentioned above, where the Hutu politician had openly explained that the message of the gospels had been changed in the Hutu Movement. Therefore, the Rwandan situation in 1992 could no longer reflect the Holy Trinity. The idea of Rwandan "Trinity" on earth needed to change in order to legitimize the extermination of one of its constituents, the Tutsi population. By evoking the divine model of the Holy Trinity as an example that cannot be applied to mundane Rwanda, this left room for interpreting its collapse (i.e. the extermination of its Tutsi population) as something which did not go against any Christian cosmic model (i.e. Trinity on earth = three populations in Rwanda).

A couple of months before, in November 1991, *Kangura* had also published an image of Grégoire Kayibanda, leader of the Hutu revolution and first President of Rwanda, next to a machete on its front page along with the

---

63. Prosecutor v. Bikindi, *Interoffice Memorandum*, ICTR-KT2-2001-72-T, 17 August 2006, Annex III.

64. Des Forges et al., *Aucun témoin ne doit survivre*, 83–87. The most important work on the role of the media in the 1994 Rwanda genocide remains Chrétien et al., *Les medias*, where a short chapter entitled "Mobilization de la religion" was very useful for the present essay (Chrétien et al., *Les medias*, 324–330). According to Chrétien et al, *Les medias*, the magazine *Kangura* was closely controlled by a small circle of the closest supporters and beneficiaries of the Habyarimana regime, and after October 1990, when RPF started the attacks against Rwanda from neighbouring Uganda, became all the more aggressive, with a public voice of hate that drove an even sharper line between Hutu and Tutsi (Chrétien et al., *Les medias*, 24–28, 33–36, 38–42).

65. Cited in Chrétien et al., *Les medias*, 325. The article was entitled "L'unité de la sainte-Trinité ne convient pas sur terre."

sarcastic slogan: "The Tutsi are God's nation" in the Kinyarwanda language ("Batutsi bwoko bw'imana")

The main question of the cover page was as follows: "What Weapons Shall We Use to Conquer the Cockroaches Once and for All?"[66] The answer expected to this rhetorical question, and with the hindsight of history and years of scholarly research, can very well be "genocide," "extermination," "ethnic cleansing," "hate propaganda," "machetes," and so forth; however, this paper sets out to expose another supplementary answer: the "weapon"

---

66. Chrétien et al., *Les medias*, 114.

of religiously-sanctioned ideology. In yet another cover page, this time in January 1991, the Holy Family is depicted with an image of the Virgin Mary asking the infant Jesus to save the Hutus of Burundi from the massacre, while the standing figure of Joseph simultaneously asks Jesus to mobilize all Hutus of the world to unite.[67]

Another extremist newspaper, *Umurava*, believed to be at the core of the Habyarimana regime, used more direct religious language. In mid-1991 it declared the God-given power of Hutu President Juvénal Habyarimana:

67. Ibid., 373. Jolyon Mitchell in his book on the role of religon and media wrote concerning this particular newspaper cover that "[t]he headline unequivocally enlists God to the Hutu cause" (Mitchell, "Cultivating Violence," 82).

"it is God who has given to Habyarimana the power to govern the country; it is He who will show the way forward."[68] However, the most effective propagandist instrument was the broadcasting of hate speeches on the radio, especially by the notorious government-funded *RTLM* which cried out for Hutu supremacy and disseminated racist messages against Tutsi. This popular Rwandan radio station began broadcasting in August 1993 its radical messages with many of its founding members from the political supporters of President Habyarimana (including members of his cabinet), as well as the vice-president of the *interahamwe*, and many of its journalists from the ranks of extremist political party *CDR*. It is not a coincidence that the New York-based NGO "Human Rights Watch" had recorded the distribution of radios to the people by the local authorities before the official beginnings of the genocide, in a country without a television network. At the same time, more than half of the houses in the cities had their own radio, often subsidized by the ruling party. The ratio in villages was much lower, but radios were also available in public places like restaurants or bars; people could also go to neighboring houses which had a radio.[69]

On April 12, 1994—(five days after the official beginning of the genocide)—*RTLM* speaker Kantano Habimana announced in relation to the alleged *RPF* assassination of the Hutu president Habyarimana:

> The Rwandan God is on our side, he is not far away and I believe he will continue to help us in our misfortune, our serious misfortune which has no parallel in the world. How can a minority, a small group of people assemble bandits to chase the authorities elected by the majority of the population out of power? That has never happened anywhere and I hope such will never happen to the Rwandans. The God of the Rwandans will save us from this. Stay tuned to free R.T.L.M. radio broadcasting from its station in Kigali.[70]

68. See Chrétien et al., *Les medias*, 46: "c'est Dieu qui a donné à Habyarimana le pouvoir de diriger le pays, c'est Lui qui indiquera la marche à suivre." For *Umurava*'s extremist tone, see ibid., 42–44. Among its founding members were the President of Rwanda himself, the director of the Rwandan Intelligence Office (*ORINFOR*), and the Seventh-Day Adventist priest Pascal Simbikangwa (Ibid., 43).

69. Des Forges et al., *Aucun témoin ne doit survivre*, 84–87; Chrétien et al., *Les medias*, 63–74, 80–82, 139–306; Mitchell, "Cultivating Violence," 78–79, 86–92; Chalk, "Hate Radio in Rwanda," 95, 97–99. For a more recent and diverse analysis (e.g. on the effect of its rhetoric of ethnic hatred in rural Rwanda), see the many contributions by specialists like Alison Des Forges, Jean-Pierre Chrétien, Marcel Kabanda, and others in Thompson, *The Media and the Rwanda Genocide*.

70. Prosecutor v. Nahimana, Barayagwiza and Ngeze, *Trial Chamber I - Prosecution Exhibit P103/4B*, ICTR-99-52-T, 2 July 2002.

RTLM never denounced brutal killings against the Tutsis; rather, it professed God's approval ("God is on our side") and aid for Hutu misfortunes ("God...will save us"). What these misfortunes are more specifically is left unexplained. But, from the historical context, we can easily understand that by this they meant the assassination of Habyarimana and the attack of the *RPF* in Rwanda. For Rwandan hardliners, and not just the *RTLM*, Rwanda was at war and not amidst genocide. In other words, the underlying message broadcast was that "the God of the Rwandans" is on their side in the war against the *RPF* and that God will save them from *RPF*'s efforts to take over the power from "the authorities elected by the majority of the population." The genocide—which was never named as such by *RTLM*—already in place by Hutu killers (representing the "majority") against the Tutsi (the "minority"), was presented as something that did not go against the plan of "the God of the Rwandans" in continuing to help the Hutu in these hours of perceived "misfortune." It is equivalent to saying that the "God of the Rwandans" was not going to save the Tutsi; he was not on their side or near them.

Ten days later, on April 22, 1994, Kantano Habimana once again appeals to the God of the Rwandans along the same lines:

> Rwanda's God is never far, is never far; I have a feeling He will continue helping us in this crisis, the terrible crisis we are in, which has never been witnessed anywhere in world history imagine a minority...a small group mobilizing here and there some people, including bandits and all, and coming to take over power from leaders representing the people who make up the majority of the population. This has never happened anywhere and I believe it will not succeed in Rwanda; Rwanda's God will ensure victory against it.[71]

It seems clear that by claiming Rwanda's God to give the victory to the Hutu, the Hutu are elected by their God to rule Rwanda. In the extremist minds, the full-fledged genocide that was taking place in order to eliminate the Tutsi could be seen as part of God's plan to ensure this victory. On an *RTLM* broadcast May 28, 1994, radio speaker Kantano Habimana used the biblical story of Solomon (1 Kgs 3:16–28) to prove that *RPF* did not really care about Rwanda. According to Habimana, since 1959, the exiled Tutsi have been acting like the false mother in the biblical story of the Judgment of Solomon where the king ruled between two women, both claiming to be the mother of a child. *RPF* prefers, much like the false mother, to destroy

---

71. Prosecutor v. Nahimana, Barayagwiza and Ngeze, *Trial Chamber I - Prosecution Exhibit P103/205B*, ICTR-99-52-T, 4 June 2003.

the cities of Rwanda than to hand them over to their real mother/owner: the Hutu population.[72] This broadcast oversees the fact that at that point (end of May 1994) a state-organized, group-perpetrated, and time-efficient killing of fellow Rwandans for their Tutsi origin or for being moderate Hutu had already taken place for the most part, which cannot be easily explained from this peculiar Hutu reading of Solomon's Judgment story. A claim against a perceived enemy (exiled-Tutsi-led *RPF*) is dressed with distorted biblical garment by the extremist-Hutu-run radio in order to justify their genocidal policy of the outmost cruelty which was aimed at eliminating the entire enemy (all Tutsi in Rwanda without exception) before the latter would have been able to carry away their assumed plan of taking Rwanda away from its real owners (the majority Hutu population).

RTLM speaker Valérie Bemeriki even broadcast on June 10, 1994—when most of the horrendous massacres of thousands of Tutsi, especially inside Christian Churches, had already taken place—that the Pope of Rome had declared that "Rwanda was a country of martyrs."[73] During that broadcast, the *RTLM* speaker made sure to name only the three Hutu bishops ("God's chosen people") that had been killed by *RPF*. In other words, any Hutu priest, chosen by God, who was killed by the *RPF*, was a martyr. However, the larger number of Tutsi priests and pastors massacred in the genocide were presented as being left outside the Pope's worries. *RTLM* was trying to convince its audience that the death of a Hutu was clearly not the same as the death of a Tutsi.

On June 13, 1994, *RTLM* speaker Kantano Habimana proclaimed that the final victory of the Hutu was the end destination of the history of Rwanda. He declared that:

> . . .MRND has given [i.e. offered] its supreme militant, as God has offered his son Jesus who died on the cross for the salvation of all sinners, all humans. The Major-General [i.e. Juvenal Habyarimana] died on the 6th of April at 20:30 in the evening, and his blood has saved all Rwandans who were condemned to death and to be killed by the *Inkotanyi* after this operation to seize power. So the MRND accepted to sacrifice this man who was a prominent militant of the MRND, in order that his blood may save a large number of Rwandans who were to perish with the seizure of power by the *Inkotanyi*.[74]

72. As cited in Chrétien et al., *Les medias*, 325–326.

73. Prosecutor v. Nahimana, Barayagwiza and Ngeze, *Trial Chamber I - Prosecution Exhibit P103/84B*, ICTR-99-52-T, 4 June 2003.

74. For the French text, see Agostini, *La pensée politique*, 108: "le MRND a donné son militant suprême, comme Dieu a donné en offrande son fils Jésus qui est mort sur

Perhaps what strikes modern audiences the most is this ability of the Hutu propaganda machine to completely ignore the killings taking place during the genocide and to present its heroic deceased leader as a "new Jesus" who had shed his blood to save his fellow Rwandans from a failed *coup d'état* by the rebels (the "Inkotanyi"), the illegitimate fighters of *RPF*. If this *coup d'état* were to succeed, "a large number of Rwandans" would have been doomed to perish. Their assassinated Major-General (and President of Rwandan Republic at that time), like God's son, saved them with the blood he shed in his airplane crash, like Jesus's blood on the cross. The interesting thing is that it is the Hutu-party *MRND* that offered its "new Jesus" to save Rwanda and that the enemy, whose plans were to seize power and kill "all Rwandans" or "a large number of Rwandans," is the Tutsi-led *RPF*. Salvation, therefore, is seen through the dichotomy of Hutu and Tutsi (despite the fact that the use of the word "Rwandans" tries to disguise this nuance). In other words, all those Rwandans, "condemned to death and to be killed by the *Inkotanyi*," must be the Hutu, but their own Hutu savior rescued them. These *RTLM* broadcasts were in perfect alliance with the Interim President Sindikubwabo, who reassured his audience via his speeches that God would help them fight their enemy. On July 2, 1994, at a time when the so-called "1994 Rwanda genocide" had claimed almost all of its victims, *RTLM* announced:

> Let us sing: "Come, let us rejoice: the *Inkotanyi* have been exterminated! Come dear friends, let us rejoice, the Good Lord is just!"
> The Good Lord really is just, these evildoers, these terrorists, these people with suicidal tendencies will end up being exterminated. When I remember the number of corpses that I saw lying around in Nyamirambo yesterday alone..."[75]

The bodies that the *RTLM* speaker has seen were almost certainly unarmed, innocent massacred Tutsi, and perhaps some *RPF* soldiers. However, if the *RTLM* joyfully claims that the good Lord is just, this means that this God is in full accordance with the extermination of the Tutsi population as an action divinely sanctioned.

---

la croix pour le salut de tous les pécheurs, de tous les hommes. Le général–major est mort le 6 avril, à 20h30 du soir, et son sang a sauvé tous les Rwandais qui étaient voués à la mort et qui devaient être tués par les inkotanyi après cette opération de prise de pouvoir. Cet homme donc qui était un éminent militant du MRND, le MRND a accepté de le sacrifier pour que son sang sauve un grand nombre de Rwandais qui devaient périr avec la prise du pouvoir par les inkotanyi."

75. Prosecutor v. Nahimana, Barayagwiza and Ngeze, *Trial Chamber I - Prosecution Exhibit P103/40D*, ICTR-99-52-T, 1 July 2002.

The victorious tone of the extermination of Tutsi with direct religious overtones was also manifested in the popular Catholic cult of the Virgin Mary at Kibeho, a hill near the center of Rwanda, which became famous for a series of miraculous apparitions of the Virgin Mary during the 1980s. Local visionaries attracted many followers and pilgrims since the first such vision in April 1982. It attracted the attention of the Bishop of Kigali, Monsignor Vincent Nsengiyumva, member of the central committee of the Hutu extremist party *MRND*, and Madame Agathe Habyarimana, wife of President Habyarima. The connection between the presidential family and the cult of the Virgin Mary at Kibeho was so strong that some called it "Our Lady of the Second Republic."[76] The apparitions were covered at length by the national radio and the government-controlled daily newspaper *Imwaho* published articles about these apparitions. Some of these visionaries were reporting that Rwanda would soon be bathed in blood. This corroborates with a document found in President Habyarimana's house concerning the prophecy of a Catholic visionary, known as Little Pebbles, who had predicted in 1987 that Jesus Christ would return on earth on Easter Sunday 1992 following a series of great catastrophes. A member of the commission on Kibeho, Bishop of Gikongoro, Monsignor Augustin Misago, had revealed to journalist Philip Gourevitch that there were visions of the Virgin Mary crying for the people killing with machetes, and for the hills which were covered with corpses.[77] The last apparition of the Virgin Mary at Kibeho was recorded on May 15, 1994, in the midst of the genocide, by the visionary Valentine Nyiramukiza. The event was reported by witnesses and broadcast by *RTLM*, according to which the Virgin Mary was reassuring that President Habyarimana was with her in heaven. Her words, according to the investigation of Gourevitch, "were widely interpreted as an expression of divine support for the genocide."[78] Indeed, *RTLM* broadcast that the Virgin

---

76. Juvénal Habyarimana had inaugurated the Second Republic after his successful seizure of power on July 5, 1973, against President Grégoire Kayibanda (who had inaugurated the First Republic), leading a totalitarian regime and ousting Kayibanda's ruling *PARMEHUTU* party.

77. Gourevitch, *We Wish to Inform*, 79, 137. Augustin Misago is often described as a Hutu power sympathizer who refused refuge to Tutsis, criticized moderate Hutus for helping the "cockroaches," and informed a Vatican emissary in Rwanda that the Rwandan people did not want Tutsi priests anymore. See also Saur, "From Kibeho to Medjugorje," 211–215, where he provides comparative material for various Marian apparitions, including those of the Virgin Mary at Kibeho, and how they have been used by totalitarian regimes for their own end at various periods in time (e.g. in Portugal, in Croatia, and in Rwanda). For more details, especially on earlier apparitions, see Getrey, *Kibeho*.

78. Gourevitch, *We Wish to Inform*, 137; Saur, "From Kibeho to Medjugorje," 215.

Mary was appearing from time to time at the Kibeho church declaring, "we will have the victory."[79]

Moving to witness accounts of Tutsi, who managed to escape the genocide or of Hutu *génocidaire*, more or less a similar picture emerges. A Tutsi woman named Théophile Zigirumugabe, who was interviewed in Kigali on June 29, 1995, by the London-based NGO "African Rights," and who survived the massacres at Kibeho, remembers an incident implicating female college students. One student of economics and two of biochemistry annoyed by the cries of a baby Tutsi which was saved a few days earlier from the notorious killings at the Kibeho church and brought to the girls' dormitory of the nearby College, had made sure that the baby was slaughtered and thrown into the toilet, while they were dancing around and saying that "God had sent all the Tutsis to their deaths."[80] "You must be eliminated. God no longer wants you" is the answer that Tutsi refugees received by the district president of the Seventh-Day Adventist Church in Mungonero when Tutsi pastors wrote to inform him that they were about to be killed. He refused to intervene for their rescue and, as a result, almost two thousand Tutsis were slaughtered on April 16, 1994.[81]

Convicted Hutu *génocidaire* Élie reveals a very interesting aspect of the power of Hutu-run and government-sponsored radio stations in general:

> On Sunday mornings the radio programs no longer broadcast masses as before. But encouraging hearsay came from well-known monsignors who arrived from Kingali. Sometimes we heard hymns and services on the radio. Those were tapes without sermons, but the religious music soothed people who felt uneasy. It reminded them of ordinary Sundays – it did them some good.[82]

---

79. Chrétien et al., *Les medias*, 327–330.

80. African Rights, *Rwanda, not so Innocent*, 69. This collection of accounts is remarkably original since it attempts to expose the role of women *génocidaire* during the 1994 Rwanda genocide, an issue as neglected as the systematic, genocidal rape cases against women Tutsi.

81. Gourevitch, *We Wish to Inform*, 25–30, 42; Prosecutor v. Elizaphan and Gerard Ntakirutimana, *Trial Chamber I - Judgement and Sentence*, ICTR-96-10-T and ICTR-96-17-T, 21 February 2003, par. 487.

82. Hatzfeld, *A Time for Machetes*, 137. This is one of the rare and certainly most controversial books, which contains testimonial texts from the killers. Some scholars have praised it, while others have attacked it. Among the former are Worms, "Les individus témoins," and Mouchard, "Absence et retour du tiers." To the latter belongs Hron, "Gukora and Itsembatsemba." Very interesting critical accounts can also be found in Kuhn-Kennedy, "À voix haute ou silencieuse," and Spiessens, "Le génocidaire parle." No doubt, this collection of testimonies is extremely valuable for historians.

Evidently, the hymns and services were not only reminding people of ordinary Sundays with broadcast masses as before, but also making them feel that God is with them or "not far", as it is recorded also in the evidence already quoted in this essay. Of course, that means that at that point God was not with the Tutsi. This is what Adalbert, a former *interahamwe* boss in Kibungo, felt when after the crash of president Habyarimana's plane, the Tutsi who were normally participating with Hutu in Sunday mass singing hymns in the choir did not show up at the appointed hour for mass:

> They had already fled into the bush in fear of reprisals, driving their goats and cows before them. That disappointed us greatly, especially on a Sunday. Anger hustled outside the church door. We left the Lord and our prayers inside to rush home. We changed from our Sunday best into our workaday clothes, we grabbed clubs and machetes, we went straight off to killing.[83]

About the Tutsi, who were hidden in the papyrus waiting to be massacred by the machetes of the Hutu killers while still praying and psalming, Élie recounts, how he and other killers were laughing "at their *Amens,*" joking about the paradise awaiting Tutsi.[84] He believes that God has turned his back on the Hutu killings and asks:

> Did He watch what was happening in the marshes? Why did He not stab our murderous eyes with His wrath? Or show some small sign of disapproval to save more lucky ones? In those horrible moments, who could hear His silence? We were abandoned by all words of rebuke.[85]

This clearly indicates that in the mind of this *génocidaire* the lack of rebuke (ecclesiastical or political) was a sign that the genocidal actions could be interpreted as enjoying God's approval. Here, we see the results of the Hutu propaganda disseminated before and during the genocide.

Similarly, Joseph-Désiré, a former teacher, waiting in prison for his capital punishment for crimes he had committed during the genocide, explains: "I did not choose this, it was God."[86] From his perspective, it is "God alone who can see it, watch over it, and guide it."[87] For him God "is the only one who could stop a genocide."[88] This is a very dangerous logic into which

---

83. Hatzfeld, *A Time for Machetes*, 132.
84. Ibid., 135.
85. Ibid., 137.
86. Ibid., 136.
87. Ibid.
88. Ibid.

young Hutu killers were purposefully left to fall; had God not wanted the genocide, he would have certainly stopped it. In other words, a genocide unfolding under his assumingly all-seeing capability, without hindrance, leaves *génocidaire* Hutu believers room for only one explanation: God's approval. Another Hutu convicted *génocidaire* Léopold makes a stunning revelation:

> We no longer considered the Tutsis as humans or even as creatures of God. We had stopped seeing the world as it is, I mean as an expression of God's will. That is why it was easy for us to wipe them out.[89]

According to Léopold, there was no problem for the killers to pray for themselves or for their crimes "to be a bit forgotten, or to get just a little forgiveness" and then to return to the marshes in the morning.[90] Following his logic, Tutsi were not God's creatures; therefore, God would not care less for them. They were beyond God's creation plans; therefore God would not intervene to save them. Even if the world was not seen any more as "an expression of God's will," for Leopold, his actions in no way were *against* God's will.

Emmanuel Murangira—a thirty-six year old at the time of the genocide who lost forty-three members of his family, in addition to all five of his children and his wife—recounts that after a meeting between the sector councilors and the *bourgmestre* in the commune of Nyamagabe, the Hutu officials went to the market of Nyarusiza to tell the Hutu population: "Go and destroy the houses of the Tutsis! Kill them! God has abandoned them!"[91] He remembers the time when he was staying outside in the open air in front of the church of Gikongoro, specifically on April 11, 1994, during the first attack of the Hutu killers blowing their whistles and chanting: "The God of Tutsis is no longer around," and "There is only the God of

89. Ibid.
90. Ibid.
91. Totten and Ubaldo, *We Cannot Forget*, 81. The remarkable aspect of this book is that it contains in-depth interviews with a wide range of survivors of the 1994 Rwanda genocide from different parts of the country, with detailed stories from before, during, and after the genocide, unlike previously accessible books with short interviews or experts interviewed (See Totten and Ubaldo, *We Cannot Forget*, 8–13). Key issues that emerge from this collection of accounts, according to the editors, are the discrimination against Tutsi, an ever-increasing violence prior to 1994, the current government's efforts to meet survivors' needs, the loneliness of survivors, an ongoing psychological suffering, a heavy burden for widows, children, and orphans, an ongoing fear for their lives, the international community's response, and so on. The editors, however, did not see the need of a specific focus on religion. (See Totten and Ubaldo, *We Cannot Forget*, 13–21).

Hutus remaining."[92] Emmanuel Muhinda, another Tutsi survivor, who was nine years old at the time of the genocide and who lost nine family members, recalls from the notorious massacre in the Ntarama church hearing the attackers singing continuously during the manslaughter, singing to God with Christian songs.[93] These examples reveal the general climate amongst Hutu killers; their actions were not against their religious beliefs since songs dedicated to their God could accompany them. There was this idea that God was on their side, while their enemy was deprived of God's protection. Paraphrasing Timothy Longman, Hutu killers were acting with this mindset (where they slaughtered and at the same time sang and praised their God), because the nature of Christianity in Rwanda was "a politicized, conservative, discriminatory faith."[94]

Overall, in a country such as Rwanda, where Christianity is the predominant religion, there is a strong feeling that we are often dealing with two different gods: the god of Hutus and the god of Tutsis. In his trial, Alphonse Nteziryayo, *préfet* of Butare in southern Rwanda who served in this position from June 1994 until he fled the country in July 1994, was accused of urging the Hutu population to kill Tutsi (even their young children) during a meeting on May 24, 1994. He is reported to have claimed that those Tutsi women who were legally married to a Hutu prior to the "war" (a not so uncommon way of referring to the genocide by participants) had to be spared, adding that they were praying to the Hutu god and not to the Tutsi god.[95] That people saw or believed in two distinct gods in Rwanda during the genocide, one for Hutu and one for Tutsi, can also be seen in a testimony of Tutsi women, victims of rape by soldiers, who reported what the perpetrators said to them:

> The God of the Tutsis has abandoned or forsaken you. I don't know how you are still alive and what are you doing here. You Tutsi women are not dying like the men because you have something to offer men.[96]

---

92. Ibid., 85.
93. Ibid., 119.
94. Longman, *Christianity and Genocide*, 197.
95. Prosecutor v. Nyiramasuhuko, Ntahobali, Nsabimana, Nteziryayo, Kanyabashi and Ndayambaje, *Trial Chamber II - Continued Trial*, ICTR-98-42-T, 8 March 2007, 48; Prosecutor v. Nyiramasuhuko, Ntahobali, Nsabimana, Nteziryayo, Kanyabashi and Ndayambaje, *Trial Chamber II - Judgement and Sentence*, ICTR-98-42-T, 24 June 2011, par. 3587.
96. Bizimungu v. Prosecutor, *Appeals Chamber - Prosecution's Additional Submissions*, ICTR-00-56B-A, 7 March 2014, par. 58. This testimony was heard at the case of Augustin Bizimungu, general in the *Rwandan Armed Forces* who briefly served as

Similarly, protected witness FAX testified on the trial Persecutor v. Idelphonse Nizeyimana,[97] that the soldiers were very young and "very, very severe, very, very harsh, insulting people, telling us that even God had cursed Tutsis."[98]

Scarce Resources in Rwanda during the 1994 Genocide

In the report of London-based NGO "African Rights" published as early as May 1994, entitled *Rwanda: Who Is Killing; Who is Dying; What Is to Be Done*, there is a small chapter called "Competition for Scarce Resources," which states:

> One of the issues most successfully manipulated by Hutu extremists was the issue of land. The extremists told peasants that the RPF was coming back to take their land, using this issue to generate fear and hostility. At the same time they also promised the land occupied by Tutsis in order to provide incentives for killing Tutsis.[99]

What if we apply this approach to religious promises? What will be the effect upon Hutu people listening that "God of the Rwandans is with us," or that "God is not far," or that "God has abandoned Tutsi"? What God thinks and believes in terms of the Hutu-Tutsi dichotomy and antagonism is completely "created" as a non-empirical scarce resource, privileging only one of the two groups which accords itself the right to exclusively interpret God's will. There is no way that any Tutsi or Hutu can disprove that this "non-verifiable religious good" was ever attributed by God to Hutu and that Hutu are self-deceived or manipulated. With no empirical grounding for claims such as "God will assist us," "God will hear our prayers," "God is by our side," "God guides us," or "God watches over us," Christianity in the mouths and minds of lay Rwandan Christians creates a powerful type of scarce resource which can be so powerful that it turns an action of outmost cruelty and the almost unimaginable savagery any human being can

---

chief of staff of the army during the genocide, and was accused of training soldiers and militiamen who carried out the genocide. He was sentenced to thirty years in prison by the *ICTR* affirmed on appeal.

97. The accused was second-in-command and in charge of the intelligence and military operations during the genocide. He was convicted by the *ICTR* for 35 years imprisonment affirmed on appeal.

98. Prosecutor v. Nizeyimana, *Trials Chamber III - Prosecution's Closing Brief*, ICTR-00-55C-T, 9 November 2011, par. 212.

99. Omaar and de Waal, *Who Is Killing*, 27-28.

commit into an acceptable action, not to say a God-sanctioned action. We have even seen, throughout this essay, how God was perceived as promising the victory to the *génocidaire*. Their life is supposed to be guided by the "Hutu Ten Commandments."

No matter how abominable these claims made by Hutu killers may be, it leads to an approach that appeared in the bibliography of the study of religions in 2005, presented for the first time by Hector Avalos in his book *Fighting Words*. Avalos argues that not only monotheistic religions, but religions in general, create scarce resources: ". . .most violence is due to scarce resources, real or perceived. Whenever people perceive that there is not enough of something they value, conflict may ensue to maintain or acquire that resource."[100] In his understanding of this issue, Avalos includes conflicts of domestic, group, national, international, and global scale over subterranean, terracentric, astrocentric, as well as transcendent resources.[101] Religions produce transcendent resources, which, according to Avalos, unlike many non-religious resources, are "wholly manufactured by, or reliant on, unverifiable premises."[102] To prove his theory, Avalos used examples where religious motives were used to "incite or maintain violence."[103] I believe that the cases brought up in this essay refer to the use of religious motives with exactly this goal.

Avalos argues that scarcity, which is an important factor of violence, is a major component of religion.[104] We can talk about scarcity in the cases brought up in this paper because none of the people who employed Christian vocabulary during the 1994 Rwanda genocide made the approval of God for their actions immediately available to all Rwandans. In other words, the killers thought they were under God's favor, while God abandoned their victims. Sometimes, they went so far as to claim that their enemies had a different God (although their enemies claimed to be Christians just like their killers) and that this God had abandoned them during the genocide. Mass killings were often aimed at depriving Tutsi victims from feeling that they had access to God's approval to survive, or to God's promise of liberation.

Since Hector Avalos's goal was to explain how religions can sometimes generate violence, the examples provided in this paper come from a specific historical event (genocide can never be a "case study"[105]) that is the cul-

---

100. Avalos, *Fighting Words*, 18.
101. Ibid., 96–99.
102. Ibid., 18.
103. Ibid., 23.
104. Ibid., 93.
105. The heroic Philippe Gaillard, head of the International Committee of the Red

mination of whatever humans perceive as violent: psychological, mental, sexual, verbal, and physical violence at the same time, in extreme quantities and monstrous quality, and targeted towards a specific group, perceived as such by genocide perpetrators. Avalos does acknowledge that political and economic factors can also lead to violence,[106] and the 1994 Rwanda genocide admittedly also had strong political and economic factors that turned ordinary men into violent killers.[107] However, I deliberately chose a historical event, which is not transparent in its form of violence. Political, economic, and religious factors created their own scarce resources and blended them together for decades in Rwanda. It is not the place here to discuss how genocide occurs, since it is one of the most complicated phenomena in human history, but one thing is clear: *the 1994 Rwanda genocide was religiously violent*. And not only violent because of the complicity of the Churches, but also because politicians, journalists, church leaders, killers, perpetrators, and even victims manufactured their own transcendent scarce resources made of Christian motifs for good or for ill.

In conclusion, the evidence available for studying the 1994 Rwanda genocide demonstrates that Avalos's theory is in need of some expansion. His arguments are often text-based and overemphasize examples about how people read and interpret their sacred books or how they act according to what they think is the right interpretation of said writings. Text interpretation can make one group feel like they are more privileged than another, but the words and deeds of the actors and participants of the 1994 Rwanda genocide reveal that the ways in which people read and understand sacred writings can be quite irrelevant in certain cases. The use of biblical motifs, as well as religious motifs in general, in the way that a religion is experienced in everyday life, even during a genocide, has much less to do with sacred books and their systematic interpretation than with their vague invocation or with general claims tentatively based on a shared religious background

---

Cross in Rwanda, who did not abandon Rwanda during the genocide and managed to save tens of thousands of lives wrote: "I still have some kind of debt, or rather duty, towards all those who died in Rwanda in 1994, who were given so little attention later that some people think that the Rwandan genocide can be considered as a 'case study.' For those who died, and especially for those who survived, the Rwandan genocide is certainly not, and never will be, a 'case study.'" See Gaillard, "Memory Never Forgets Miracles," 111.

106. Avalos, *Fighting Words*, 21.

107. Two important works can be outlined here for their significant field-work and outstanding quality of research: that of Scott Strauss (Strauss, *The Order of Genocide*) and that of Lee Ann Fujii (Fujii, *Killing Neighbors*). Although both are trying to answer the thorny question concerning why ordinary people committed genocide in Rwanda, none of them makes any single mention of religious factors.

that people should have in a certain culture at a given time and place. Real people create or choose to sustain a religion within their specific historical environment and in as much as these real people are to be blamed for violent episodes in the course of their history, whatever ideology they produce, uphold, and follow, including religious beliefs, is to be blamed as well.

Bibliography

African Rights. *Rwanda, not so Innocent: When Women Become Killers.* London: African Rights, 1995.

Agostini, Nicolas. *La pensée politique des génocidaires Hutus.* Paris: L'Harmattan, 2006.

Alston, Philip, and Sara Knuckey, eds. *The Transformation of Human Rights Fact-Finding.* Oxford: Oxford University Press, 2016.

Avalos, Hector. *Fighting Words: The Origins of Religious Violence.* Amherst, New York: Prometheus Books, 2005.

Berry, John A., and Carol Pott Berry, eds. *Genocide in Rwanda: A Collective Memory.* Washington: Howard University Press, 1999.

Bizimana, Jean Damascène. *L'Église et le génocide au Rwanda: Les pères et le négationnisme.* Paris: L'Harmattan, 2001.

Bjørnlund, Matthias, et al. "The Christian Churches and the Construction of a Genocidal Mentality in Rwanda." Pages 141–167 in *Genocide in Rwanda: Complicity of the Churches?* Edited by Carol Rittner, John K. Roth, and Wendy Whitworth. St. Paul: Paragon House, 2004.

Braeckman, Colette. *Rwanda: Histoire d'un génocide.* Paris: Fayard, 1994.

———. *Terreur Africaine: Burundi, Rwanda, Zaïre: Les racines de la violence.* Paris: Fayard, 1996.

Bührer, Michel. *Rwanda: Mémoire d'un génocide.* Paris: Éditions Unesco, 1996.

Burnet, Jennie E. *Genocide Lives in us: Women, Memory, and Silence in Rwanda.* Madison: University of Wisconsin Press, 2012.

Carney, James Jay. *Rwanda before the Genocide: Catholic Politics and Ethnic Discourse in the Late Colonial Era.* Oxford: Oxford University Press, 2014.

Chalk, Frank. "Hate Radio in Rwanda." Pages 93–107 in *Path of a Genocide: The Rwanda Crisis from Uganda to Zaire.* Edited by Howard Adelman and Astri Suhrke. New Brunswick: Transaction, 1999.

Chrétien, Jean-Pierre, et al. *Rwanda: Les médias du génocide.* Paris: Karthala, 1995.

Clark, Phil and Zachary D. Kaufman, eds. *After Genocide: Transitional Justice, Post-Conflict Reconstruction and Reconciliation in Rwanda and Beyond.* New York: Columbia University Press, 2009.

Combs, Nancy Amoury. *Fact-Finding without Facts: The Uncertain Evidentiary Foundations of International Criminal Convictions.* Cambridge: Cambridge University Press, 2010.

de Brouwer, Anne-Marie, and Sandra Ka Hon Chu. *The Men Who Killed Me: Rwandan Survivors of Sexual Violence.* Vancouver: Douglas & McIntyre, 2009.

Des Forges, Alison, et al. *Aucun témoin ne doit survivre: Le génocide au Rwanda.* Human Rights Watch. Fédération internationale des ligues des droit de l'homme. Paris: Karthala, 1999.

Essoungou, André-Michel. *Justice à Arusha: Un tribunal international politiquement encadré face au génocide Rwandais.* Paris: L'Harmattan, 2006.

Fujii, Lee Ann. *Killing Neighbors: Webs of Violence in Rwanda.* Ithaca: Cornell University Press, 2009.

Gaillard, Phillipe. "Memory Never Forgets Miracles." Pages 111–125 in *Genocide in Rwanda: Complicity of the Churches?* Edited by Carol Rittner, John K. Roth, and Wendy Whitworth. St. Paul: Paragon House, 2004.

Getrey, Gérard. *Kibeho ou la face cache de la tragédie Rwandaise.* Paris: F.-X. de Guibert, 1998.

Gourevitch, Philip. *We Wish to Inform you that Tomorrow we will be Killed with our Families: Stories from Rwanda.* New York: Farrar Straus & Giroux, 1998.

Grele, Ronald J. "Oral History as Evidence." Pages 43–101 in *Handbook of Oral History.* Edited by Thomas L. Charlton, Lois E. Myers, and Rebecca Sharpless. Lanham: Altamira, 2006.

Guichaoua, André, ed. *Les crises politiques au Burundi et au Rwanda (1993–1994).* Lille: Université des Sciences et Technologies de Lille, 1995.

Guichaoua, André, and René Dégni-Ségui. *Rwanda, de la guerre au génocide: Les politiques criminelles au Rwanda (1990–1994).* Paris: la Découverte, 2010.

Hatzfeld, Jean. *Life Laid Bare: The Survivors in Rwanda Speak.* Translated by Linda Coverdale. New York: Other Press, 2006.

———. *A Time for Machetes: The Rwanda Genocide: The Killers Speak.* Translated by Linda Coverdale. London: Serpent's Tail, 2008.

Hoyweghen, Saskia. "The Disintegration of the Catholic Church of Rwanda: A Study of the Fragmentation of Political and Religious Authority." *African Affairs* 95 (1996) 379–401.

Hron, Madelaine. "Gukora and Itsembatsemba: The 'Ordinary Killers' in Jean Hatzfeld's Machete Season." *Research in African Literatures* 42:2 (2011) 125–146.

Janzen, John M., and Reinhild Kauenhoven Janzen. *Do I Still Have a Life? Voices from the Aftermath of War in Rwanda and Burundi.* Publications in Anthropology Series 20. Lawrence: University of Kansas, 2000.

Jones, Nicholas A. *The Courts of Genocide: Politics and the Rule of Law in Rwanda and Arusha.* Abingdon: Routledge, 2010.

Kabagema, Edouard. *Carnage d'une nation: Génocide et massacres au Rwanda 1994.* Paris: L'Harmattan, 2002.

Karemano, Charles. *Au-delà des barrières: Dans les méandres du drame Rwandais.* Paris: L'Harmattan, 2003.

Kehrer, Brigitte. *Rwanda: Part de dieu part du diable.* Paris: L'Harmattan, 2002.

Kuhn-Kennedy, Fleur. "À voix haute ou silencieuse: Dans *le nu de la vie* de Jean Hatzfeld et les médiations du témoignage." *Cahiers ERTA* 8 (2015) 89–100.

Linden, Ian. *Church and Revolution in Rwanda.* Manchester: Manchester University Press; New York: Africana Publishing Company, 1977.

Longman, Timothy. *Christianity and Genocide in Rwanda*. African Studies Series. Cambridge: Cambridge University Press, 2010.

———. "Church Politics and the Genocide in Rwanda." *Journal of Religion in Africa* 31:2 (2001) 163–186.

———. "Churches and Social Upheaval in Rwanda and Burundi: Explaining Failures to Oppose Ethnic Violence." Pages 82–101 in *Religion and African Civil Wars*. Edited by Niels Kastfelt. New York: Palgrave Macmillan, 2005.

Longman, Timothy, and Théonèste Rutagengwa. "Religion, Memory, and Violence in Rwanda." Pages 132–149 in *Religion, Violence, Memory, and Place*. Edited by Oren Baruch Stier and J. Shawn Landres. Bloomington: Indiana University Press, 2006.

Lumurerwa, Marie-Aimable. *Comme la langue entre les dents: Fratricide et piège identitaire au Rwanda*. Paris: L'Harmattan, 2000.

Malagardis, Maria, and Pierre-Laurent Sanner. *Rwanda, le jour d'après: Témoignages au lendemain du génocide*. Paris: Somogy, 1995.

Maynes, Mary Jo, Jennifer L. Pierce, and Barbara Laslett. *Telling Stories: The Use of Personal Narratives in the Social Sciences and History*. Ithaca: Cornell University Press, 2008.

McCullum, Hugh. *The Angels have left us: The Rwanda Tragedy and the Churches*. Geneva: WCC Publications, 2004.

Mitchell, Jolyon P. *Promoting Peace, Inciting Violence: The Role of Religion and Media*. Media, Religion, and Culture. London: Routledge, 2012.

Moghalu, Kingsley Chiedu. *Rwanda's Genocide: The Politics of Global Justice*. New York: Palgrave Macmillan, 2005.

Mouchard, Claude. "Absence et retour du tiers." Pages 185–190 in *Rwanda 1994–2004: Des faits, des mots, des œuvres*. Edited by Laure Coret. Paris: L'Harmattan, 2005.

Mujawayo, Esther, and Souâd Belhaddad. *Survivantes: Rwanda, histoire d'un génocide*. La Tour d'Aigues: l'Aube, 2004.

Nolan, Francis. *Les Pères Blancs entre les deux guerres mondiales: Histoire des missionnaires d'Afrique (1919–1939)*. Paris: Karthala, 2015.

Omaar, Rakiya, and Alex de Waal. *Rwanda: Who Is Killing; who is Dying; what is to be Done: A Discussion Paper*. London: African Rights, 1994.

———. *Rwanda: Death, Despair and Defiance*. 2nd edition. London: African Rights, 1995.

Prunier, Gérard. *The Rwanda Crisis: History of a Genocide*. New York: Columbia University Press, 1995.

Reyntjens, Filip. *L'Afrique des grands lacs en crise: Rwanda, Burundi, 1988–1994*. Paris: Karthala, 1994.

Saur, Léon D. "From Kibeho to Medjugorje: The Catholic Church and Ethno-Nationalist Movements and Regimes." Pages 211–227 in *Genocide in Rwanda: Complicity of the Churches?* Edited by Carol Rittner, John K. Roth, and Wendy Whitworth. St. Paul: Paragon House, 2004.

Semujanga, Josias. *Récits fondateurs du drame Rwandais: Discours social, idéologies et stéréotypes.* Paris: L'Harmattan, 2000.

Semujanga, Josias, et al. *Le Manifeste des Bahutu et la diffusion de l'idéologie de la haine au Rwanda (1957–2007).* Butare: Éditions de l'Université Nationale du Rwanda, 2010.

Shorter, Aylward. *Les Pères Blancs au temps de la conquête coloniale: Histoire des Missionnaires d'Afrique 1892–1914.* Paris: Karthala, 2011.

Spiessens, Anneleen. "Le génocidaire parle: Mise en texte et mise en scène chez Hatzfeld et Gatore." Pages 199–211 in *J'ai tué: Violence guerrière et fiction.* Edited by Déborah Lévy-Bertherat and Pierre Schoentjes. Romanica Gandensia 40. Geneva: Droz, 2010.

Strauss, Scott. *The Order of Genocide: Race, Power, and War in Rwanda.* Ithaca: Cornell University Press, 2006.

———. *Intimate Enemy: Images and Voices of the Rwandan Genocide.* Photographs by Robert Lyons. New York: Zone Books, 2006.

Strizek, Helmut. *Geschenkte Kolonien: Ruanda und Burundi unter deutscher Herrschaft.* Schlaglichter der Kolonialgeschichte 4. Berlin: Links, 2006.

———. *Der Internationale Strafgerichtshof für Ruanda in Arusha/Tansania: Eine politisch-historische Bilanz.* Berliner Studien zur Politik in Afrika 19. New York: Peter Lang, 2015.

Taylor, Christopher C. *Sacrifice as Terror: The Rwandan Genocide of 1994.* Global Issues Series. Oxford: Berg, 1999.

Taylor, Lisa, Umwali Sollange, and Marie-Jolie Rwigema. "The Ethics of Learning from Rwandan Survivor Communities." Pages 88–118 in *Beyond Testimony and Trauma: Oral History in the Aftermath of Mass Violence.* Edited by Steven High. Vancouver: University of British Columbia Press, 2015.

Theunis, Guy. "Le rôle de l'église catholique dans les évènements récents." Pages 289–298 in *Les crises politiques au Burundi et au Rwanda (1993–1994): Analyses, faits et documents.* Edited by André Guichaoua. Villeneuve d'Ascq: Université des Sciences et Technologies de Lille, 1995.

Thompson, Allan, ed. *The Media and the Rwanda Genocide.* Ottawa: International Development Research Centre, 2007.

Totten, Samuel, and Rifiki Ubaldo, eds. *We Cannot Forget: Interviews with Survivors of the 1994 Genocide in Rwanda.* New Brunswick, New Jersey: Rutgers University Press, 2011.

Ugirashebuja, Octave. "The Church and the Genocide in Rwanda." Pages 49–63 in *Genocide in Rwanda: Complicity of the Churches?* Edited by Carol Rittner, John K. Roth, and Wendy Whitworth. St. Paul: Paragon House, 2004.

Williams, Paul D. *War and Conflict in Africa.* Cambridge: Polity, 2011.

Wilson, Richard Ashby. *Writing History in International Criminal Trials.* New York: Cambridge University Press, 2011.

Worms, Frédéric. "Les individus témoins." Pages 177–184 in *Rwanda 1994–2004: Des faits, des mots, des œuvres.* Edited by Laure Coret. Paris: L'Harmattan, 2005.

Case Documents

Bizimungu v. Prosecutor, *Appeals Chamber - Prosecution's Additional Submissions*, ICTR-00-56B-A, 7 March 2014.

Prosecutor v. Akayesu, *Trial Chamber I - Prosecutor's Exhibit 74*, ICTR-96-4-T, 11 May 1998.

Prosecutor v. Akayesu, *Trial Chamber I - Judgement*, ICTR-96-4-T, 2 September 1998.

Prosecutor v. Bikindi, *Interoffice Memorandum*, ICTR-KT2-2001-72-T, 17 August 2006, Annex III.

Prosecutor v. Bizimungu, Mugenzi, Bicamumpaka and Mugiraneza, *Trial Chamber II - Continued Trial*, ICTR-99-50-T, 22 November 2005.

Prosecutor v. Bizimungu, Mugenzi, Bicamumpaka and Mugiraneza, *Trial Chamber II - Continued Trial*, ICTR-99-50-T, 19 April 2006.

Prosecutor v. Bizimungu, Mugenzi, Bicamumpaka and Mugiraneza, *Trial Chamber II - Continued Trial*, ICTR-99-50-T, 22 October 2007.

Prosecutor v. Nahimana, Barayagwiza and Ngeze, *Trial Chamber I - Prosecution Exhibit P103/40D*, ICTR-99-52-T, 1 July 2002.

Prosecutor v. Nahimana, Barayagwiza and Ngeze, *Trial Chamber I - Prosecution Exhibit P103/4B*, ICTR-99-52-T, 2 July 2002.

Prosecutor v. Nahimana, Barayagwiza and Ngeze, *Trial Chamber I - Prosecution Exhibit P103/84B*, ICTR-99-52-T, 4 June 2003.

Prosecutor v. Nahimana, Barayagwiza and Ngeze, *Trial Chamber I - Prosecution Exhibit P103/205B*, ICTR-99-52-T, 4 June 2003.

Prosecutor v. Nizeyimana, *Trials Chamber III - Prosecution's Closing Brief*, ICTR-00-55C-T, 9 November 2011.

Prosecutor v. Nyiramasuhuko, Ntahobali, Nsabimana, Nteziryayo, Kanyabashi and Ndayambaje, *Trial Chamber II - Continued Trial*, ICTR-98-42-T, 8 March 2007.

Prosecutor v. Nyiramasuhuko, Ntahobali, Nsabimana, Nteziryayo, Kanyabashi and Ndayambaje, *Trial Chamber II - Judgement and Sentence*, ICTR-98-42-T, 24 June 2011.

Prosecutor v. Elizaphan and Gerard Ntakirutimana, *Trial Chamber I - Judgement and Sentence*, ICTR-96-10-T and ICTR-96-17-T, 21 February 2003

Prosecutor v. Ntawukulilyayo, *Trial Chamber III - Judgement and Sentence*, ICTR-05-82-T, 3 August 2010.

Prosecutor v. Nyiramasuhuko et al., *Trial Chamber II - Exhibit D357(b)*, ICTR-98-42-T, 28 September 2005.

Prosecutor v. Muvunyi, *Trial Chamber II - Prosecutor's Closing Brief*, ICTR-2000-55A-T, 15 June 2006.

Prosecutor v. Muvunyi, *Trial Chamber II - Final Brief*, ICTR-2000-55A-T, 15 June 2006.

5

Discourse of Sacrifice

Religious Studies and Violence against Animals

Marion Achoulias

Hector Avalos's critique of the ideology of the theological establishment in academia creates nothing less than the conditions for new types of knowledge in the study of society's relations with biblical texts. It is the type of knowledge that for Habermas is gained by self-emancipation through reflection and dialogue, indeed a hermeneutic of suspicion, leading to a transformed consciousness or *perspective transformation,* opening up new avenues for positive change.[1] First, we can detect a shift in Avalos himself towards a more inclusive understanding of violence. While the definition of violence in his contribution to *The Blackwell Companion to Religious Violence* (2011) refers to humans exclusively,[2] three years later, a considerable section of his recent work, *The Bad Jesus* (2014), carefully examines Jesus's harsh attitudes towards animals[3] and nature.[4] Indeed, justice-oriented and socially responsible scholarship should take the problematization of violence seriously enough to consider all victims, including those sentient nonhumans capable of suffering. In addition, we might entertain the question: are we, as scholars, unwitting participants in structural violence against other species?[5] This author proposes that the careful application of

---

1. See Habermas, *Theory and Practice,* 253–282. Habermas's work on reason is a good example of bridging two opposing Enlightenment legacies: reason in the service of justice *and* the risk of using reason to "transcend" or even subdue nature or what we today call human animality.
2. Avalos, "Explaining Religious Violence," 145.
3. Avalos, *The Bad Jesus,* 326–343.
4. Ibid., 343–357.
5. Structural violence is defined by David A. Nibert as the, "physical and

Avalos's theory of religious violence to the situation of the animals we eat, wear, and use might bring about a much needed shift in perspective *vis-à-vis* other animals. In the framework of scarcity theory, religious violence is understood as avoidable conflict between competitors over valuables that only exist in the imaginary and is thus inherently unethical.[6] It appears that at least three of the four components on Avalos's list of artificially created resources are denied to all animals, namely divine communication, group privileging, and salvation.[7] Religious violence against animals in its secularized or ideological form is no different in that it is based on the magical idea of human exceptionalism. Most atheists—no different from religionists—deny animals the status of inherent value, due to the idea that only humans have speech or access to what seems to be considered "divine" communication (*logos*), speciesist group privileging, and salvation or transcendence of the body through consciousness or mind. Typically, these resources are considered so valuable and so scarce that they are not only denied to animals. In the context of divine communication, Avalos offers the example of inscripturation as a scarce resource denied broadly to those individuals that cannot read.[8] Those who lack literacy—the quintessential marker of civilization as cultural capital—have historically been considered less than human and closer to brute nature; indeed, as closer to the animal. In general terms, the dynamics of group privileging that Avalos outlines generally involve the *dehumanization* of the other, of all others denied access based on class, race, gender, culture/religion, ability, and so on. Those members of the hegemonic group tend to construct narratives of their own supernaturally (as in unreasonably) favorable status.

Thus, the "humanist machine"[9] of sacrifice, its very structure that arguably continues to shape western civilization to this very day, is oppressive of and cruel to all alterity; in its total denial of our own mortality and animality as embodied and vulnerable beings. Note the self-destructiveness of our religion/ideology of human superiority in the context of the market, which will be outlined below. Just as alarming—even though animals cannot fight back or wage war against humanity—is our obsession with transcending the animal. Such denial of human animality has trapped us in an extremely dangerous spiral of environmental and social self-destruction. Not only

---

psychological harm experienced by humans and other animals that results from societal, economic and political policies and practices." Nibert, *Animal Oppression*, 276.

6. See Avalos, "Religion and Scarcity," 557.
7. Ibid.
8. Ibid., 558.
9. Georgio Agamben coined this term. Agamben, *The Open*, 77.

is human superiority imaginary, but the application of Avalos's theory of religious violence to the case of the subjection of the animal will also show that contemporary speciesist discourse has religious overtones; in its very dismissal of the interests of other animals the human is divinized, his desire for dominating nature is enshrined in every institution of society, and his appetite for meat as a manufactured necessity is construed as sacred.

The appreciation of the point that the global phenomenon of violence against animals cuts through all layers of society and not only the fundamentalist religious faction might lead to a conceptual narrowing of the gap between the religious and the secular. Indeed, the problematization of the industrialized treatment of animals leads us to a reflective critique of hegemonic ideologies, which might beneficially be linked to the multi-layered interactions of biblical discourse, ideas, images, and values with non-biblical ideologies such as economic and cultural forces. In this attempt, I found that the demarcations between the religious and the secular, and the religious versus the secular, are far from clear. Notably, with respect to the animal question, these interactions are highly charged as they affect our everyday economic, social, and moral behavior. With Avalos's critique as starting point, religion scholars can do much to contribute to a better understanding of the religious/ideological aspects of structural violence against animals.

One important method is the study of the Bible as a socio-cultural text that conceals and exposes ideological—and often violent—taxonomies, which structure the ways we perceive and treat animals. If we agree that our deeply disturbed relations with the natural world is in large part shaped by biblical notions, we may trace how these notions have historically interacted with philosophical-scientific discourses, technology, and the science-industry-economy complex of our present world.[10] The biblical text, as ideological material, is thus a system of representation that can be read as a "text" of the power relations of a society's ability to instantiate and empower certain notions of truth. Considering, however, that there exist biblical images and values that can be understood as eco-friendly (e.g., Gen 1:22, 2:15; Prov 12:10; Isa 11:6–9; Hos 2:18–22), it might be important to appreciate the importance of the possible internal changes within religious traditions, such as the introduction and contributions of animal rights theologies. This author, however, focuses on the question as to why the more belligerent passages seem to have had the greater impact on society and human behavior while the benign texts have been widely ignored except in the focused readings of

---

10. See Avalos, *The Bad Jesus*, 378. Avalos points to the biocidal ideologies that the Bible can espouse.

environmental and animal rights activists. The reason appears to lie in the secularized and economic continuation of ancient religious ideas of human supremacy.

The status of animals *vis-à-vis* the human, indeed the valuation of the otherness of animals, is an ancient concern. But today's society seems to be at a turning point due to our historical context of the "unprecedented proportions"[11] of animal manipulation, subjection, and suffering through the rise of concentrated animal feeding operations after World War II. For Derrida, our context involves an awareness of the "alarming rate of acceleration"[12] of the change of relations to other animals; something close to a mutation of our understandings and limits of the human, the animal, life versus death; biology versus technology.[13] These relations have been transformed radically through technology and the practice of industry, by way of "joint developments of zoological, ethological, biological, and genetic forms of knowledge."[14]

Importantly, in keeping with Derrida, "[t]his new situation can be determined only on the basis that is most ancient."[15] Hence, for a better understanding of where we stand in relation to the animal, Derrida invites us, "to move continuously along the coming and going between the oldest and what is coming,"[16] to trace the interrelationships and interactions between old ideas, relations, and behaviors with new technologies, new means, and new manifestations.[17] It seems that the joint efforts of scholars of culture, religion, and history might come to share Derrida's conclusion that, "No one can deny seriously anymore, or for very long, that men do all they can in order to dissimulate this cruelty or to hide it from themselves; in order to organize on a global scale the forgetting or misunderstanding of this violence."[18] Importantly, this dissimulation, denial, and disavowal have given rise to much of our cultural heritage, from the sacrificial altar to the vivisection table. Hence, the problem of violence perpetuated against animals in slaughterhouses, laboratories, and factory farms can, perhaps, be understood as a modern and utterly extreme manifestation of a combination of major material and symbolic factors: biblical human-centrism;

11. See Derrida, *The Animal*, 25; Nibert, *Animal Oppression*, 236.
12. Derrida, *The Animal*, 25.
13. Ibid.
14. Ibid.
15. Ibid., 24.
16. Ibid.
17. Ibid.
18. Ibid., 26.

notions of progress in history (linear time); the taxonomies found in the books of Genesis and Leviticus mixed with other problematic forces of industrialization; the rise of meat consumption; technology and the complex, often hidden, forces of our globalized economy.

Where religious ideology intersects with secular capitalist notions of human desire as "sacrosanct," scholarly analysis of the problem of everyday violence becomes messy. The historical tendency of human "group privileging" against all other species has given rise to the contemporary consequences of speciesist ideology. In other words, the dismissal of non-human interests as perpetuated by carnist hegemony can be defined in the Western context of easy access to sustainable plant-foods as the belief and institution that eating meat is necessary—despite the scientific evidence to the contrary[19]—as well as being both desirable and a symbol of power.[20] Carnism,[21] the principle that certain animals exist to be bred, used, and eaten, is a material practice that structures not only human relations to other animals, but also our economy, infrastructure, and our ecological footprint; a network of relations that we are largely only semi-conscious about. Importantly, this ideology persists even in light of mounting evidence revealing its global violence perpetrated against worker's rights, the climate, the world's hungry and thirsty, and other animals. The manufactured necessity of animal products can be understood as culturally constructed and perpetuated by aggressive lobbying of the meat and dairy industries,[22] leading to the "meatification of diets" globally,[23] contributing to public health threats,[24] climate change,[25] extreme cruelty, and desensitization to violence in our very midst. Animal flesh that is labeled and sold as "meat" is, after all, a socio-cultural construct with far-reaching material consequences. Fifty-nine billion land animals slaughtered globally each year involve a vast infrastructure of confinement, transport, and killing.

19. Craig and Mangels, "Position of the American Dietetic Association," 1266.

20. Derrida and Nancy, "Eating Well," 113.

21. A term coined by American psychologist Melanie Joy in 2003. However, this paper uses the term in a broadened sense.

22. Perlo, *Kinship and Killing*, 6.

23. Weis, *The Ecological Hoofprint*, 17, 20.

24. Such as Zoonotic epidemics, viral mutations caused by animal agriculture; diseases of civilization, e.g., elevated cancer risk, coronary heart disease due to consumption of red meat. See World Health Organization (WHO), "International Agency for Research."

25. See Food and Agriculture Organization of the United Nations, "Livestock's Long Shadow."

Therefore, in light of "sacrifice" being central to contemporary philosophical thinking about violence, it is vital for theologians and religion scholars to join the discussion. In *Au nom du marché: Regards sur une dimension méconnue du liberalisme économique: sa violence sacrificielle*, Nelson Tardif describes the current market operations as sacrificial of vulnerable human populations.[26] But the myth of limitless progress equally depends on the mass multiplication of animal bodies; the emblematic "reproducible resource" with the real costs disavowed. Of similar significance, Lawrence Schmidt in *The End of Ethics in a Technological Society*[27] lays out the way in which the myth of progress through technology originated in the Abrahamic concept of linear time, which was transmuted into the paradigm of relentless progress. Hence, our secular cosmology of development towards perfection retains those religious elements that now serve the industry in its incremental control of animal and human bodies.

But, as one might ask, are there any historical and semantic connections between ancient animal sacrifice *per se* and the contemporary mass slaughter of animals? What are the potential political implications of sacrifice apologetics? Can we speak of nonhuman animals at all in the field of the Humanities? As Avalos proposes, the study of violence requires interdisciplinary approaches.[28] As we will see, this demand could not be more relevant in the case of carnist/speciesist violence. Further, Avalos's call for the acknowledgment that empirical evidence should inform all ethical decision-making is critical.[29] While philosophers have debated the gap between the "is" (ontology) and the "should" (ethics) for centuries, we cannot ignore the weight of facts in reasonable decision making. For example, the devastating global effects of cycling large amounts of water, grains, and energy through the bodies of cattle to be killed are tangible and very real. These facts should inform our behavior. To go further, Avalos's theory on artificial scarcity produced by religious modes of thinking should alert us to other forms of artificially constructed conflicts that are no less dangerous. Carnism produces an artificial scarcity of arable land, clean water, grain,

---

26. Tardif, *Au nom du marché*, 64.

27. Schmidt, *The End of Ethics*, 11–21. I would like to thank Paul York at the University of Toronto for drawing my attention to this source, and the many helpful comments on an early draft of this paper.

28. Avalos, "Explaining Religious Violence," 145. This paper refers exclusively to those studies on violence determined to identify solutions. The study of violence must go beyond any fetishistic fascination and focus on the reduction of suffering in the world; anything less than these amounts to pornographic exploitation of the subject as much as the victims.

29. Avalos, *The Bad Jesus*, 378.

as well as inequities based on climate change, all on the shakable grounds of "manufactured necessity."[30] Religion, economics, and other forms of ideologies thus intersect in problematic ways. In addition, the acknowledgment of the empirical evidence about animal sentience, consciousness, and intelligence should play a role in the framing and study of animal sacrifice. One might even entertain the possibility that there is a contemporary continuation of the sacrificial principle that we are participating at in an individual and societal level.

Religion Turning into Ideology

Even though one might be tempted to believe that our enlightened minds have overcome religion as much as the past ideologies of the twentieth century, this self-assurance might very well stem from the phenomenon of consumerism having usurped them all. A functional definition of religion reveals to what extent "producing to consume" can be considered a para-religious paradigm; a *nomos*, in fact, effectively hiding its own constructed nature. Framing cultural practices as informed by ideologies helps examine how they are interwoven with power and how the relation between thought and social reality is structured. The classical Marxist/Althusserian definition of ideology sees it as a system of representation, located in everyday embodied practices, and inscribed in signifying practices and in discourses exercising an important role in naturalizing "the way things are."[31] While we never stand outside ideology, we occupy different positions in its socio-symbolic system. Some are killed, some are doing the killing, and some benefit from the violence inherent in these relations.

What then might the role of the intellectual in dismantling unjust relations be? First, the injustice needs to be acknowledged as existent. This, of course, is no easy task due to what Peter Ludwig Berger considers the hallmark of nomos in *The Sacred Canopy*—namely, its invisibility.[32] Carnism, as a dominant social imaginary, creates an invisible subject, utilizing the absent referent behind "meat."[33] Note, that carnism is the inherent reduction of the sentient and conscious creature to a substance to be ingested and thus annihilated. This corresponds directly to the idea that animals have no soul, consciousness, and spirit or mind worthy of the status of inviolability that is associated with something akin to salvation.

30. Perlo, *Kinship and Killing*, 6.
31. See Althusser, *Lenin and Philosophy*, 155–159, 276.
32. See Berger, *The Sacred Canopy*, 3–28.
33. See Adams, *The Sexual Politics*, 20–26, 42, 64, 141.

While carnism can be understood as an ongoing form of religious violence, it can also be helpfully framed as a textbook example of a social symbolic system governed by practical interests and "imaginary relations."[34] These relations are imaginary in the sense that the connection between one's steak and the individual animal that suffered and died for it is not made. Neither is the connection made to the forests that were cut down, the workers that suffered physical and psychological harm, nor those people who are going hungry because their government switched agricultural structures to cash crops for animal feed. Thus, recognition of the reality of unequal social relations in production processes will remain incomplete without considering human interactions with other animals that are literally the flesh, skin, and bone of our globalized economy. Animals are part of our social reality and we, as consumers and scholars, are linked to their realities on many levels with the slaughterhouse at the centre of the knot. The denial of that link is a misperception of the relation between self and world, our fateful relations to all these different beings, their biographies, their situation, and ours. However, the sheer attempt to think through these social realities is a difficult undertaking. Language can be used to rationalize, even explain away, the contradictions we sense intuitively. As we will see, the relationship between reality and language can indeed be a violent one, especially in the form of the world creating *logos* that is denied to all nonhumans.

As Althusser proposes, we must nevertheless try to understand the conditions and meaning of our existence. A sincere attempt includes reducing the gap between the euphemizing language of ideology and the harsh realities borne in the psyche and body of those at the bottom of the established order. It will also be necessary to keep in mind that ideologies tend to naturalize existing power relations, explain away, and resist or co-opt critique and problematization. It seems that atheists especially do well to consider their necessary entanglement in ideology.[35] If ideology is the way that truth is produced and reproduced in discourse, body and institution, then the scholar's labor consists precisely of a rigorous scientific approach to society, economics, and history and, of course, through the study of culture and its founding texts. Now that scholars are called upon to scrutinize ecocidal ideologies of human superiority, we begin to realize how little about nature and about animals we actually know. This lack of knowledge or "this not wanting to know" empirical facts about the animals we use, poses an ethical, if not also intellectual problem as much as this not knowing distorts

34. See Althusser, *Lenin and Philosophy*, 153–156.

35. This serves as a reminder that freedom is worked for since no one is born outside ideology.

our view of the reality of our impact on the lives of others.[36] But, do we even dare to know?[37]

Religion scholar Paul Waldau calls such "self-inflicted ignorance"[38] with respect to animals a particularly problematic form of violence as it perpetuates harmful power relations that enable exploitation. It is thus a radical act indeed for a theologian (or anyone working in the field of Humanities) to ask what are the animal industry mass-slaughters really like? What is the social and emotional life of a calf? What are the intelligence and capabilities of animals typically sacrificed? To be sure, biology, genetics, and ethology are important scientific tools in the challenge of carnist ideologies that systematically indoctrinate false ideas such as the unchallenged myth of the plain stupor of farmed animals. Waldau goes even further and challenges us to perform a type of "personal archeology" to probe the many layers of our own views on the animals we have learnt to use and consume.[39] As Noam Chomsky outlines in 1967 with respect to the responsibility of intellectuals from a historical perspective, "our basic concern must be their role in the creation and analysis of ideology."[40] The scholar is called upon to stop maintaining the illusion of ethical neutrality on questions we all take position on through our silence, our consent, and our self-inflicted ignorance. This point is very much in line with Avalos's challenging message to the effect that neutrality is impossible.[41]

Ideological Bible Criticism

Waldau concludes from his analysis of the historical transmission of images and stories that religious traditions have been the *principal vehicle* by which the status of animals was evaluated not only by believers, but entire cultures and institutions.[42] Other thinkers propose that it is the religious adherents' contradictory attitudes to animals, their paradoxical feelings that may include fear, respect, and the awareness that the animal can be "of use,"

---

36. Waldau, "Seeing the Terrain," 42.

37. Habermas, *Theory and Practice*, 256. He stresses the importance of genuine dialogue in society as, "This civilization is no more rooted in the knowledge and conscience of its citizens."

38. Waldau, "Seeing the Terrain," 47.

39. Ibid., 43.

40. Chomsky, "The Responsibility of Intellectual."

41. Avalos, "Religion and Violence."

42. Waldau, "Seeing the Terrain," 42.

which shaped religious thought in complex ways.[43] Considering these internal conflicts and accepting the view that human needs and attitudes have historically been projected both on the natural and the metaphysical realm, there might be a dialectic relationship between human attitudes to the natural world with the metaphysical or divine realm as an extension of this.[44] Not to forget, religion had, until the Enlightenment period and beyond, the special role of creating, transmitting, and shaping cosmologies that were tightly linked to ethical systems guiding society's views of the natural world. Until that period, religion was inseparable from Western culture and only in the seventeenth century was taken as a separate category from both culture and state. In truth, of course, we are inheritors of cosmologies that are traceable to religion, namely human superiority. Importantly, as we will see, while Abrahamic religions have welfare elements in them, they are missing from the mechanistic Cartesian worldview that helped shift theocentric human superiority—that is, as projection—to anthropocentric human superiority by advancing the status of the human to that formerly occupied by the divine. Similarly, the Enlightenment ideal of the autonomous subject has been described as a displacement of the sacred; the "human sublime" as god-like. Thus, for Kant, sublimity was a becoming conscious of human superiority of nature "within us" and "thereby also to nature outside us."[45] Therefore, with respect to the question about whether atheists have freed themselves of harmful religious myths, the animal question might be the ultimate litmus test.

Ultimately, what this means is that we are not likely to transcend our culture as enmeshed and based on structural violence by putting aside the Bible or by pointing blame to religionists without acknowledging our commonalities as they stand in this historical moment. To get at the problem of sanctioned everyday violence, it might be risky to exaggerate the gap and the differences between the religious and the secular. Yet, the critical study of biblical texts—taken as self-reflexive practice—has the chance of becoming cultural critique, a practice invigorated with a keen eye on those traces in us that are the heritage of a problematic past leading to our problematic present.

Even from a secular point-of-view, it should be stressed that to classify, "the Bible as source and origin to human centrism," and to violence, is a problematic idea.[46] "[T]he Bible is no magical point of origin for vio-

43. Perlo, *Kinship and Killing*, 2.
44. Ibid.
45. Kant, *Critique of Judgement*, 94.
46. Strommen, "Beastly Questions," 15.

lence, neither is it a stable artifice;"[47] rather, these texts merely mythologize existing worldviews and solidify them—thus slowing down change. To be sure, one of history's lessons appears to be that the Bible, as the dynamic matrix of culture, cannot be contained. Indeed, "[w]e are all affected by biblical ontologies, our scriptural histories and its afterlives."[48] Yet, there exists in this very tension the possibility to use the text as a tool, index, and mirror of cultural change as interconnected to past and present texts of word, life, and body. The large gray zone of continuation and interaction between traditional religious images and the secular might give us clues as to what makes our current and ever-changing worldviews. Religion scholar Jennifer L. Koosed, for example, offers the helpful image of Torah as expansive textuality, as enmeshed in materiality; crisscrossing and shaping life as much as its reading is shaped by lived experience.[49] Similarly, Yvonne Sherwood, scholar of biblical cultures, considers the study of Bible and religion as a unique opportunity wherein, "[t]he text comes out of its historicized box and becomes paradigmatic of certain ways of thinking, certain structures, that are not simply or dismissively "religious" or simply and dismissively "past."[50] The text becomes material to think with, to think about how we think and categorize, divide, and decide."[51] Indeed, the question of the animal stands, "at the strange point of intersection and continuity between so-called pre-modern and the modern, thereby exposing shared exclusions and occlusions around those cardinal modern virtues of "life" and "rights."[52]

What does it mean for the scholar who is operating at this intersection between the "pre-modern and the modern," a historical situation structured by carnist ideologies that necessitates taking a stance? While one could argue that we live in a post-Christian era due to global demographic shifts, we also carry on the Enlightenment project of deconstructing ancient traditions, paradoxically disguised and yet amplified by the forces of industrialization, technology, and capitalism. It is also hard to ignore that the project of animal rights involves political struggle and pushback by industry and state repression. The simple fact that questioning the dairy and meat industries may put one at the receiving end of repressive tactics is an indication of its revolutionary potential. A prominent example of this is that

47. Ibid., 26.
48. Ibid.
49. Koosed, "Conclusion," 328.
50. Sherwood, "Cutting Up Life," 251.
51. Ibid. In fact, the deep paradigm shift toward a less violent world that truly values "otherness" requires that we wrestle with texts as much as we examine ourselves.
52. Ibid., 285.

Biblical Accounts and Taxonomies

an increasing number of U.S. states are pushing for so-called Ag-Gag laws, seeking to criminalize undercover investigations on factory farms.[53] These events stand against the legal background that nonhuman animals are still considered objects of property over which the owner has complete power.

The biblical texts reflect an ancient agrarian society concerned with the "proper use" of animals that includes at the same time a concern for their abuse. Indeed, compared with other ancient Near Eastern systems of the same period, this explicit interest is unusual.[54] According to the priestly authority in Genesis 1, animals are not in "the image of God," while the second Genesis account, both humans and animals are made of earth, indicating ontological likeness. While Israelites obviously cared about animals and the animal question, the reader nevertheless readily detects human jealousy over divine favor, the constructed scarce resource of divine communication.

> Then the Lord God said, 'It is not good that the man should be alone; I will make him a helper as his partner.' So out of the ground the Lord God formed every animal of the field and every bird of the air, *and brought them to man to see what he would call them* [my italics]; and whatever the man called every living creature, that was its name. The man gave names to all cattle, and to the birds of the air, and to every animal of the field" (Gen 2:18–21).[55]

Just as God speaks the world into existence, the account portrays human beings as the extension of his *logos*, the vice-regent over the animals who lack speech. The animal—that is, the *alogon*—passively bears human projections reified and justified through language and, in Derrida's words, "[f]inding oneself deprived of language, one loses the power to name, to name oneself, indeed to answer (*répondre*) for one's name."[56] One should note that this classification is based on the instrumental relation human civilization has to animals. The docile and useful "domestic cattle" are construed God-created when it is in fact a product of sustained force. We find a remarkable silence with respect to the origins of animal husbandry in the account—the hegemonic extension of exploitation of other species through

---

53. Lin, "Ag-Gag Laws," 466.
54. Freund, *Understanding Jewish Ethics*, 172.
55. All scriptural translations are from the NRSV.
56. Derrida, *The Animal*, 19.

domestication—a much more violent process than the conventional "benign partnership" storyline reveals.[57] Yet, exploitation is what lies at heart of the operation Pierre Ducos defines as the integration of, "living animals as objects into the socio-economic organization of the human group, in the sense that, while living, those animals are objects for ownership, inheritance, exchange, trade."[58] Thus, in the Genesis story, it is their use value that becomes animal ontology—"this is what they are"—and their teleology—"this is what they were made for." Today, the biblical theocentric ontology has shifted to the anthrocentric declaration, "this is what animals are *bred*, indeed *genetically designed* for." For Derrida, it seems as if God has created man in his likeness so that man will subject, tame, dominate and control the animals born before them and assert his authority over them (Gen 2:19).[59] "God destines the animals to an experience of the power of man, *in order to see* the power of man in action, in order to see the power of man at work, in order to see man take power over all the other living beings."[60] Importantly, in part, through speech and, of course, because God told him to. Derrida identifies the direct connection between naming, classifying, fixing and killing: as "God prefers the sacrifice of the very animal that he has let Adam name—*in order to see* [my italics]."[61]

Is this the first moral test of man? How do humans tend to treat those who lack the power to talk back?[62] How to study this passage in a university class while keeping in mind Avalos's warning that, "[a]ny solution to the problem of violence should also be cognizant about how scholars of religion have been complicit in promoting views of the Bible or of religion that may be unhelpful or harmful."[63] One responsible approach might be to remind students of the multiplicity of voices found in the Bible, as it is indeed an "artefact" full of paradox. Perhaps a reminder is called for that whatever the Bible says it lies still in the reader's conscience as to how the

---

57. Nibert, *Animal Oppression*, 11. For example, excavations from 8500 BCE revealed bone pathologies in goats and cows indicating physical trauma, poor diet, chronic arthritis, and high levels of stress.

58. Ducos, "'Domestication' Defined," 53. In light of the force and violence inherent in such processes, Nibert proposes the term "domesecration." See Nibert, *Animal Oppression*.

59. Derrida, *The Animal*, 42.

60. Ibid., 16.

61. Ibid., 19, 42.

62. There are other tests: Do humans listen to God's speechless voice in creation? One example of a biblical space for transmission of knowledge about God without speech can be found in Ps 19:1–4, whereby God's glory can be experienced in creation.

63. Avalos, "Explaining Religious Violence," 145.

text is used. It lies in the reader's responsibility to abstain from using the texts to justify oppression of the disempowered. Reading Ecclesiastes alongside Genesis we encounter a different voice; the contemplative voice of the teacher (*Qoheleth*):

> I said in my heart with regard to human beings that *God is testing them to show that they are but animals* [my italics]. For the fate of humans and the fate of animals is the same; as one dies, so dies the other. They all have the same breath, and humans have no advantage over the animals; for all is vanity. All go to one place; all are from dust, and all turn to dust again. Who knows whether the human spirit goes upward and the spirit of animals goes downward to the earth? (Eccl 3:18–21).

We can see that humanity failed the test. Humans lack humility. Most of us lack the heart to face our shared mortality with nonhuman life in a nonviolent way. Rather, historically, humans have jealously and anxiously prayed, bartered, and killed for divine favor. The practice of sacrifice is thus the construction and maintenance of the divinely favorable status and amounts to what Avalos describes as the "expense" required in the acquisition of that resource.[64] Accordingly, all animal taxonomies in the Bible are aligned with a sacrificial structure condemning them to use value by paradoxically assigning them importance while enabling utter objectification. The emblematic text of this is Deuteronomy 14:3–20, the quintessential division of the animal world into eatable and not eatable. Bourdieu's insight into the inherent violent structure of all symbolic systems due to economic basis is helpful in understanding the Leviticus taxonomy as an account of its own symbolic/material economy of sacrifice.[65] The animal that cannot speak thus has no inherent value, but only carries symbolic, economic, or sacrificial worth. Considering the situation that human-animal relations are always structured by the possibility of the acceptable killing of the latter, we will see that the only ethical difference is between killing "done right" and killing "done wrong."

However, we do find spaces in the text for symbolic care of animals. As domesticated animals participate in the Sabbath rest along with the slaves and all other members of the family unit, they are truly made part of the extended household. Furthermore, we could interpret this inclusion as the recognition for animal labor and the ability and need of working bodies to rest. During the sabbatical year, even wild animals partake of the produce from fields lying fallow; a remarkable law indeed, considering the marginal

---

64. Avalos, "Religion and Scarcity," 557.
65. Bourdieu, *Outline of a Theory*, 177–197.

status of the wild and the fact that many undomesticated species are seen as a threat to civilization (Exod 23:11).

Knowledge about Animals

For Waldau, "[o]ne peculiar form of human-on-nonhuman harm, indeed, violence—a form which has, sadly, been institutionalized to an extraordinary degree—occurs when authorities of any kind, religious or not, pass along human caricatures and ignorance of nonhuman animals' actual realities."[66] Against the background of inherited unverifiable myths about the animals we sacrifice, what is needed, it seems, is a set of interrogatories of an ethic in the responsibly and scholarly sound engagement with other animals in the study of religion, especially sacrifice. Continental philosopher Dominick LaCapra acknowledges that we are certainly limited in our abilities "to know" other animals due to the problem of determining rigorously the inner realities of other individuals' inner lives. Yet, he observes that the construal of animals as eternal enigma or forever "opaque" while seeing no problem in the continued use in them is unethical.[67] Therefore, social science scholars might want to begin asking questions that have until now only been considered proper subject matter of the sciences as these questions bear upon our own research in important ways.[68]

Scientific Language/Consciousness/Disavowal

Charles Darwin, the epitomic figure of reference for many humanist neo-atheists, was aware that most people have all kinds of preconceived ideas about animals that they were reluctant to challenge. But Darwin's approach of impartial, non-reductionist, and rigorous observation of animals did just that. For example, he noted on many occasions that the behavior to "pause, deliberate and resolve" is observable in a variety of species.[69] Darwin was fully aware of the moral implications of the fact that mammals and even birds differ from humans not essentially, but only in degree. He writes, "[t]he sufferings of millions of the lower animals throughout almost

66. Waldau, "Seeing the Terrain," 3.
67. LaCapra, *History and its Limits*, 154.
68. See Habermas's compelling critique of the intellectual division of labour and its complicity in technocratic society, *Theory and Practice*, 253–282.
69. Darwin, *The Descent of Man*, 96. For remarkable statements on similarities between human and animal faculties and abilities see Darwin, *Charles Darwin's Notebooks*, 564, 567, 582, 588.

endless time is apparently irreconcilable with the existence of a creator of 'unbounded goodness.'"[70] Emphasizing that no species exist for any other species as all struggle to adapt or perish, Darwin wrote: "Animals whom we made our slaves, we don't like to see them as equals."[71] Consequently, *The Origin of Species* has also been attacked by neo-Cartesians on the basis that "if his theory was true, it would mean that animals could suffer."[72] When it comes to animal consciousness and the ethical dimension of its reality many atheists are just as seriously challenged by Darwin as the next creationist. Therefore, in the specific case of animals, scientific language freed from technocratic reductionism can be surprisingly liberating.[73] As such, the "Cambridge Declaration on Nonhuman Consciousness" of 2012, presided over by physicist Stephen Hawking, can be understood as a *scientific-political-ethical stance*, in its purpose comparable to the statement on the non-existence of race by the American Anthropological Association (AAA) from 1998. The declaration merits quoting:

> [c]onvergent evidence indicates that non-human animals have the neuroanatomical, neurochemical, and neurophysiological substrates of conscious states along with the capacity to exhibit intentional behaviors. Consequently, the weight of evidence indicates that *humans are not unique* [my italics] in possessing the neurological substrates that generate consciousness. Nonhuman animals including all mammals and birds, and many other creatures, including octopuses, also possess these neurological substrates.[74]

"Neurological substratum" is an *ahuman* and thus neutral term that opens up a space urgently needed to speak of ethically relevant capabilities that are not weighed down by a humanist legacy of the glorification of human faculties, alongside the dismissal of animal capabilities.

Another important example of the liberating potential of the scientific method is to reframe language, as it is in philosophical humanism, as a "well-nigh magical property" that ontologically separates Homo sapiens from every other living creature. Indeed, it is effectively reframed as an

---

70. Darwin and Seward, *More Letters*, 94. Darwin also spoke out against animal cruelty in his pamphlet "an appeal" written and distributed with his wife Emma. See "'An Appeal,'" Darwin Correspondence Project.

71. Darwin, *Metaphysics, Materialism*, 187.

72. Rachels, *Created from Animals*, 131. See also Murray, *Nature Red*.

73. The humanities and social sciences have their role to play in order to guide science in the direction of emancipation in dialogue with citizens who refuse to be reduced to consumers.

74. Low, *The Cambridge Declaration*, 2.

ahuman emergence of "linguistic domains" from longer processes of social interaction and communication that many animals share and, thus, are not limited to Homo sapiens.[75] In the study of humans interacting with nonhumans in religious ritual, these terms may serve as a tool as they can be employed in addition, and sometimes as an alternative to, certain mystical approaches that may be informed by distorting projections of the *nomos* of human superiority that fail to do justice to the animal subject. Animals clearly communicate their pain and joy; all we have to do is look and listen. To adapt Avalos's call for activist scholarship to the case of the human denial of animal communication as mythically linked to the divine *logos*, one might suggest, "Nonbelievers must challenge believers to explain why they believe in such resources in the first place."[76] The humanist/religious belief in language/logos is a strange thing indeed, considering that communication is not something to "believe in," but rather a tool or resource for the goal of *understanding*.

Sacrificial Apologetics

Unfortunately, most condemnation of animal sacrifice is not consistent from an ethical point-of-view. While killing animals for religious purposes is construed as "barbaric," their exploitation for economic or aesthetic reasons is considered commonsense. To correct such contradictions one important stream in anti-speciesist ethics strives to be intersectional in its outlook,[77] in that it considers the historical and discursive connections between violence against animals with the oppression of the "dehumanized" (or indeed animalized) human other.[78] The intersectional lens is thus sensitive to the fact that critiques of animal sacrifice are quite often launched and/or appropriated within discourses informed by supersessionist Christian, racist, and colonialist religio-phobic discourses that refuse to self-reflexively analyze their own violent cultural practices against the nonhuman other. Therefore, it should be stressed that an ethical critique of religious violence must be clearly differentiated from religio-phobic or colonialist attacks on the imagined "irrational" other. Similarly, Avalos notes that much scholarship on religious violence after 9/11 can indeed be seen as ethnocentric.[79]

75. Wolfe, *Zoontologies*, 45, 54.
76. Avalos, "Religion and Scarcity," 566.
77. See Nocella II et al., *Defining Critical Animal Studies*, 5.
78. Ibid., 53.
79. See Avalos, "Explaining Religious Violence," 137.

In his chapter, "The Eco-Hostile Jesus," Avalos addresses the other side of the debate; the quite remarkable phenomenon of contemporary apologetics of ancient animal sacrifice.[80] Among those scholars working for positive change for animals, Avalos notes Andrew Linzey's attempts to identify animal-friendly traces in biblical texts on sacrifice in order to construct a coherent Christian animal ethics.[81] Similar work has been done from the Jewish perspective.[82] Curiously, however, some apologies of sacrifice display much more empathy to the sacrificer than the animal victim. That is understandable, given that human-centered disciplines employ anthropocentric tools. The stated goal of the social sciences, after all, is to understand human behavior. However, ignoring the fact that in the sacrificial ritual human subjects interact not only with inert objects, but also with animal subjects who have an interest in continuing their lives, participates in the invested practice of reality distortion.

To identify with the human agent, especially if the observing scholar herself eats meat and has no interest in animal subjectivity, is tempting—or perhaps it is with the shared and familiar practice of meat eating that the scholar identifies. In other words, the observer is not neutral, but rather biased as a result of her own behavioral practices of discriminating against animals.

Religion scholar Jonathan Klawans has no patience for the squeamish and exclaims, "[w]hoever feels smug about the elimination of sacrificial altars can just visit a slaughterhouse or laboratory: neither is a more welcome place for an animal than an ancient temple...[t]he elimination of sacrifice is not an ethical development, but an aesthetic one."[83] This might be true, however, his chapter does not contain any critique of the latter and the reader gains the impression that slaughterhouses are accepted as "normality." In a similar tone, Kimberley Christine Patton calls for more empathy with the one who kills, to appreciate their narratives and point-of-view: in the sacrificer's eyes, "[a]nimals are seen as active subjects from start to finish in the sacrificial process, glorified mediators between realms, whose cooperation is essential to the efficacy of the ritual, whose forgiveness is often sought from kinship groups to avert vengeance."[84] Even further, the sacrificial animal is construed as *benefitting* from the process in that it is symboli-

---

80. Avalos, *The Bad Jesus*, 335.

81. Ibid., 330. See also Linzey, *Christianity and the Rights*, 42.

82. For example, the idea of the exclusive sacrifice of plants in the Messianic period. See Sears, *The Vision of Eden*. See also Kalechofsky, *Haggadah*; Schwartz, *Judaism and Vegetarianism*.

83. Klawans, "Sacrifice in Ancient Israel," 66.

84. Patton, "Animal Sacrifice," 393.

cally elevated as "theophoric subject that has metaphysical standing in its own right." Patton seems to uncritically accept that the victim is portrayed as a willing, active participant that is "rescued from inconsequentiality as one of a multitudinous herd;"[85] symbolically empowered and transformed into a state of deathlessness. However, to construe these points as genuinely "beneficial" for the animal victims, the scholar must not only dismiss the possibility that the lamb's "multitudinous herd" actually had meaning to her. One must also assume that the animal is indeed a religious subject *and* that Patton knows what animal religiosity is all about, in this case the animal dedicating her own death to the gods and appetites of humanity, indeed to entering deathlessness—whatever that means. Lest we forget, this very same narrative appears in hunting societies, with the animal imagined giving herself over to their own killers who will perform rituals of thanksgiving. In light of the evident expressions in animals of a desire to live, we might identify a very common pattern of anthropomorphic projections on the side of the killer to assuage feelings of guilt, which are, from a socio-evolutionary point-of-view, emotional warning signs for wrongdoing. To conclude, the study of sacrifice should not entail the participation in sacrifice, as Aaron S. Gross reminds us in *The Question of the Animal and Religion*.[86]

The extraordinary complexity of relationships between killer and victim is one conclusion we can surely draw from the study of violence against animals in sacrifice. Humans do not have to hate to kill; humans may very well identify with the victim on a deep level. For example, Eilberg-Schwartz's anthropological study of Israelite sacrifice indicates a common occurrence of ritually expressed identification with the victim. In this, the person on whose behalf the animal dies may place his hands on the victim's head (Exod 29:10, 15, 19; Lev 3:2, 8, 13; 4:4, 15, 24).[87] While in this case we can speak of a quite abstract and metaphorical type of identification, Eilberg-Schwartz points to an almost intimate relationship between Israelites and their cattle. In fact, it is those animals that are slaughtered and eaten that they identify with the most. The construction of human identity as ingested, eaten, and embodied gives the animals significance in their very objectification and destruction. Indeed, solely animals that serve as metaphors for Israelites, the docile herds and flocks, can serve as sacrificial substitutes.[88] For this identification to be possible, of course, the idea of animal consciousness,

---

85. Ibid., 397.
86. Gross, *Question of the Animal and Religion*, 122.
87. See Eilberg-Schwartz, *The Savage in Judaism*, 135.
88. Ibid.

their distinct interests, and perhaps even their own stakes in the notion of salvation must be subsumed into human embodied religiosity.

Another example of problematic framing of sacrifice is religion scholar McClymond's detaching of the category violence from sacrifice so that we can appreciate the many intriguing details of the ritual dance of sacrifice. Without acknowledging it, she takes the emic or sacrificing culture's point-of-view when she states, "Sacrifice often involves multiple activities, and frequently the victim's death carries *less significance* [my italics] than other procedures."[89] One could argue that for the victim losing his life is the ultimate significance while religious symbolism could fare very well without killing.

On a more balanced note, McClymond remarks that, "[a]ctivities that would, in any other context, be characterized as violent often described with ritual language that negates any apparent violence."[90] One strategy to neutralize violence, atomization, is looking at the ritual as made up of a multitude of discrete acts through time, each of which is named and invested with significance. The organization of space, the division of labor, and the rhetoric employed in today's slaughterhouses seem to have the same purpose.[91] However, to genuinely tackle the problem of our culture of violence, it is important to deconstruct such rhetoric and to always remain skeptical with regard to what extent it matters if the one who kills truly "means well." The ritualized nullification of violence was already noted by Mary Douglas: "it may please the butcher to disguise the violence with rites and pretend that the animal consented to its death, but why it is killed makes no difference to the victim."[92] A consistent ethical critique and factual analysis does not minimize the issue of violence, but is rather informed by the suffering it causes in the one hurt, broken, and silenced.

To conclude this section, it appears that sacrifice apologists write to respond to those secular critics, who assumingly eat meat and who criminally charge sacrifice with "senseless" killing. The moral high ground operative here is that animals "should not die for nothing"[93] and religion is nothing. Seemingly, to save human religiosity from such reductionism, Patton makes the point that such killing indeed does have meaning for the sacrificer. One might even say that the human agent means well, performs gestures

---

89. McClymond, "Sacrifice and Violence," 324.
90. Ibid., 327.
91. Pachirat, *Every Twelve Seconds*, 9–11, 13, 251.
92. Douglas, *Leviticus as Literature*, 66.
93. Sherwood, "Cutting Up Life," 286.

of empathy, and care. The result, however, is a skewed kind of love,[94] as already noted by feminist thinkers and reminiscent of the infamous situation of domestic violence in which the husband beats his beloved wife into submission. In other words, such rationalizations are a device of structural violence. Indeed, this account is quite close to the belief of one's own atonement or salvation requiring the destruction of those outside one's group who lack such access to salvation, an important criterion to be considered a typical case of religiously motivated violence amplified through *logos*. Those in pain do not have the luxury of refined speech.[95] Ultimately, the acceptability of the killing of an animal really hinges on the violent potential of language to rationalize force, to add a layer of rhetoric in order to conceal the sheer cruelty of killing someone who does not want to die. It is also the refusal to encounter the other, to allow oneself "to be seized by a foreign being, a fellow subject"[96] in the revelation of the suffering animal other.[97]

The Perpetual Sacrifice—Meanings Past and Present

Investigating the possible connections between ancient sacrifice and contemporary slaughter, one might be surprised when we learn that the past was perhaps less brutal than today, at least when it comes to the treatment of animals. The Israelites considered neither divine nor animal otherness as absolute. As much as humans were God's chosen creatures, humans and animals shared in life though the blood (the Hebrew *nefesh*). *Nefesh* indeed becomes a powerful "signifier for divine animation of creation."[98] This view of shared "creatureliness" is to be clearly distinguished from the Aristotelian thought of the human soul as radically different from the animal. Despite the problematic taxonomies of the Bible, it seems that sacrifice amounts to a type of *negotiation* of hierarchies, with a deep sense of shared corporality and mortality. The process of slaughter brings to the forefront the blood as signifier of the commonality of human sacrificer and animal victim. All flesh (*col basar*) is like grass, and all those fantasies of man's dominion—all those acts of naming the animals, of placing one's hands on the head of the animals—can be read as defense mechanism against the truth of the human animal, as meat, as dust, as vulnerable.[99] Genesis famously points

---

94. Adams, *The Sexual Politics*, 55.
95. Scarry, *Body in Pain*, 27–59.
96. Gross, *Question of the Animal and Religion*, 128.
97. Ibid.
98. Seesengood, "What Would Jesus Eat?" 232.
99. Sherwood, "Cutting Up Life," 270.

to the ontological distinction humans and animals, as only humans were created in God's image (Gen 1:26–27). However, Robert Paul Seesengood notes ambivalence about this "semipermeable boundary" between humans, animals, and gods in Leviticus 17 with respect to the anxiety-provoking issue of improper slaughter.[100] Similarly, Sherwood notes that, "sacrifice is a site where strange oscillations in the unstable flux of the "theo-anthropo-zoomorphic" are produced.[101] Anxiety over the human place in the cosmos was thus both expressed and dealt with through the meticulously prepared sacrificial event that served as the marker of a culture that stood in divine favor. In other words, even though animals do not actively compete for the scarce resource over the privileged "divine connection," in ancient times, sacrifice might be understood as a site of struggle over divine favor. In order to keep such anxieties under control animal killing was to proceed in a tightly controlled and orderly way.[102] Sources indicate that a distinction was indeed made between the proper sacrifice of an animal and something akin to animal murder.[103] For example in Leviticus, the improper slaughter and consumption of the animal, outside the sacrificial system, is condemned: "he shall be held guilty of bloodshed; he has shed blood" (Lev 17:4). Controversies around meat eating after the destruction of the sacred killing space of the temple encompass the vegetarian option favored by several communities including the Essenes and the Therapeutae. The very existence of these practiced alternatives to killing animals indicate that Israelites "sincerely believed" in their sacrificial morality. It is relevant to point out that the dietary and historical context was shaped by real scarcity of nutrition. For the general population, hunger was a painful fact of daily life. Animal meat was not eaten frequently; it was a rare and priced source of protein. Indeed, a piece of meat could take away that pain instantly.

The paradox of sacrifice now comes into view: on the one hand we see performance of dominance and control while on the other we sense human anxiety, vulnerability, and a hunger both for sustenance and transcendence. It is the quintessential site of lack and excess that is brought into tension when in the sacrificial moment, humankind expresses both need and greed whether he wills or not. Man, the pinnacle of creation, the creator's vice-regent, wants something and lacks something the animal has. Indeed, it is a moment when man has to admit that his own life is parasitical to animal

---

100. Seesengood, "What Would Jesus Eat?" 233.

101. Sherwood, "Cutting Up Life," 247.

102. An order, that in today's language we might call "civilized" and "rational." See Pachirat, *Every Twelve Seconds*, 9–11, 251.

103. See Seesengood, "What Would Jesus Eat?" 237.

life; or, in Derrida's words, "sacrifice as a sign of the nakedness and deficit that is intrinsic and essential to man."[104] As Giorgio Agamben, theorist of biopolitics states in *The Open*, the human is always more and less than the animal and his own animality at the same time: "[h]umanitas is produced in sacrifice, by deciding, at every moment, every sacrifice between animal and man."[105] Bringing into focus the links between ancient sacrifice and the modern sacrificial structures of Western culture, Derrida's diagnosis is a cruel state in which both humanist conceptions of the rational unified subject, as much as religious views of human as "*imago dei*" are pushed to sacrifice what is reminiscent of the animal in the human. This is how precious, how rare, salvation is from worldly existence. In this process of human auto-aggression, non-human animals are sacrificed in violent, hegemonic, and canonized Western metaphysics and religions.[106] For Agamben, the anthropological machine of humanism is "an ironic apparatus that verifies the absence of a nature proper to *Homo*, holding him suspended between a celestial and terrestrial nature, between animal and divine— and, thus, his being always more and less than himself."[107] It is the humanist sacrificial machine that expresses the paradoxical desire for solid conceptual and emotional ground, a full belly, and transcendence, carried forward historically in the Promethean development of the Enlightenment subject, motivated by a fear of and rage at uncontrollable nature.[108] Thus, it is imagined human lack that informs his tense relations to the animal. Tellingly, the Bible links animal death to human transgression. When humans lack, fail and sin, animals die.

Girard suggests that domestication could be seen as a side effect to building an easy access-reserve of sacrificial victims.[109] In this functionalist view, the killing of defenseless lambs appears to be a rather indolent exercise, craven indeed. But, in paradoxical ways, the sacrificer is "hurting" too. The one who kills empathizes or identifies with the victim and yet the victim must perish. One might even say that controlled ritual must be accompanied by gestures of regret and empathy or it is not acceptable to the gods involved. Humans surely can be seen as compartmentalizing their own identifications and emotions, but there is more to it than cognitive dissonance. In keeping with Bourdieu's insight into an economic logic underlying all symbolic systems, it

---

104. Derrida, *The Animal*, 270.
105. Agamben, *The Open*, 77.
106. Derrida and Nancy, "Eating Well," 113.
107. Agamben, *The Open*, 29.
108. Bell, "Dialectic of Anthropocentrism," 164.
109. Girard, *Things Hidden*, 129.

makes sense to think that the empathy and even regret that must accompany sacrifice ultimately raises the victim's sacrificial value; it raises the stakes. Sacrifice always entails loss, a destruction or surrender of something valued for the sake of something having a higher or more pressing claim: human pity for the animal other and full acceptance of human "creatureliness" for the sake of salvation and the dream of transcendence. Thus, every time, man sacrifices a piece of himself even at the same moment of auto-empowerment. Yet, the one who cuts animals at the sacrificial altar of human civilization becomes the quasi-divine "endowing source"[110] of value for the victim's life, flesh, and death. This is the paradox of violating those that are denied speech and subjectivity by dismissing their inarticulate cries.

Sacrifice is productive of gods. After all, sacrifice is for the gods only. The construction of animal sacrifice, the destruction of a valued animal that is justified through the narrative of necessity and privilege always conceals a hidden exploitation enabled by the transmutation of economic into symbolic capital.[111] Thus, the application of Avalos's theory of religious violence exposes the economic layers of conflicted human nature, imagination, and jealousy that continue into our times.

Thinking about the force we exercise over other species, I have come to think that today, as in the past, the most fundamental two categories in the ideological taxonomy are the "sacrificable" and "nonsacrificable." In the context of advanced capitalism, sacrifice for Sherwood, "presses the darker side of modern biopolitical and biocultural economies. . .[as it] presses the question of how, and where, we make cuts in life" as individuals and societies.[112] This involves the management of life through sacrifice; the demarcation between "bare," almost undifferentiated life, or *zoe*, and on the protected side of the moral divide, *bios*. The latter denotes the individualized, worthy, and politically relevant life of the human subject that counts. In this tension, all animals are forced into the dangerous and paradoxical position of "bare life, raw material, or in specific circumstances, as scapegoated victim."[113] Of course, discourse about animals is often contradictory. Indeed, in the neutralized or euphemized discourse of pure instrumentality, the same species may be reduced to "sub-ethical status," as raw material, whereas in the sacrificial context it is elevated to a supra-ethical position as unique and special. Note that the outcome is always death.

110. LaCapra, *History and its Limits*, 162.
111. Bourdieu, *Outline of a Theory*, 196.
112. Sherwood, "Cutting Up Life," 251.
113. LaCapra, *History and its Limits*, 151. This particular critical use of the ancient Greek distinction between *bios* and *zoe* was coined by Giorgio Agamben. See Agamben, *Homo Sacer*.

We can see sacrificial ideologies of different times converging in that, "modernity and biopolitics seem...compressed together with ancient forms of life management,"[114] when scientists frame as "sacrifice" the act of guillotining a genetically modified rat previously used in painful radiation experiments. Not to forget, the "higher purpose" may involve "saving humanity," but it also stretches to include grants, prestige, and sheer curiosity.[115] In the humanist machine of sacrifice there exist only two underlying human motives: progress, development, or transcendence and all programs associated with it are thus "sacred-untouchable-unquestionable." The other side of the binary is dismissed as inferior, simple, and animalistic. The effect is not merely a justification, but indeed a sacralization of violence against those whose life, growth, and desire to flourish is dismissed as unimportant; a "space in which the supreme value of the human leads to the sanctioning of violence to animals,"[116] even a hallowed requirement for domination. Continental philosopher LaCapra sums it up this way:

> Violence is postulated as legitimate in unqualified or even absolute terms, whether by an appeal to God, the sovereign state, natural law, the terroristic threat of an elusive enemy, the maintenance of an imperial order, or the good, even the transcendence, of the human with respect to the animal.[117]

In sum, pretty much any purpose humans can find for the use of animals that can be couched in rational language thus stands a good chance to be promoted to the level of "justified."

In sharp contrast to ancient sacrifice, twentieth-century automated mass slaughter is a mundane operation—rationalized, cold, and "necessary." Animal life is cheap, but curiously, with the increased awareness of animal intelligence and suffering, a new economic niche is being exploited that seems to satisfy the human desire to sacralize violence. The oxymoron of "happy" or "humane" or "ethical" meat is indeed a misleading label seeking to raise the value and the price of products in the industry's very return to the sacrificial frame. Never mind that the ultimate byproducts of animal suffering and death are mundane and not needed for living.

Thus, the sacrificial discourse of "humane meat" works itself out by an acknowledgement, even amplification, of the individuality of the animal

114. Sherwood, "Cutting Up Life," 251.

115. Not to forget, the very same vivisection industry that has quite effectively appropriated the sacrificial frame also routinely tests on the life animals for the sake of "higher purposes" of cosmetics, artificial sweeteners, and weapons.

116. Gross, *Question of the Animal and Religion*, 138.

117. LaCapra, *History and its Limits*, 94.

victim through cultural, ritual, rhetorical, and cosmetic means especially in advertising. In the context of the recognition that certain value is produced, LaCapra observes that animals have been elevated to a "supra-ethical status" as sacrificial or quasi-sacrificial victim.[118] Advertising depicts cows and chickens with grotesque grins eager to land on the barbecue to be grilled alive. Yet, these grins are perversely anthropomorphized.[119] In the same context, more stringent laws on animal welfare or cameras in farms are rejected: farmers are construed as loving, even adoring their animals and not in need of outside control. Their sacrificial relationship is untouchable.

Engaging animal slaughter in Avalos's theory of religious violence brings to the fore the economic nature of human symbolic systems. In the background of the many elaborate and sophisticated stories and rituals there looms the specter of human lack, vulnerability, and mortality. The secularly manufactured necessity of meat was not only made possible by the religious construction of the false scarcities of salvation, transcendence, and divine favor, it also amplifies the risk of the inherent self-destructive tendencies of the humanist machine of sacrifice that must deny and destroy human animality/vulnerability. Now, in the twenty-first century and at the brink of global environmental destruction, it seems high time to systematically challenge the sacrificial taxonomy, to question inherited ideologies that harm human relations to the nonhuman world, and to think through the implications of the Darwinian realization that we all share ethically relevant features with those other animals we routinely exploit and kill.

Reading Avalos is a challenge to the reflective student of religion and inspires the following types of questions: How committed am I really to ending violence? What is the mission of the university and of religious studies in the historical moment of environmentally caused human conflict, migration, and climate change; indeed human misery that is deeply entangled with the reality of the twenty-four hour slaughterhouse? What should professors profess?[120] Perhaps, not surprisingly even for the atheist, studying and teaching human culture, politics, and symbols also implies "doing theology" in the sense of understanding, even wrestling with our "faith" in knowledge, dialogue/speech, and reason. Historically, we have frequently misused these capabilities to perpetuate oppression and violence. It seems that it is our responsibility to use these very real resources to labor for peace.

---

118. Ibid., 159.

119. For numerous examples of such images used in meat advertising see suicide-food.blogspot.ca.

120. Derrida, "The University," 214.

Bibliography

Adams, Carol J. *The Sexual Politics of Meat: A Feminist-Vegetarian Critical Theory*. New York: Bloomsbury Revelations, 2015.

Agamben, Giorgio. *Homo Sacer: Sovereign Power and Bare Life*. Translated by Daniel Heller-Roazen. Stanford: Stanford University Press, 1998.

———. *The Open: Man and Animal*. Translated by Kevin Attell. Stanford: Stanford University Press, 2004.

Althusser, Louis. *Lenin and Philosophy and Other Essays*. Translated by Ben Brewster. London: New Left, 1971.

"'An Appeal' against Animal Cruelty." Darwin Correspondence Project. https://www.darwinproject.ac.uk/topics/life-sciences/darwin-and-vivisection/appeal-against-animal-cruelty.

Avalos, Hector. *The Bad Jesus: The Ethics of New Testament Ethics*. Sheffield: Sheffield Phoenix, 2015.

———. "Explaining Religious Violence: Retrospects and Prospects." Pages 137–146 in *The Blackwell Companion to Religion and Violence*. Edited by Andrew R. Murphy. Oxford: Wiley-Blackwell, 2011.

———. "Religion and Scarcity: A New Theory for the Role of Religion in Violence." Pages 554–570 in *The Oxford Handbook of Religion and Violence*. Edited by Mark Juergensmeyer, Margo Kitts, and Michael Jerryson. Oxford: Oxford University Press, 2013.

———. "Religion and Violence: A New Theory for an Old Problem." Paper presented at the Colloquium: Religion, Violence and the Ethics of Biblical and Religious Studies." in Honor of Dr. Hector Avalos. Montreal, Canada. June 16, 2015.

Bell, Aaron. "The Dialectic of Anthropocentrism." Pages 163–176 in *Critical Theory and Animal Liberation*. Edited by John Sanbonmatsu. Maryland: Rowman & Littlefield, 2011.

Berger, Peter Ludwig. *The Sacred Canopy: Elements of a Sociological Theory of Religion*. New York: Anchor Books, 1990.

Bourdieu, Pierre. *Outline of a Theory of Practice*. Translated by Richard Nice. Cambridge: Cambridge University Press, 1977.

Chomsky, Noam. "The Responsibility of Intellectuals." *New York Review of Books*. February 23, 1967. http://www.nybooks.com/articles/1967/02/23/a-special-supplement-the-responsibility-of-intelle/.

Craig, Winston J. and Ann Reed Mangels. "Position of the American Dietetic Association: Vegetarian Diets." *Journal of the American Dietetic Association* 109:7 (2009) 1266–1282.

Darwin, Charles. *Charles Darwin's Notebooks, 1836–1844: Geology, Transmutation of Species, Metaphysical Enquiries*. Transcribed and Edited by Paul H. Barrett et al. London: British Museum (Natural History), 1987.

———. *The Descent of Man, and Selection in Relation to Sex.* London: Penguin Books, 2004.

———. *Metaphysics, Materialism, and the Evolution of Mind: The Early Writings of Charles Darwin.* Edited by Paul E. Barrett. Commentary by Howard E. Gruber. Chicago: Chicago University Press, 2011.

Darwin, Francis, and Albert C. Seward, eds. *More Letters of Charles Darwin, Volume I.* London: Murray, 1903.

Derrida, Jacques. *The Animal that Therefore I Am.* Edited by Marie-Louise Mallet. Translated by David Wills. New York: Fordham University Press, 2008.

———. "The University without Condition." Pages 202–280 in *Without Alibi.* Edited and Translated by Peggy Kamuf. Stanford: Stanford University Press, 2002.

Derrida, Jacques, and Jean-Luc Nancy. "Eating Well or the Calculation of the Subject." Pages 96–119 in *Who Comes After the Subject?* Translated by Peter Connor and Avita Ronell. Edited by Eduardo Cadava, Peter Connor, and Jean-Luc Nancy. New York: Routledge, 1991.

Douglas, Mary. *Leviticus as Literature.* Oxford: Oxford University Press, 1999.

Ducos, Pierre. "'Domestication' Defined and Methodological Approaches in its Recognition in Faunal Assemblages." Pages 53–56 in *Approaches to Faunal Analysis in the Middle East.* Edited by R.H. Meadow and M.A. Zeder. Boston: Harvard University Press, 1978.

Eilberg-Schwartz, Howard. *The Savage in Judaism: An Anthropology of Israelite Religion and Ancient Judaism.* Bloomington: Indiana University Press, 1990.

Food and Agriculture Organization of the United Nations. "Livestock's Long Shadow: Environmental Issues and Options." Rome: FAO, 2006. http://www.fao.org/docrep/010/a0701e/a0701e00.HTM.

Freund, Richard A. *Understanding Jewish Ethics: Major Themes and Thinkers.* Volume II. New York: Edwin Mellen, 1993.

Girard, René. *Things Hidden since the Foundation of the World.* Translated by Stephen Bann and Michael Metteer. Stanford: Stanford University Press, 1978.

Gross, Aaron S. *The Question of the Animal and Religion: Theoretical Stakes, Practical Implications.* New York: Columbia University Press, 2015.

Habermas, Jürgen. *Theory and Practice.* Translated by John Viertel. Boston: Beacon, 1988.

Kalechofsky, Roberta. *Haggadah for the Liberated Lamb.* Marblehead, Massachusetts: Micah, 1988.

Kant, Immanuel. *Critique of Judgement.* Translated by James Creed Meredith; Revised and Edited by Nicholas Walker. Oxford: Oxford University Press, 2007.

Klawans, Jonathan. "Sacrifice in Ancient Israel: Pure Bodies, Domesticated Animals and the Divine Shepherd." Pages 65–80 in *A Communion of Subjects: Animals in Religion, Science and Ethics.* Edited by Paul Waldau and Kimberley Christine Patton. New York: Columbia University Press, 2006.

Koosed, "Conclusion." Pages 327–330 in *The Bible and Posthumanism*. Edited by Jennifer L. Koosed. Atlanta: Society of Biblical Literature, 2014.

LaCapra, Dominick. *History and its Limits: Human, Animal, Violence*. Ithaca: Cornell University Press, 2009.

Lin, Doris. "Ag-Gag Laws and Farming Crimes against Animals." Pages 466–478 in *The Routledge International Handbook of the Crimes of the Powerful*. Edited by Gregg Barak. London: Routledge, 2015.

Linzey, Andrew. *Christianity and the Rights of Animals*. New York: Crossroad, 1989.

Low, Philip. *The Cambridge Declaration on Consciousness*. Edited by Jaak Panksepp et al. July 7, 2012. http://fcmconference.org/img/CambridgeDeclarationOnConsciousness.pdf.

McClymond, Kathryn. "Sacrifice and Violence." Pages 320–330 in *The Blackwell Companion to Religion and Violence*. Edited by Andrew R. Murphy. Oxford: Wiley-Blackwell, 2011.

Murray, Michael J. *Nature Red in Tooth and Claw: Theism and the Problem of Animal Suffering*. Oxford: Oxford University Press, 2008.

Nibert, David. A. *Animal Oppression and Human Violence: Domesecration, Capitalism, and Global Conflict*. New York: Colombia University Press, 2013.

Nocella II, Anthony J., et al., eds. *Defining Critical Animal Studies: An Intersectional Social Justice Approach for Liberation*. New York: Peter Lang, 2013.

Pachirat, Timothy. *Every Twelve Seconds: Industrialized Slaughter and the Politics of Sight*. New Haven: Yale University Press, 2011.

Patton, Kimberley Christine. "Animal Sacrifice: Metaphysics of the Sublimated Victim." Pages 391–405 in *A Communion of Subjects: Animals in Religion, Science and Ethics*. Edited by Paul Waldau and Kimberley Christine Patton. New York: Columbia University Press, 2006.

Perlo, Katherine W. *Kinship and Killing: The Animal in World Religions*. New York: Colombia University Press, 2009.

Rachels, James. *Created from Animals: The Moral Implications of Darwinism*. Oxford: Oxford University Press, 1990.

Scarry, Elaine. *The Body in Pain: The Making and Unmaking of Worlds*. Oxford: Oxford University Press, 2003.

Schmidt, Lawrence. *The End of Ethics in a Technological Society*. Montreal: McGill-Queens University Press, 2008.

Schwartz, Richard H. *Judaism and Vegetarianism*. New York: Lantern Books, 2001.

Sears, David. *The Vision of Eden: Animal Welfare and Vegetarianism in Jewish Law and Mysticism*. Revised Edition. Meorei Ohr, 2015.

Seesengood, Robert Paul. "What Would Jesus Eat? Ethical Vegetarianism in Nascent Christianity." Pages 227–246 in *The Bible and Posthumanism*. Edited by Jennifer L. Koosed. Atlanta: Society of Biblical Literature, 2014.

Sherwood, Yvonne. "Cutting Up Life: Sacrifice as a Device for Clarifying and Tormenting Fundamental Distinctions between Human, Animal, and Divine." Pages 247–300 in *The Bible and Posthumanism*. Edited by Jennifer L. Koosed. Atlanta: Society of Biblical Literature, 2014.

Strommen, Hannah M. "Beastly Questions and Biblical Blame." Pages 13–28 in *The Bible and Posthumanism*. Edited by Jennifer L. Koosed. Atlanta: Society of Biblical Literature, 2014.

Suicidefood Blog. "Suicidal Tendencies." http://suicidefood.blogspot.ca.

Tardif, Nelson. *Au nom du marché: Regards sur une dimension méconnue du liberalisme économique: sa violence sacrificielle*. Montreal: MNH, 2013.

Waldau, Paul. "Seeing the Terrain we walk." Pages 40–64 in *A Communion of Subjects: Animals in Religion, Science and Ethics*. Edited by Paul Waldau and Kimberley Christine Patton. New York: Columbia University Press, 2006.

Weis, Tony. *The Ecological Hoofprint: The Global Burden of Industrial Livestock*. London: Zed Books, 2013.

Wolfe, Cary. *Zoontologies: The Question of the Animal*. Minneapolis: University of Minnesota Press, 2003.

World Health Organization (WHO). "IARC (International Agency for Research on Cancer) Monographs Evaluate Consumption of Red Meat and Processed Meat." Press Release 240. October 26, 2015. https://www.iarc.fr/en/media-centre/pr/2015/pdfs/pr240_E.pdf.

6

Is There Such a Thing as a Radicalized Brain?

Marc-André Argentino and Dalia Sabra

In his work *Fighting Words*, Hector Avalos sets out a new theory to explain how and why religion is prone to lead some people to violence. It is with this question in mind that he presents his scarce resource theory to explicate why violence occurs:

> 1) Most violence is due to scarce resources, real or perceived. Whenever people perceive that there is not enough of something they value, conflict may ensue to maintain or acquire that resource. This can range from love in a family to oil on a global scale. 2) When religion causes violence, it often does so because it has *created new scarce resources*."[1]

According to Avalos, people are more likely to fight, and to fight more brutally, when a scarce resource is at stake. In many cases the scarce resources are genuine (food, water, land, and so forth); however, in some cases they are not and this is where religion comes into play. Religions, argues Avalos, have created scarce resources where in reality there is no scarcity and this is what has and continues to cause people to fight over them. Once a religious group or individual claims to have the one true interpretation of a sacred text, decides that a particular location is a sacred site, or dictates the parameters for salvation, it is often made clear that access to such resources is limited to a privileged few. If a site is limited to one faith or belief system, then another cannot access it; if salvation does not extend to all equally, then only the initiated and true practitioners can acquire it. As a result, the uninitiated and unbelievers will not be saved.

---

1. Avalos, *Fighting Words*, 18.

The concept of scarce resources led us to contemplate the psychological factors related to scarcity as well as the evolutionary processes of fight and flight. What Avalos presents in his work can also play a role in the process behind radicalization. We believe that scarce resource theory can offer more than merely explaining why religion is prone to violence. As we have been developing a process by which to examine the ways young adults become radicalized, it has been made clear that a multi-disciplinary approach is needed. Many fields can examine and explain parts of the problem, but a complete approach has not yet been developed. We propose that the concept of gene and environment interaction be used as a way to approach and examine the process of radicalization, and the violent behaviour linked to this process. Violence and radicalization can be associated to a multiplicity of biological and environmental factors that can affect an individual or a group in a variety of ways. This is where Avalos's scarce resource theory can play a part in the larger frame of gene and environment interaction. In this essay, we first examine some possible genetic, biological, and neurochemical sources of violent behaviours. We then see how these biological factors can interact with environmental factors in order to shape the plasticity of the brain. The key environmental factor to be considered amongst others is the scarce resource theory.

Gene and Environment Interplay

Neurobiological[2] or psychological[3] explanations alone cannot answer why religious beliefs or practices can, in some cases, lead to violent behavior in human beings. Rather, the lacunae left behind by the solitary use of these methods indicate the need for a multi-disciplinary approach.[4] In light of this, we examine the problem of religion and violence through the lens of gene and environment interplay in order to provide a more comprehensive picture of what religion has to do with violence and what our brain and genes have to do with this behavior.

How do genes and environment interact together to shape human behavior? Both play equally important roles. A general fear held by many humans is that their behavior is solely pre-determined by their genetic

---

2. See Teehan, "The Evolved Brain;" Jalain, "The Impact of Serotonin and Dopamine."

3. See Orsini, "Poverty, Ideology and Terrorism;" Rice, "Emotions and Terrorism Research;" McGregor et al., "Motivation for Aggressive Religious Radicalization."

4. Reif et al., "Nature and Nurture."

makeup, which is their complete heritable genetic identity.[5] Evolution has acted so that genes capture the evolutionary responses to selection on particular behaviors that are crucial for survival.[6] The environmental context, on the other hand, is the surrounding, or the immediate condition, in which a person operates. A person's interaction with their surrounding environment gives them the ability to adjust adaptively, or change their behavior, during their developing years. Moreover, some environmental effects may be seen only under certain genetic conditions whereas some genetic effects may be seen only under certain environmental conditions. It is clear that the relationship between our genetic makeup and the environment we are exposed to is not a cause and effect relationship.

The contribution of genes and environment varies immensely among individuals. In general, genes and environment act independently, but can also interact in order to produce a wide range of behavioral traits that we see among individuals. An individual may have a genetic predisposition to violent behaviors, but may not show this trait unless he or she experiences environmental risk factors at an early age. However, some environments serve as a protective factor and prevent future behavioral problems among humans whereas others can amplify the risk of acting on those behaviors. The interplay of genes and environment on children's development is dynamic, but there are four main variations of nature-nurture interplay that clearly explain how environmental factors can directly or indirectly influence the expression of a genetic predisposition.[7] The most common interplay is the usual gene-environment interaction, where the environment of an individual can help or facilitate the risk of enhancing that genetic predisposition and vice-versa.[8] The second type of nature-nurture interplay is known as passive. In this scenario, biological parents may pass genotypes onto their children, as well as provide home environments that correlate with their genotypes.[9] For instance, the biological relatives may have a genetic predisposition to the MAOA[10] gene and provide an unstable environment for their offspring, putting their offspring at a higher risk for developing aggressive tendencies. Thirdly, evocative nature-nurture interplay refers to the association between the genotype of an individual and the environment

---

5. Breed and Sanchez, "Both Environment and Genetic Makeup," 68.
6. Ibid.
7. Dodge, "Mechanisms of Gene-Environment."
8. Hernandez, "Genetics and Health."
9. Lemery-Chalfant et al., "Childhood Temperament."
10. The X-linked monoamine oxidase A (MAOA) gene has previously been associated with impulsive aggression in animals and humans.

in which the child is raised.[11] It is the association between an individual's genetically influenced behavior and others' reactions to that behavior.[12] This entails that a child who is genetically predisposed to be aggressive may evoke aggressive reactions from their environment. Lastly, active nature-nurture interplay emphasizes the common perception that individuals seek an environment or a niche that is related to their genetic makeup.[13] Thus, individuals who are characteristically aggressive tend to select an aggressive environmental niche. All in all, different types of nature-nurture interplays demonstrate that some genetic effects may be seen under certain environmental contexts and some environmental effects may be only seen under certain genetic conditions.

Aggression during adolescence has become a multimodal problem in the world because of its deep-seeded roots in the neuro-chemical pathways of the human brain and its environmental influences. One biological implication is the neurotransmitter serotonin, which has been implicated in the modulation of aggression because of its inhibitory action in the brain.[14] Decreased serotonin function has consistently been shown to be highly correlated with impulsive aggression. Research has found associations between serotonergic dysfunction, especially low levels of the serotonin genotype and criminal behavior.[15] More specifically, serotonin hypofunction may represent a biochemical trait that predisposes individuals to unprovoked aggressive behavior.[16] How does an individual come about having depleted levels of serotonin? The precursor for the molecule serotonin is essentially the amino acid tryptophan, which happens to be found in our day-to-day diets. Normal healthy individuals who have a low tryptophan diet exhibit a significant increase in aggressive behavior since they are lacking the amino acid tryptophan. Though there is evidence that tryptophan is a key player in aggression, the development may vary from one person to another depending on their environmental circumstances. Nonetheless, medical research suggests that a balanced, protein rich diet is especially important during early childhood development.

The dopaminiergic system is composed of nerve cells, which originate in the midbrain. This group of nerve cells, which send their axons to different parts of the forebrain, has been highly correlated with aggression. The

11. Jaffee and Price, "Genotype–Environment Correlations."
12. Ibid.
13. Ibid.
14. Seo et al., "Role of Serotonin," 384.
15. Ibid., 385.
16. Ibid.

neurotransmitter dopamine itself is a neurochemical made in the brain that is involved in many activities including emotion and reward processing.[17] In humans, hyperactivity in the dopamine system is followed with a heightened response to impulsive aggression.[18] Various studies on aggressive behaviors involving rodents have shown that elevated levels of dopamine were seen before, during, and after an aggressive act.[19] In addition, hyperfunction of the dopamine system has been associated with impulsivity and emotional disturbances in patients with borderline personality disorders.[20] Overall, evidence from various studies acknowledges that dopamine plays an active role in the regulation of aggressive behaviors.

Let us take a further look at the role of gene and environment interplay by taking the previously mentioned MAOA gene as an example. The monoamine oxidase enzyme works by breaking down important neurotransmitters including dopamine and serotonin.[21] Further evidence comes from MAOA deficient mice that lack the enzyme responsible for the inhibition of certain neurotransmitters. As a result, elevated levels of serotonin and norepinephrine were observed, which led the mice to exhibit an overabundance of aggressive behavior.[22] Consequentially, people with the low activity form of the MAOA gene produce less of the enzyme responsible for the breakdown of those neurotransmitters, while the high-activity form of the gene produces more of the enzyme. This particular gene has been linked to impulsive, as well as delinquent behavior among adolescents.[23] This suggests that low-activity of the MAOA gene may lead to a disruption in mood and behavior during early childhood, which in turn can predict the aggressive and dysfunctional behaviors seen during early adulthood. Over the years, multiple studies[24] have tested the authenticity of the MAOA gene and its ability to predict violent behavior in humans. The evidence as a whole continuously shows that other factors besides low MAOA go into the making of aggressive individuals. An interaction with early life adversities such as abuse in childhood, a dysfunctional upbringing, and/or alienation from parents, increases the likelihood for future violent tenden-

17. Fundukian, *Gale Encyclopedia*, 74.
18. Seo et al., "Role of Serotonin," 386.
19. Ibid.
20. Ibid.
21. Cases et al., "Aggressive Behavior."
22. Merriman and Cameron, "Risk-Taking," U2240.
23. Baker et al., "Behavioral Genetics," 16.
24. Meyer-Lindenberg et al., "Neural Mechanisms;" McDermotta et al. "Monoamine."

cies. In a particular study, Caspi and his colleagues investigated the role of genotype in the cycle of violence in maltreated children. Their objective was to determine why some children who were maltreated grow up to develop antagonist behavior, whereas others do not. Their findings concluded that a polymorphism in the MAOA gene was found to moderate the effects of maltreatment.[25] Thus, children who were maltreated and had a genotype consisting of high levels of MAOA were less likely to develop aggressive behavior.[26]

Humiliation and Victimization

The findings suggest that aggressive behavior is being moderated through the interaction between genotype and environment. By itself, the genetic makeup of an individual is only a small proportion of the risk involved in violent behavior. The interaction with other biological, neurobiological, sociobiographical, and environmental factors is crucial. There is an interaction of multiple risk factors that give rise to deceitful, aggressive, and even violent behaviors among adolescents. Approaching the problem from the "genes" perspective alone does not provide us with answers. It is, however, crucial that we adopt a multi-disciplinary approach that examines both facets of biology and social science since nearly all behaviors result from a complex interaction between an individual's genetic makeup and the environmental influences that he or she has been exposed to since childhood. To demonstrate this, we use the effect of humiliation and victimization on human beings as an example of how environmental factors play their role in violent behavior.

Both the concepts of humiliation and victimization have been widely studied as important psychological factors that lead up to violent behavior, terrorism, extremism, and radicalization. What is humiliation? From an affective perspective:

> Humiliation, derived from the Latin humiliatus (made to lose self-respect) appears to have a strong aversive quality and to be significant across cultures; words that literally translate into the English "humiliation" and have the same connotation of lowering of status are found in languages as distinct as Hebrew, Polish, German, Hindi, Chinese and Urdu. Humiliation has been assumed to explain a variety of negative interpersonal and intergroup behaviors such as school related difficulties, psychological

25. Caspi et al., "Role of Genotype," 851.
26. Ibid.

disorders, marital discord, domestic violence, poverty, as well as intergroup conflict and violence. Despite its apparent real world importance across cultures, there is a paucity of empirical research into the experience of humiliation [19–20].[27]

Neil Walsh and Judy Kuriansky state that, "humiliation occurs when members of one group feel that they are not allowed to live life in a dignified way because of a perceived lack of recognition and respect from another group."[28] David Lacey explains humiliation as:

> . . .the emotion associated with being treated disrespectfully and undeservedly by others. 'How dare they treat me like that?' Humiliation occurs when others treat a group as if they perceive their worth or status to be lower than the group perceives it to be. What the group believes others think about them intensifies the emotion.[29]

The concepts of humiliation and shame are characterized as the result of a shame-inducing event,[30] depriving the subject of self-value, or self-respect, and ultimately inducing feelings of rejection. Furthermore, humiliation is a process of subjugation that damages or strips away a person's pride, honor, dignity, and their self-esteem. Humiliation destroys social hierarchy by demeaning and degrading; humiliation is the result of a forced lowering of a person or group of people.[31] Therefore, humiliation is the perception of an event as shameful; it depends on cultural parameters.

In *The Psychology of the Global Jihadists*, Farhad Khosrokhavar highlights three types of humiliation, some of which have already been mentioned: 1) physical, transcultural humiliation; 2) humiliation by proxy, which is the most universal in the Muslim world; and 3) humiliation based on its ideological justification through reference to the sacred register of jihad.[32]

As he elaborates, the first type of humiliation is one that is aimed at the body of another; this type of humiliation is found in warzones or during crisis situations. Khosrokhavar gives body searches as an example of this

---

27. Leidner et al., "Affective Dimensions." See also Klein, "Humiliation Dynamic;" Duhl, "Superfluous People;" Atran, "Genesis of Suicide;" Atran and Stern, "Small Groups."

28. Lindner et al., "Humiliation or Dignity," 99.

29. Lacey, "The Role of Humiliation," 78. See also Juergensmeyer, *Terror in the Mind of God*; Hassan, "Suicide Terrorism."

30. Wurmser, *Mask of Shame*, 51, 76.

31. Lindner et al., "Humiliation or Dignity," 100.

32. Khosrokhavar, "Psychology of the Global Jihadists," 144–145.

such as, an Israeli soldier that would stop and search Palestinians at check points, or an American that does the same to a Pakistani, or even Europeans that are stopping and searching Syrian refugees. Humiliation by proxy is exemplified by Muslims living in the West, who believe that they are humiliated in a similar manner to Muslims in a warzone. A Western Muslim, who sees examples of physical humiliation or the way that Syrian refugees are treated like cattle at the borders or processing stations,[33] feels downgraded in a similar fashion. It is an imaginary humiliation that stems from real underlying layers of shame, discrimination, racism, etc. However, this type of humiliation is created by the proxy of the media: news, television, social media, internet, etc. The third type of humiliation "shifts from individual and personal to general and holistic."[34] Ultimately, this type of humiliation "transforms stigma into absolute enmity toward the society. The aim is to destroy a society that is impious and godless and hates Muslims because of their faith."[35]

The role of humiliation and victimization can be caused by different situations. The three types of humiliation that Khosrokhavar presents can be the result of either conflict or globalization. Humiliation and victimization are mentioned as some of the important stepping-stones that lead to conflict and terrorism. This is something that has been clearly demonstrated in the role played by these processes in the Palestinian-Israeli conflict. In his work on this conflict, David Lacey mentions that:

> ...the daily humiliations of the people of Gaza helps to build a pool of resentful young men and women, and that this becomes a fertile recruitment ground for resistance organizations, and this recruitment can be described in terms of Moghaddam's staircase metaphor. Retaliation against aggression results in deeper humiliation and the cycle of violence continues.[36]

Zones of intense conflict create a perfect environment for the process of humiliation and victimization to operate: one will either be an oppressor or a victim/humiliated. Outside of a warzone, as Ömer Taspınar explains, globalization is a source of humiliation and victimization:

> Globalization creates an acute awareness about opportunities available elsewhere. This leads to frustration, victimization,

---

33. See the BBC News report "Migrant Crisis;" Bacchi, "EU Migrant Crisis;" Wilgress, "Forced into a Makeshift Enclosure."
34. Khosrokhavar, "Psychology of the Global Jihadists."
35. Ibid.
36. Lacey, "The Role of Humiliation," 77.

and humiliation among growing cohorts of urbanized, undereducated, and unemployed Muslim youth who are able to make comparisons across countries. The scale of youth frustration is compounded by a demographic explosion, growing expectations, weak state capacity, and diminishing opportunities for upward mobility in most parts of the Muslim world. Globalization further exacerbates this situation because restive Muslim masses of both genders are caught in the growing tension between religious tradition and western modernity.[37]

As Brown demonstrated in his classic study, social humiliation is associated with retaliatory behavior, even at an additional cost to the retaliator.[38] When an individual or a group feels humiliation, an appetite for revenge is felt. As Muenster and Lotto highlight in their examination of the psychology of humiliation: "The self, it is feared, will never be the same unless such injustice is appropriately addressed. What renders humiliation such a dangerous source for generating violence is the fact that such experiences are often fueled by long-lasting and extremely negative emotions."[39] These emotions are important to consider. Thus, when looking up the immediate and long term effect of racism and discrimination, which is something that plays an important role in humiliation via globalization as well as conflict, we can see that:

> Immediate emotional reactions can include fear, anger, confusion, sadness, humiliation, and shame. Longer-term emotional styles can also develop in reaction to cumulative experiences of racism and discrimination. These include bitterness, hostility, numbness, irritability, apathy, pessimism, suspiciousness, and agitated hypervigilance. These emotional styles represent adaptations to living in the context of racism, and their ultimate function is protective. However, prolonged exposure to racism, for someone who may have existing psychological vulnerabilities and inadequate resources, can contribute to increased risk for psychopathology, violence, or self-destructive behaviors.[40]

In the context of religious violence, the behaviors of violence or self-destruction that are a result of humiliation and victimization can express themselves through acts of terrorism or religious war.

---

37. Taspinar, "Fighting Radicalism," 78.
38. Brown, "Effects of Need to Maintain Face."
39. Muenster and Lotto, "Social Psychology," 72.
40. Jackson, *Encyclopedia*, 399.

Humiliation leads to a sense of victimization, which motivates avoidant behavior[41] as well as retaliative anger.[42] When an individual feels humiliation, there is an initial response of self-deprecation. The person who has been humiliated scrutinizes themselves as they feel that they did something wrong or that they are a bad person. This self-deprecation leads the humiliated individual to feel trapped and overwhelmed; thus, in such a situation human beings will tend to engage in defensive exercises. One manner in which control and agency are regained is to redirect the self-deprecation—an internal schema—towards an external force via anger and retaliation, as many studies have shown.[43] The risk of the humiliation process, for the Palestinian, the second or third generation migrant in the West, for the Syrian refugee, or any human being, is that humiliated individuals can manage this external schema of anger in an unconstructive fashion. In some cross-sectional developmental studies of children, adolescents, college students, and adults, proneness to shame was consistently related to malevolent intentions, direct, indirect and displaced aggression, self-directed hostility, and projected negative long-term consequences of everyday episodes of anger.[44]

If we take into account all of this information and return to our example of second or third generation migrants living in the West, this self-deprecation turned to anger will be aimed at the source of their humiliation and victimization. This is where the danger in humiliation and victimization is made present, in light of the narrative of jihadism and the quest for recognition that is present for some migrants living in the West:

> In Europe, where a large proportion of Muslims, mainly second- or third-generation migrants, are economically excluded and culturally stigmatized, jihadism is part of a narrative to demand recognition for those who believe they are denied recognition, as much in the Muslim world as in European societies. It is the inversion of the quest for recognition. Since Muslims are not recognized as full-fledged citizens, they opt for a jihadist identity that pushes them to the zenith of violence by which they will be recognized as villains and dreaded instead of despised. Inspiring fear is ersatz for the lack of recognition as respected citizens, mainly in Europe where radicalized Muslims believe that they are unwelcome, even more, rejected and scorned. In

---

41. Holtfortha, "Avoidance Motivation."
42. Leidner et al., "Affective Dimensions."
43. See Leidner et al., "Affective Dimensions;" Seo et al., "Role of Serotonin," 386. See also Klein, "Humiliation Dynamic;" Duhl, "Superfluous People;" Atran, "Genesis of Suicide;" Atran and Stern, "Small Groups."
44. Tangney et al., "Relation of Shame and Guilt."

the Muslim world it is the lack of recognition as political citizens with a say in social and political matters that pushes some to become jihadists.[45]

The quest for recognition and the narrative of jihad are elements that counter the sentiment of humiliation and turn it into glory through martyrdom; in turn the humiliator becomes the humiliated. Terrorism and religious violence, in this case, that stem from victimization and humiliation, turn "private action into collective action in the name of a radical version of Islam; aggressivity becomes boundless, confined by no frontier, its only limit the physical capacity of inflicting death through 'human bombs' who die in the name of a radical version of religion."[46]

What this implies is that a sense of injustice is the basis of all revenge; it is a primary cause of anger and rejection. The humiliated that retaliate perceive the self as victimized in order to conjure up a solid justification for violent conduct.[47] Furthermore, Pratyusha Tummala-Narra explains that:

> Collective trauma can be further understood through Volkan's conceptualization of "chosen trauma," which refers to the mental representation of an event that caused a large group of people to feel victimized, to be humiliated by another group, and to suffer losses, especially the loss of self-esteem. Although a particular ethnic group does not choose to be victimized, it does consciously and unconsciously attach significance to certain events. These traumas are linked with an inability to mourn or a disruption in a group's mourning of the experience.[48]

To summarize, both the effects of genes and the environment in an individual way can be a cause for violent and aggressive behavior; together they create the worst-case scenario. If we have an individual who has a neurochemical imbalance of dopamine or serotonin, or is found to have the MAOA gene, who has gone through either a process of humiliation and victimization, this individual is very likely to react in a violent or aggressive fashion. If, on the other hand, the same individual has a neurochemical imbalance or the individual's MAOA gene does not go through the psychological trauma of victimization of humiliation, then they are less likely to express violent behavior. Also, an individual who does not have a neurochemical imbalance or the MAOA gene, but goes through the process of

---

45. Khosrokhavar, "Psychology of the Global Jihadists," 143.
46. Ibid., 147.
47. Muenster and Lotto, "Social Psychology," 76.
48. Tummala-Narra, "Addressing Political and Racial Terror," 21.

being humiliated or victimized can also react with violent behavior, more so than only possessing the biological factors. Finally, an individual who does not have the MAOA gene and does not suffer through victimization or humiliation can either express violent behavior or not. What this implies is that there are multiple factors that must be considered in the gene and environment interplay that cannot simply be numbered one after another. As human beings we do not live in a vacuum; therefore, we must also take into consideration how our environment plays into the plasticity of our brain.

Neuroplasticty

When an individual is being radicalized, especially when we are concerned with a youth or a young adult, the plasticity of the brain can factor into the outcome of whether this individual will be violent or not. The brain's plasticity allows adolescents to learn and adapt, but by the same token it can also pose dangers. The adolescent years are noted to be a time of dramatic transformation in body and behavior; it is also the time when the human brain undergoes the most changes. Consequently, different rates of development can lead to increased risk-taking behavior and more importantly, poor decision making. From childhood through adolescence, the human brain alters in many significant ways. A notable difference can be observed in neurotransmitters since they peak during childhood then decline during adolescence.[49] Most important are changes in brain structures that are crucially involved in the regulation of aggressive behavior. Studies of glucose metabolism assessed with PET reveal prefrontal abnormalities in individuals more prone to impulsive aggression.[50]

Children and adolescents become better able to regulate their own thoughts, emotions, and behaviors as they develop. One of the most complex and important regions of our brain is the limbic system. This system is composed of evolutionary structures that are involved in the regulation of many of our emotions. Specifically, this region of our brain allows us to feel guilt, anger, and is related to many behaviors that are crucial for our survival. It includes structures such as the amygdala, the hippocampus, and the basal ganglia, which are all implicated in various aspects of emotion regulation and affective style.[51] One important component of the basal ganglia is a structure called the nucleus accumbens, which plays a significant role in the processing of pleasure and reward to risk-taking. In addition, the frontal

49. Johnson et al., "Adolescent Maturity."
50. Davidson et al., "Dysfunction in the Neural Circuitry," 593.
51. Ibid., 591.

lobe is an upper area of the cortex, which is responsible for executive control and functions to carry out higher order mental processes such as decision-making and planning. This division of the cerebral cortex is among the last areas of the brain to mature.[52] Similarly, part of the frontal lobe called the prefrontal cortex coordinates specific cognitive processes such as response inhibition, which allows an individual to pause and assess a situation, assess his or her options, plan a course of action, and execute it.[53] Damage or underdevelopment of the prefrontal cortex can lead to difficulty with mental inflexibility all of which could undermine judgment and decision-making.[54]

During the adolescent years, the brain areas that are involved in emotion and executive control are the ones that undergo the most changes. Due to its comprehensive cognitive complexity and its unlimited potential for neuronal plasticity, the brain has the ongoing ability to continuously rewire its cognitive functions. Studies that consistently show the interplay between different anatomical structures help us understand the emergence of new cognitive and behavioral changes that we see in adolescence. In addition, the constant interplay between the socio-emotional system of the brain and the cognitive control system of the brain help us to understand some aspects of risk-taking behavior that we see emerge during adolescence.[55] To further illustrate, one study compared brain activation during various cognitive tasks in thirty-seven participants ranging between seven to twenty-nine years of age. In this particular experiment, they were able to explore risk-taking behavior in adolescents by exploring the development of the nucleus accumbens relative to the orbitofrontal cortex.[56] Their findings showed that the response to rewards in the nucleus accumbens of adolescents was equivalent to that of adults, but the activity in the adolescent orbitofrontal cortex was similar to that seen in children.[57] The results of this study highlight the problematic reality that most, if not the majority, of adolescents have not yet fully cognitively matured; attributed in part to their underdeveloped frontal lobes. This earlier development of the accumbens relative to the orbitofrontal cortex may serve as a primary risk factor, making these individuals more prone to risk taking behavior due to their lack of impulse control and inadequate decision-making.

---

52. Johnson et al., "Adolescent Maturity," 216.
53. Ibid., 218.
54. Ibid.
55. Ibid.
56. Galvan et al., "Earlier Development," 6885.
57. Ibid.

For youths aged thirteen to twenty, the experiences they live or the environment they are raised in plays an important role in the psychological make-up since they are more vulnerable to their environment. Consequentially, their environment has to be protective rather than a risk factor due to the vulnerability of their brain during the adolescent years (the prefrontal cortex stops growing approximately at the age of twenty). In light of this, psychological factors found in their environment can play an important role in the process of radicalization and ultimately violent behavior. Potentially, this can be activated by a multiplicity of social and psychological factors, which can prompt one's inherent violent tendencies. Human beings are victims of their social-psychological environment, part of which is the concept of ideology[58] or religious belief. How is it that an ideology can affect and shape the psychological construct of our brains? In a 2009 experiment by Dimitrios Kapogiannis et al., the cognitive and neuronal foundations of religious belief were examined. The aim of their experiment was to, "define the psychological structure of religious belief, based on fundamental cognitive processes, and to reveal the corresponding pattern of brain activation to determine the relevance of evolutionary theories of cognitive development to the development of religious beliefs."[59] Their experiment was concerned with an examination of three key components: First, ideology/religious belief presupposes intent-related and emotional theory of mind being applied to supernatural agents, a fact that links fundamental aspects of social cognition to religious belief.[60] Secondly, any belief system relies on a body of semantic and event knowledge. One source of semantic knowledge for religious belief is doctrine. Aspects of doctrine may be rooted in intuitive world-theory creation inherent in all humans, such as belief in the existence of nonmaterial agents. However, doctrine, which has abstract linguistic content, is for the most part specific to various institutionalized religions and is culturally transmitted. Finally, another source of religious knowledge is event knowledge stemming from personal experiences explicitly religious, but also from multiple social and moral events influenced by religion, religious beliefs, or ideology. In this view, religious knowledge forms a continuum from doctrinal to experiential, and most beliefs draw from both sources.[61] The results found that "religious belief engages well-known brain networks performing abstract semantic processing, imagery,

58. We understand ideology to be a set of ideas, doctrines, and beliefs that characterize the thinking of an individual or group and may transform into political and social plans, actions, or systems.
59. Kapogiannis et al., "Cognitive and Neural Foundations."
60. Ibid., 4876.
61. Ibid.

and intent-related and emotional theory of mind, processes known to occur at both implicit and explicit levels."[62] In light of this, the process of adopting religious beliefs or an ideology depends on cognitive-emotional interactions. The experiment concludes:

> ...religiosity is integrated in cognitive processes and brain networks used in social cognition, rather than being sui generis. The evolution of these networks was likely driven by their primary roles in social cognition, language, and logical reasoning. Religious cognition likely emerged as a unique combination of these several evolutionarily important cognitive processes.[63]

This experiment shows the important cognitive effect that religious belief can have. Furthermore, religious belief is an important evolutionary process in human beings. The cognitive psychological impact on religious beliefs are very real as religious ideologies have a greater explanatory reach than most other ideologies because they address questions of existence, ultimate causality, and absolute morality. The fact that there are no objectively correct or scientifically verifiable answers to such questions, religious ideologies invoke a rich symbolic and supernatural universe prescribing appropriate emotions and behaviors. They also specify normative practices relating to daily life; although the framing, to a varying degree, is in terms of the sacred or divine, the focus is on everyday life choices and behavioral routines. However, when approaching the problem of religious violence and extremism, we have to emphasize the "group" nature of the phenomenon. Part of this group phenomenon is the central role played by belief and ideology for the group, as well as for the individuals that make up the group; for whom ideology is of prodigious importance. Nehemia Friedland states that when the ideology of a group is threatened, the concept of ideology can be a real source of deeply felt anger and frustration.[64] Mark Juergensmeyer echoes this as he states that:

> ...religious terrorists themselves have fostered: the image of a world at war between secular and religious forces. A belligerent secular enemy has often been just what religious activists have hoped for. In some cases it makes recruitment to their causes easier. For it demonstrates that the secular side can be as brutal as it has been portrayed by their own religious ideologues.[65]

62. Ibid., 4879.
63. Ibid.
64. Friedland, "Becoming a Terrorist."
65. Juergensmeyer, *Terror in the Mind of God*, 235.

What this implies is that the individuals in a group of religious terrorists sincerely believe that their ideals are under siege. "The cultures (in the sense of a social group with an ideology) have the perception that their communities are being violated and their acts are simply a response to the violence they have experienced. Humiliation and revenge are key motivators."[66] This is where Hector Avalos's scarce resource theory comes into play in an important way. When considering the importance of ideology and religious belief on the cognitive and neuronal functions of an individual, the doctrinal system of religious terrorists creates a scarce resource of belief, salvation, sacred space, and group privileging. As he states:

> Islam is many things, and violence has been part of its theology from the beginning. As is the case with Christianity and Judaism, Islam has created scarce resources that always have the potential for violence. Muslim scriptural traditions have been held to be sufficiently valuable to kill others who may challenge their authority as indicated by the Qurayza massacre. Sacred spaces have been created, and many Muslims feel that death is part of the price of defending them. Group privilege has resulted in oppression and violence toward non-Muslims. Salvation is premised on the existence of a torturous and eternalized violence called hellfire. Above all, Muhammad, who is held to be the paradigm of Muslim behavior, committed acts of unspeakable violence that are still imitated today.[67]

This concept of scarce resource is not limited to Islam, but also applies to Judaism and Christianity. Avalos examines the effect of scarce resource theory in relation to the ideology of Nazism and Stalinism. What this implies is that if one's ideology or religious belief—that is an integral part of a person's evolutionary makeup and part of their social cognitive construct—is under attack then that person will want to fight and defend their belief system. It becomes part of the fight or flight mechanism; one's identity, social group, and reason for existing are attacked by an external force. These environmental factors will affect the plasticity of the brain. They will interact with possible biological and genetic dispositions; they will shape the neurological, cognitive, and psychological structures and thus influence a person's behavior and actions to their core.

Avalos's work plays a role in the larger image of the radicalized brain. It is an important environmental factor that has a significant impact on the individual and group psychology of religious practitioners and ideological

---

66. Terman, "Theories of Group Psychology," 26.
67. Avalos, *Fighting Words*, 274.

believers. However, on its own, scarce resource theory does not cover all elements that lead to violence. It is a piece of the larger puzzle of how religion can lead to violence, yet one that cannot be ignored. The ultimate problem is that there is probably no single methodological approach, model, or theory that can explain violent behaviors or radicalization found in religious or ideological belief. Each stratum has its own psychological and environmental factors to be considered and on the individual level we have the biological factors that can play into the ultimate result. This is why we believe that gene and environment need to be considered in the examination of radicalization, terrorism, and religious violence. It can provide the most complete set of tools that scholars and researchers can use in order to examine the issue at hand; however, it also requires that scholars and researchers depart from their siloed practices, approaches, and methods. As we have shown, biological, sociological, psychological, philosophical, or environmental factors alone cannot account for, or encompass, all possible explanations. A multi-disciplinary approach is the only solution that is viable, as there is a multiplicity of causes and consequences that can lead to one same result: violence sourced by a particular religious belief or ideology.

Bibliography

Atran, Scott. "Genesis of Suicide Terrorism." *Science* 299 (2003) 1534–1539.

Atran, Scott, and Jessica Stern. "Small Groups Find Fatal Purpose through the Web." *Nature* 437 (2005) 620.

Avalos, Hector. *Fighting Words: The Origins of Religious Violence.* Amherst, New York: Prometheus Books, 2005.

Bacchi, Umberto. "EU Migrant Crisis: Hungary Refugee Camp like 'Cattle in Pens.'" *International Business Times.* September 11, 2015. http://www.ibtimes.co.uk/eu-migrant-crisis-hungary-refugee-camp-like-cattle-pens-video-reveals-1519383.

Baker, Laura A., et al. "Behavioral Genetics: The Science of Antisocial Behavior." *Law and Contemporary Problems* 69:1–2 (2006) 7–46.

Breed, Michael D., and Leticia Sanchez. "Both Environment and Genetic Makeup Influence Behavior." *Nature Education Knowledge* 3:10 (2010) 68.

Brown, Bert R. "The Effects of Need to Maintain Face on Interpersonal Bargaining." *Journal of Experimental Social Psychology* 4 (1968) 107–122.

Cases, Olivier, et al. "Aggressive Behavior and Altered Amounts of Brain Serotonin and Norepinephrine in Mice Lacking MAOA." *Science* 268:5218 (1995) 1763–1766.

Caspi, Avshalom, et al. "Role of Genotype in the Cycle of Violence in Maltreated Children." *Science* 297:5582 (2002) 851–854.

Davidson, Richard J., et al. "Dysfunction in the Neural Circuitry of Emotion Regulation: A Possible Prelude to Violence." *Science* 289:5479 (2000) 591–594.

Dodge, Kenneth A. "Mechanisms of Gene-Environment Interaction Effects in the Development of Conduct Disorder." *Perspectives on Psychological Science* 4:4 (2009) 408–414.

Duhl, Leonard. "Superfluous People in Tomorrow's Society." *Journal of Primary Prevention* 12 (1992) 243–254.

Friedland, Nehemia. "Becoming a Terrorist: Social and Individual Antecedents." Pages 81–93 in *Terrorism: Roots, Impact, Responses.* Edited by Lawrence Howard. New York: Praeger, 1992.

Fundukian, Laurie J. *Gale Encyclopedia of Medicine.* Detroit: Cengage Gale, 2008.

Galvan, A., et al. "Earlier Development of the Accumbens Relative to Orbitofrontal Cortex Might Underlie Risk-Taking Behavior in Adolescents." *The Journal of Neuroscience* 26:25 (2006) 6885–6892.

Hassan, Nasra. "Suicide Terrorism." *The Roots of Terrorism.* Edited by Louise Richardson. New York, New York: Routledge, 2006.

Hernandez, Lyla M. "Genetics and Health." Pages 44–67 in *Genes, Behavior, and the Social Environment: Moving Beyond the Nature Nurture Debate.* Edited by Lyla M. Hernandez and Dan G. Blazer. Washington: National Academies, 2006.

Holtfortha, Martin Grosse. "Avoidance Motivation in Psychological Problems and Psychotherapy." *Psychotherapy Research* 18:2 (2008) 147–159.

Jackson, Yolanda Kaye. *Encyclopedia of Multicultural Psychology*. London: Sage, 2006.

Jaffee, Sara R., and Thomas S. Price. "Genotype–Environment Correlations: Implications for Determining the Relationship between Environmental Exposures and Psychiatric Illness." *Psychiatry* 7:12 (2008) 496–499.

Jalain, Caroline Isabelle. "The Impact of Serotonin and Dopamine on Human Aggression: A Systematic Review of the Literature." Master's Theses. University of Southern Mississippi, 2014.

Johnson, Sara B., et al. "Adolescent Maturity and the Brain: The Promise and Pitfalls of Neuroscience Research in Adolescent Health Policy." *Journal of Adolescent Health* 45:3 (2009) 216–221.

Juergensmeyer, Mark. *Terror in the Mind of God: The Global Rise of Religious Violence*. Los Angeles: University of California Press, 2003.

Kapogiannis, Dimitrios, et al. "Cognitive and Neural Foundations of Religious Belief." *Proceedings of the National Academy of Sciences* 106:12 (2009) 4876–4881.

Khosrokhavar, Farhad. "The Psychology of the Global Jihadists." Pages 139–155 in *The Fundamentalist Mindset: Psychological Perspectives on Religion, Violence, and History*. Edited by David M. Terman, et al. New York: Oxford University Press, 2010.

Klein, Donald C. "The Humiliation Dynamic: An Overview." *Journal of Primary Prevention* 12:2 (1991) 93–121.

Lacey, David. "The Role of Humiliation in the Palestinian/Israeli Conflict in Gaza." *Psychology & Society* 4 (2011) 76–92.

Leidner, Bernhard, et al. "Affective Dimensions of Intergroup Humiliation." *PLoS One* 7:9 (2012) 1–5.

Lemery-Chalfant, et al. "Childhood Temperament: Passive Gene-Environment Correlation, Gene-Environment interaction, and the Hidden importance of the Family Environment." *Development and Psychopathology* 25 (2013) 51–63.

Lindner, Evelin Gerda, et al. "Humiliation or Dignity in the Israeli-Palestinian Conflict." Pages 99–106 in *Terror in the Holy Land: Inside the Anguish of the Israeli-Palestinian Conflict*. Edited by Judith Kuriansky. Westport, Connecticut: Praeger, 2006.

McDermotta, Rose, et al. "Monoamine Oxidase A Gene (MAOA) Predicts Behavioral Aggression Following Provocation." *Proceedings of the National Academy of Sciences of the United States of America* 106:7 (2008) 2118–2123.

McGregor, Ian, et al. "Motivation for Aggressive Religious Radicalization: Goal Regulation Theory and a Personality x Threat X Affordance Hypothesis." *Frontiers in Psychology* 6:1325 (2015) 1–18.

Merriman, Tony, and Vicky A. Cameron. "Risk-Taking: Behind the Warrior Gene Story." *The New Zealand Medical Journal* 120:1250 (2007) U2440.

Meyer-Lindenberg, Andreas, et al. "Neural Mechanisms of Genetic Risk for Impulsivity and Violence in Humans." *Proceedings of the National Academy of Sciences of the United States of America* 103:16 (2005) 6269–6274.

"Migrant Crisis: People Treated 'Like Animals' in Hungary Camp." BBC News. September 11, 2015. http://www.bbc.com/news/world-europe-34216883.

Muenster, Bettina, and David Lotto. "The Social Psychology of Humiliation and Revenge." Pages 71–81 in *The Fundamentalist Mindset: Psychological Perspectives on Religion, Violence, and History*. Edited by David M. Terman, et al. New York: Oxford University Press, 2010.

Orsini, Alessandro. "Poverty, Ideology and Terrorism: The STAM Bond." *Studies in Conflict & Terrorism* 35:10 (2016) 665–692.

Reif, Andreas, et al. "Nature and Nurture Predispose to Violent Behavior: Serotonergic Genes and Adverse Childhood Environment." *Neuropsychopharmacology* 32 (2007) 2375–2383.

Rice, Stephen K. "Emotions and Terrorism Research: A Case for a Social-Psychological Agenda." *Journal of Criminal Justice* 37 (2009) 248–255.

Seo, Dongju, et al. "Role of Serotonin and Dopamine System Interactions in the Neurobiology of Impulsive Aggression and its Comorbidity with other Clinical Disorders." *Aggression and Violent Behavior* 13:5 (2008) 383–395.

Tangney, June Price, et al. "Relation of Shame and Guilt to Constructive Versus Destructive Responses to Anger Across the Lifespan." *Journal of Personality and Social Psychology* 70:4 (1996) 797–809.

Taspinar, Ömer. "Fighting Radicalism, Not 'Terrorism': Root Causes of an International Actor Redefined." *SAIS Review of International Affairs* 29:2 (2009) 75–86.

Teehan, John. "The Evolved Brain: Understanding Religious Ethics and Religious Violence." Pages 233–254 in *The Moral Brain: Essays on the Evolutionary and Neuroscientific Aspects of Morality*. Edited by Jan Verplaetse, et al. New York: Springer, 2009.

Terman, David M. "Theories of Group Psychology, Paranoia, and Rage." Pages 16–28 in *The Fundamentalist Mindset: Psychological Perspectives on Religion, Violence, and History*. Edited by Charles B. Strozier, et al. New York: Oxford University Press, 2010.

Tummala-Narra, Pratyusha. "Addressing Political and Racial Terror in the Therapeutic Relationship." *American Journal of Orthopsychiatry* 75 (2005) 19–26.

Wilgress, Lydia. "Forced into a Makeshift Enclosure and Thrown Food like Animals in a Pen: Shocking Footage Shows Hungarian Police in Hygiene Masks Hurling Sandwiches at Hungry Migrants who Scramble for the Bags of Food." Mailonline. September 11, 2015. http://www.dailymail.co.uk/news/article-3230425/Desperate-migrants-forced-makeshift-enclosure-thrown-sandwiches-like-animals-pen-Hungarian-police-shocking-footage-reveals.html.

Wurmser, Leon. *The Mask of Shame*. Baltimore, Maryland: Johns Hopkins University Press, 1981.

7

Religion and Violence

Rethinking the Role of the Biblical Scholar in the Contemporary World

CALOGERO A. MICELI

IN HIS BOOK *THE End of Biblical Studies*, Hector Avalos puts forth a radical critique of the field of biblical studies because, in its current state, he views it as a religionist and apologetic operation which primarily seeks to maintain the value of the Bible in the present day.[1] He argues,

> Many persons in the modern world still hold to biblical ideas (e.g., creationism)...because academic biblical scholars are not sufficiently vocal about undermining outdated biblical beliefs. Instead, such scholars concentrate on maintaining the value of the biblical text in modern society.[2]

The following essay is directly related to exploring this particular issue and asks a very important question for the field of biblical scholarship: what is the role of the biblical scholar in relation to maintaining or disavowing, for contemporary readers, the value of texts like those contained in the Bible (or other religious texts)? This question is further complicated when we consider the issue of biblical texts used to commit or promote violent actions. At the core of our question is the extent to which biblical scholars should or should not interject themselves in what they are writing for and teaching to the public.

Following some explanations of the field of biblical studies and a brief definition of the biblical scholar more broadly, this essay surveys some of

---

1. Avalos, *The End of Biblical Studies*.
2. Ibid., 18.

the recent contentious debates that have emerged in relation to the field of biblical studies and how these intersect with faith and secularism. As we shall see, the field of biblical studies has, in recent years, been the subject of re-examination by a number of scholars including Hector Avalos, Philip Davies, and others. After briefly overviewing these current shifts, the essay turns to exploring the role of modern-day biblical scholars who, in researching, writing, and teaching others about the Bible, must position themselves with respect to the value of these ancient texts for today's audiences. Three positions are outlined: those who maintain the value of biblical texts, those who disavow their value for the present day, and finally, a neutrally inclined stance, advocated by this paper.

The essay argues that today's academics have a social responsibility to the public and, as a result, should strive to be as objective as possible. The role of the academic biblical scholar should *no longer be* to maintain the value of the biblical texts, or any religious texts (ancient or modern) for that matter. By the same token, this paper questions whether that should be taken to the other extreme, as Avalos does, in trying to end the practice of modern readers who continue to find meaning in these texts. Taking the stance of explicitly ending or maintaining the value of the New Testament or other biblical or religious texts is deemed too forceful a stance; rather, the role of the biblical scholar should be to explain how ancient audiences—those for whom and by whom the biblical texts were written—found value in these writings and also how they have and continue to be infinitely re-appropriated with each passing generation by people in every corner of the world. Even today, two-thousand years after they were first penned, there are still large numbers of people who read and use religious texts, like the Bible, as a means of guiding and governing their lives. This happening can be academically studied and critiqued without necessarily being promoted or rejected. While those biblical scholars who maintain the value of the Bible today are mistaken for doing so, the rejection or condemnation of the men and women who continue to use the Bible as a guide for their lives is also unsuitable. The ambition of the academic discipline of biblical studies should be to study and critique all areas of biblical and religious studies from as objective a standpoint as possible. Though it is impossible to be wholly objective or neutral, the biblical scholar should try to stand on the outside looking in. The chief exceptions to this tenet, I argue, are in cases when religious texts are used to promote, incite, or justify forms of violence in the world. In such instances, the duty of the biblical scholar must unreservedly be to intervene and strongly disavow the use of religious texts in such deplorable manners.

Biblical Studies & Biblical Scholars

What is the field of biblical studies and who are its specialists? According to Judith Lieu and J. W. Rogerson in their preface to *The Oxford Handbook of Biblical Studies*, biblical studies is defined as, "a collection of various, and in some cases independent, disciplines clustering around a collection of texts known as the Bible whose precise limits (those of the Bible) are still a matter of disagreement among various branches of the Christian churches."[3] Thus, from this definition, we can infer that a biblical scholar is one who undertakes these disciplines and applies them in the study of the Bible, which consists of the Hebrew Bible (referred to by some as the Old Testament) and the New Testament. For the purposes of this paper we limit our discussion to biblical scholars, but note that an understanding of the role of the biblical scholar is nevertheless applicable and relevant to how we understand the role of religious studies scholars more generally.

Michael Legaspi, in his book *The Death of Scripture and the Rise of Biblical Studies*, explores how the Bible was reconceived during the advent of modern biblical criticism.[4] For most of the history of the Christian faith, the biblical texts were read from a confessional perspective; its authority embedded in the Christian Church. This type of reading, however, was unsettled during the Reformation period when more academic ways of reading the Bible emerged. Modern biblical studies, then, has its origins in the eighteenth century CE where German Enlightenment scholars such as Gotthold Lessing, Johann Semler, and Johann Michaelis sought to interpret the Bible, not in a confessional context as had been done previously, but from a historical and cultural perspective.[5]

Today, in universities, colleges, and divinity schools around the world, the Bible is still very much the focus of investigation and study. In many of these institutions the field of biblical studies is taught as an academic discipline. However, while the rise of biblical criticism liberated the Christian Church's authority over the Bible, there are differing approaches for studying the Bible academically, several of which cling to faith. There are some scholars and academics that even today adhere to the authority of the Bible and uphold it as the word of God or as divinely inspired, while others are committed to a humanistic understanding of the Bible and religions in general. These two opposing camps are often labeled as conservative/evangelical biblical scholars and liberal/academic biblical scholars respectively.

3. Rogerson and Lieu, *Oxford Handbook of Biblical Studies*, xvii.

4. Legaspi, *Death of Scripture*. See also Morrow, "The Enlightenment University," 897–922.

5. Legaspi, *Death of Scripture*, 26.

Intersections of Biblical Studies, Secularism, and Faith

As it stands today, the field of biblical studies is struggling to find its footing between the boundaries of the confessional and the academic. In recent writings and publications, many scholars have interjected their opinions on the current field of biblical studies and have argued contentiously about its future. The discipline finds itself caught in-between two modes of thinking. As Simkins explains:

> [There has been] a long-running debate within biblical studies. Unlike the fields of religious studies and theology, the role of faith and theology remains unsettled in biblical studies. Religious studies, for example, has been defined as a secular discipline that examines religious beliefs and practices from an external, objective position. It is a widely accepted academic discipline at most universities, and the religious studies professor is like the historian, sociologist, anthropologist, or psychologist who studies religious subjects. Theologians, in contrast, tend to be adherents of the faith they study. Theology is generally thought to be a religious academic discipline – "faith seeking understanding," as first articulated by Anselm – and is largely relegated to religiously affiliated universities and seminaries. The secular status of biblical studies within the academy and university, however, is not clearly defined. It functions within both religious studies and theology, and so the discipline's relationship to secularism and faith remains disputed.[6]

Simkins effectively points out one of the major issues plaguing biblical studies today, which is that in the academic university setting, it is struggling to find its place either as Theology or as Religious Studies. As a result of this tension, what we are now seeing are scholars weighing in on the place and nature of biblical studies. There are those who would want to see a secular brand of biblical studies with no ties or relationship to faith, while others who posit for more confessional biblical scholarship upholding the place of theology and faith in the field.[7]

Among those who advocate that faith and theology are necessary for the discipline of biblical studies,[8] is Jim West. West writes that the field today is too atheistic in its approach and, as a result, is what has led to an

---

6. Simkins, "Biblical Studies," 1.

7. See Gross, "The Place of the Personal," 168; Simkins, "Biblical Studies;" Simkins, "Scientific Nonsense."

8. See Bulkeley, "The No-man's-land."

ignorant population. For West, the Bible is the Christian Church's book and faith is the glue of the books therein.[9] He writes:

> Atheists and unbelievers didn't write a word of [the Bible], transmit it, preserve it, or pass it along. No one can argue with the fact that the Bible is the book of the people of faith. It belongs to us. Not to the atheists. They are now and have been and always will be outsiders to it. Their point of view, then, is as mere observers.[10]

In my opinion, West's ideas are utterly senseless and without basis. The Bible, as it is, does not belong to anyone, be it people of faith or people without faith. His arguments are both untenable and illogical. The notion that those who do not have faith should be excluded from studying or working with biblical texts is an utterly unsustainable proposition.

A more sound promotion of the idea that secularism does not preclude faith can be found in the writing of Simkins.[11] Of particular interest is the argument that since a majority of the world's population has faith, in some form or another, then faith should hold a place in the academic study of the Bible.[12] This faith, however, need not be tied to the Christian Church. In essence, those who recognize the place of faith and theology in the university see this as free from religious authority. This brand of biblical studies, which embraces theology and faith, is understood as keeping in-line with the academic study of the Bible that emerged and flourished during the eighteenth and nineteenth centuries CE. For such advocates, there is need for a place like the academic forum where higher truths can be freely discussed.

On the other hand, we have those who argue for a more secular brand of academic biblical studies. One such proponent is Philip Davies whose book, first published in 1996, *Whose Bible is it Anyway*, stands out as a call for a genuinely academic discourse on the Bible removed from confessional studies.[13] Davies suggests that confessional and non-confessional approaches to studying the Bible are so different that they require separate disciplines.[14] Though not always entirely the same, there have been other scholars who have argued, in one form or another, for a move away from faith in biblical studies.[15] Although an exhaustive exploration into each of

9. West, "The Sackgasse."
10. Ibid.
11. Simkins, "Biblical Studies."
12. Ibid., 14.
13. Davies, *Whose Bible*.
14. Ibid., 13.
15. See Berlinerblau, *Secular Bible*.

these pieces and opinions is beyond the scope of this essay, I mention some of the authors whose works have stood out. One of these is Ronald Hendel who, in 2010, published an opinion piece in *Biblical Archeology Review* entitled, "Farewell to SBL: Faith and Reason in Biblical Studies," where he openly criticized the SBL (Society of Biblical Literature) for blurring the distinction between secular biblical studies and faith-based biblical studies.[16] More recently, Roland Boer has edited a volume of essays in a book entitled, *Secularism and Biblical Studies*.[17] The book represents the most wide-ranging exploration of the topic to date. Finally, Hector Avalos has also contributed to the discussion on the state of biblical studies in many of his works, the most notable being his book *The End of Biblical Studies*.[18] His thesis is further explored below.

The problem of reconciling secular or devotional biblical studies in academic institutions is not a simple task given the fact that many institutions were founded by religious denominations and some are still religiously affiliated today. In many cases, biblical scholars are employed at religiously sponsored seminaries and colleges with expectations that their work (in research and teaching) contributes to the religious life of the students, the institution, and the community. Some professors are expected to teach in accordance with the religion affiliated with the college or seminary. Many are even required to sign faith statements before they can accept a position to work at such institutions. Academic freedom, then, can be very restrictive in these cases.[19] As a result, the religious institution largely regulates what can or cannot be publicly taught and written about the Bible.

Role of the Biblical Scholar Today

As it has been shown, the current state of affairs in the field of biblical studies is complex. It is inundated with a variety of approaches to studying the Bible, which intersect faith and secularism.[20] The issue extends from individual academics to institutions as a whole. All of this is relevant for the question at hand, which asks about the role of the biblical scholar in main-

16. Hendel, "Farewell to SBL," 28–29.

17. Boer, *Secularism*.

18. Avalos, *The End of Biblical Studies*.

19. See Davis, "Academic Freedom," 76–80; Withrow and Wecker, *Consider no Evil*.

20. Similarly, there have also been recent debates on the question of the religious studies scholar's role in the field. Are scholars to be viewed as caretakers of the religious traditions and their aspects or are they critics of these faiths? See McCutcheon, *Critics Not Caretakers*.

taining or ending the value of biblical texts. Of course, the answer provided to the question may be heavily shaped by one's own views on how biblical studies more generally should be conducted today. But, for those who study the Bible from an academic perspective, in the classrooms and seminars of academic institutions, not the churches or the synagogues, what position should be taken in regards to biblical texts? Should biblical scholars maintain the value of these texts today, which were and still are being used and highly regarded by groups of men and women (some of which are the ones studying these texts themselves), or should scholars disavow their usefulness in the present age? As it pertains to answering this question, I see three possible positions. Through teaching, researching, and writing, the biblical scholar can either choose to uphold the value of the ancient texts, disavow their usefulness and importance, or stand neutral.

Those who would wish to maintain the value of the Bible are sympathizers who see it as beneficial for the modern world. They see the biblical texts as having purpose and meaning for the lives of modern readers. No doubt, this view is shared among religious believers as well. Millions of Jews, Christians, Muslims, Hindus, and so forth, all believe that their religious texts hold significance since the core of their beliefs and practices are shaped and informed by the sacred religious texts they hold dear. This acclaim for the writings is shared by some scholars who themselves may adhere to a particular religious tradition or sympathetically value the usefulness of religious texts for guiding one's life no matter what religious tradition they may or may not associate with. Since many biblical scholars are themselves believers they evidently uphold the importance of religious texts for other believers as well.

So then, what is the role of the biblical scholar for those who maintain the value of biblical texts today? For Michael Lafargue, the answer is clear:

> . . .the role of the biblical scholar, as scholar, is to be a servant of the biblical text, to guard its otherness, to help make its substantive content something modern people can in some way experience and understand, in its particularity and in its otherness. As scholar, the biblical researcher has this invaluable and irreplaceable expertise and role to perform, and it should be done self-effacingly.[21]

This stance, in my opinion, is fraught with many flaws. The biblical scholar's role or responsibility is not and should not be as a servant to the biblical texts in any way, shape, or form. We need to make the texts of the Bible understandable for modern audiences, but always in context. They

21. LaFargue, "Are Texts Determinate?" 355.

were written at a different time and place. As a result, they reflect ideas, worldviews, and concepts from when they were conceived. That being said, there are components in the texts, like those in literary works, that transcend time and space and that can be read and appreciated by modern audiences. They speak, in some ways, to the human condition and even today people can and do connect their lives with the characters, stories, and events they hear or read about in religious texts. However, we must be conscious of the fact that the same approach is generally not taken with other ancient works. Most people in the world today do not use the literary works of Shakespeare or other ancient texts like the *Epic of Gilgamesh* as a guide for living their lives though the same cannot be said about religious texts. People are free to choose to live their lives by adhering to these religious books if they so please, but it is *not* the responsibility of the academic biblical scholar to help promote this endeavor. The scholar's role should be to explain, study, and understand the practices of those who did and continue to use these texts without promotion.

Unfortunately, we can easily find numerous examples of authors writing about biblical texts from an academic perspective, but they also try to extend such works by helping to find meaning in religious texts for modern audiences. A recent example of this can be seen in a work entitled *Short Stories by Jesus: The Enigmatic Parables of a Controversial Rabbi*, by Amy-Jill Levine. In it, the author works to salvage the parables of Jesus for modern Christian readers. She writes, "The parables, if we take them seriously not as answers but as invitations, can continue to inform our lives, even as our lives continue to open up the parables to new readings."[22] Here, we find an outright example in recent scholarship—one of very, very many—where the author's stated goal is for modern readers to find new meaning in ancient biblical texts. This type of approach is no doubt common within religious communities and is realized by religious people who look to Scripture in order to find meaning for their own lives; however, I do not believe this should be advanced in an academic book written by an academic biblical scholar. This is not meant as an attack of Levine or her work because there are many other biblical scholars writing other books that promote the same type of religionist approaches. The mention of her book serves as an example of the type of research that is being produced in the academy, which clearly demonstrates that some scholars endorse the value of biblical texts for modern readers. The scholar should not be involved in the process of finding meaning in religious texts for modern audiences. There are religious professionals and religious laypeople that strive to accomplish this. The role of the bibli-

---

22. Levine, *Short Stories by Jesus*, 427.

cal scholar should be to investigate, analyze, and understand those who are finding the meaning in these texts. It should not be to participate in process of meaning making. The biblical scholar should strive to study religious traditions and practitioners without involving oneself in the practice.

It is precisely this type of scholarship that Hector Avalos criticizes in his works as he argues that trying to find meaning in the text for modern readers should not be a part of biblical studies. For Avalos, it is clear that the Bible is a product of a bygone era which should not be employed or have any meaningful relevance in the modern world. After outlining a number of problems within the field, he comes to the conclusion that change is necessary. Avalos has called for an end to the field of biblical studies, not as an entire abandonment of the discipline, but to alter the way that it currently exists and is carried out. That is, Avalos does not think that people today should stop studying the Bible (his view is quite the opposite), but that scholars must redefine the purposes for studying these texts. They should not be trying to find meaning and relevance in the biblical texts for people's lives today.[23] Rather than altogether dismissing the field of biblical studies or simply admitting that it is religionist in its endeavor, he calls for a retention of biblical studies, but with a new purpose: to completely eliminate the Bible's influence in the modern world.[24] The radical nature of Avalos's suggestion for what the purpose or definition of biblical studies should be is highlighted here:

> So our purpose is to exercise from modern life what little of the Bible is being used and also to eliminate the potential use of any sacred scripture as an authority in the modern world. What I seek is liberation from the very idea that *any* sacred text should be an authority for modern human existence.[25]

The reason that it needs to be expulsed as a guide for human existence is that it is a danger to human civilization. The Bible, as Avalos demonstrates in his research, has in the past and continues today to be used for violence.[26] His argument about the ways in which religious violence has been espoused is elaborated in his book *Fighting Words: The Origins of Religious Violence*.[27] Here too, he comes to the conclusion that, "given the violence in scriptures. . .Our job as biblical scholars is to undermine the value of

---

23. Avalos, *The End of Biblical Studies*. See also Avalos, "Philip Davies on the End."
24. Avalos, *The End of Biblical Studies*, 341.
25. Ibid., 342.
26. Ibid.
27. Avalos, *Fighting Words*.

any scripture that endorses violence."[28] According to Avalos, today's biblical scholars should not continue to maintain the value of biblical writings. The mission of biblical studies should be to end the Bible's influence in the modern world.

Not surprisingly, some scholars have been critical of this forceful position.[29] One such scholar is Elisabeth Fiorenza who, in her book *Democratizing Biblical Studies*, critiques Avalos's motives to end religious interest in studying biblical texts as a product of his atheistic agenda.[30] For Fiorenza, the displacement of the Bible does not ensure an end to violence.[31] She writes, "We need to develop a critical pedagogy that teaches people, who love Scripture and accord it great authority for their lives, to read the Bible in a way that enables them to critically assess its ethos and vision."[32] It is true that the transposition of the Bible would not bring with it an end to all violence; however, this is not what Avalos argues. Avalos writes about religious violence, which is different than all types of violence more generally. Also, that Avalos is an atheist should bear no relevance to the question at hand. Any attack on a scholar's religious beliefs (be they Christian, Jewish, Hindu, Atheist, and so forth) is unwarranted and out of place. The issue has little to do with the fact that scholars are Christians, Jews, Muslims, Atheists, or anything else. Rather, what is at stake is the type of research and teaching in the field of biblical studies and the involvedness of scholars.

Luke Timothy Johnson would likely disagree with Avalos's take on the relevance of Scripture as he argues that in today's world the New Testament is still very pertinent.[33] Despite the charges against the New Testament (which the author does not name specifically) Johnson finds fault, not with the violence in the texts, but with those who would carry out violence because their dispositions inclined them to do so.[34] For Johnson, the books of the New Testament should be considered like the plays of Shakespeare or like other great literary works in that they are capable of stirring human hearts and speaking to the human condition. Despite their use for violence and tyranny, which Johnson does not deny, the author finds that from a historical perspective the books of the New Testament have also been used

28. Ibid., 382.

29. See Boer, "Elitism, Colonialism;" Davies, "Whose Bible;" Lemche, "Guns do not Kill;" Simkins, "Biblical Studies." Avalos offers a response to Davies: see Avalos, "Philip Davies on the End."

30. Fiorenza, *Democratizing Biblical Studies*, 38–41.

31. Ibid., 40.

32. Ibid.

33. Johnson, *New Testament*.

34. Ibid., 125. See Boer, "Elitism, Colonialism."

to help humanity. He writes: "If the New Testament has been the tool of tyranny in the hands of the wicked, so has it been the great resource of those saints whose energies were bent to the liberation of others."[35] For Johnson, we must take the good with the bad.[36] This standpoint—that though the New Testament has been used for violence when in the wrong hands, but is still valuable today because of its usefulness for good in the right hands—is admittedly quite problematic. As Avalos points out in response to these types of arguments:

> But suppose now that someone argued that there were *some* good things within *Mein Kampf*. Hitler, after all, said he stood for family values. He said he was following God's wishes. He said he loved his fellow community members. I would speculate that most people would still not be convinced that we should keep any part of *Mein Kampf*, even if there were 'good' chapters. The genocide committed under Hitler is so heinous that it would outweigh any supposed good in *Mein Kampf*.[37]

For Avalos, the reasoning espoused by those like Johnson is flawed. If a work like *Mein Kampf* should be rejected because it is racist and genocidal in its policies, then the Bible too should be rejected for its own genocidal policies.[38] Avalos argues that the biblical texts have and continue to endorse negativity and violence in the world, a strong reason for why they should be rejected, not glorified. In arguing against the preservation of the value of biblical texts, Avalos suggests that the opposite should be the objective of biblical studies scholars. The role of the biblical studies scholar should not be to promote or endorse these texts today, but it should be to eliminate the Bible's influence in the world altogether.

A Neutral/Objective Inclined Stance

In regards to keeping or disavowing the value of biblical or religious texts today, we have on the one hand those who wish to maintain the value of the Bible in the world because they believe that these writings have important lessons and elements which are useful. On the other hand, we have those

---

35. Johnson, *New Testament*, 125.

36. In a similar fashion, Rita Gross has argued that the job description of a religious scholar is not only to evaluate religious phenomena, but also to discuss which religious beliefs and behaviors are likely to promote good in humans and in the world. See Gross, "The Place of the Personal," 168.

37. Avalos 2005, 360–361.

38. Avalos, *Fighting Words*, 361.

who see no value in keeping alive biblical texts and have called for an end to such assertions and practices. An alternative approach to either of these positions, advocated here, is for biblical scholars to remain neutral and objective, to a certain extent, on this issue.

The biblical scholar, like other ideal professionals in the social sciences—historians, psychologists, sociologists, anthropologists, etc.—need to adhere to a secular approach for studying religious phenomena. Keeping in-line with the field of religious studies, the academic and non-faith based approach to the discipline should not be aimed at promoting or suppressing religions, but rather on observing, understanding, and critiquing religious phenomena.[39] As Dessì writes:

> ...the scope of Religious Studies is to analyze, describe, and explain various religious phenomena as objectively as possible. The fact that a degree of accuracy such as that of the natural sciences is never achievable in this field is acknowledged by scholars in Religious Studies, and in no way undermines their effort, as it is also the case, for example, for historians and sociologists.[40]

The aim is to be as objective as possible even if we must admit that true objectivity is ever elusive. Of course, that does not mean that we should go as far as William Kristensen, who maintained that as far as the researcher is concerned, religious believers are 'completely right' because, "only after we have grasped this can we understand these people and their religion."[41] This statement is problematic since one need not attribute correctness onto the other in order to properly understand their position. For example, a historian does not need to agree with what Hitler believed or carried out in order to achieve an understanding of him. We may assert that Hitler believed that what he said and did was for the better, but that is merely conjecture. The error in such an approach is what leads to lack of objectivity.

Most academics are already conscious of the fact that 'true objectivity'—that is, to be completely bias free—is unattainable because, as Gross points out:

> ...the scholar inevitably brings his or her own outlook, his or her experience, training, life situation, and values into the study, making objectivity and neutrality impossible. One cannot get completely outside one's skin and one's culture to observe

---

39. See Dessì, "Objectivity and Belief," 60.
40. Ibid.
41. Waardenburg, *Classical Approaches*, 396.

religion from some neutral nowhere, reporting what is, completely separate from one's own observing viewpoint.[42]

The presuppositions, background, and life experiences of a researcher are such that their worldview is always affected and their objectivity is always tainted. However, this problem is not debilitating or insurmountable. That we cannot achieve complete objectivity does not entail that our subjectivities are warranted. Biblical scholars need a conscious awareness of their biases and presuppositions in order to help them navigate their study of religions and religious phenomena. The remedy to the problem of true objectivity is, "self-consciousness and self-awareness, and the modesty to admit that one may not be seeing everything."[43] Therefore, an objective or neutral stance means that one neither favors maintaining or ending the value of the biblical or religious texts for the modern world. In that way, the scholar is able to observe and understand the ancient audiences of the texts (by whom and to whom they were written) and also be understanding of the reality of the current global situation which is that modern religious individuals and communities have in the past and continue to re-appropriate religious texts for guiding their lives. Is it right that they do so? That depends. It may be that these modern religious people do not comprehend the meaning of the texts they read as they were originally written and intended for ancient audiences, but that fact does not make it right or wrong for them to read and apply these texts to their lives. Essentially, people can do and still do what they want and lead their lives how they wish. Our role as biblical scholars is to understand these religious texts in their contexts and to study the ancient and modern people who hold to these writings and the practices that they generate.

The proposition put forth, then, is for the biblical scholar to take a neutrally inclined position and remain outside of the group of believers under study. One should not be an advocate for or a deterrent of religions, no matter the personal faith or lack thereof of the biblical scholar. As an example, in teaching a biblical studies or religious studies course, one explains to the students the meaning and understanding of religious texts for the people (authors and audiences) during which time these texts were written. Regarding modern religious believers, one would explain that there are modern Christians, Jews, Buddhists, etc. who still hold these texts in high regard within the various denominations of the faiths and who read these texts in a number of differing ways as a means of guiding their lives without commenting, one way or the other, about whether or not they should

---

42. Gross, "The Place of the Personal," 168.
43. Ibid.

be doing so. If a teacher is asked in class about their personal opinion on a particular religious matter or questioned about their personal faith it is up to said teacher to determine whether or not they wish to disclose such information to the students. It is not expected that a teacher lie about what religious tradition they adhere to or why they may not be religious followers themselves. What the biblical scholar believes or does not believe, their religious faith or lack thereof, is a part of their background and undoubtedly informs their worldviews. That being said, one's personal faith should not have any bearing on what is being taught; they should be aware that their personal faith or lack of faith is an important part of what influences and shapes their perspectives. The teacher can be honest about their personal views/background while trying to stay neutrally inclined on the topic of study. The same neutral approach applies to academic publications. Scholars can explore religious texts within the framework of their creation and reception throughout history while trying to avoid interjecting their personal opinions or experiences on whether it is acceptable or not acceptable for people to have found value and meaning in these texts in the past or for those who continue to find meaning in them today.

Some of the principal issues and concerns in contemporary religious studies deal with the issue of neutrality in the field. The question posed by this paper about the practical position and role of the biblical scholar in many ways echoes such ongoing methodological discussions taking place in religious studies. Scholars have, for years, questioned the type of approach they ought to take in investigating religious traditions. Peter Berger proposed a method for the sociological study of religion termed "methodological atheism," which he described as follows:

> In all its manifestations, religion constitutes an immense projection of human meanings into the empty vastness of the universe — a projection, to be sure, which comes back as an alien reality to haunt its producers. Needless to say, it is impossible within the frame of reference of scientific theorizing to make any affirmations, positive or negative, about the ultimate ontological status of this alleged reality. Within this frame of reference, the religious projections can be dealt with only as such, as products of human activity and human consciousness, and rigorous brackets have to be placed around the question as to whether these projections may not also be something else than that (or, more accurately, refer to something else than the human world in which they empirically originate). In other words, every inquiry into religious matters that limits itself to

the empirically available must necessarily be based on 'methodological atheism.'[44]

In response to Berger, Ninian Smart preferred to talk about "methodological agnosticism," which implies that scholars need not deny or be skeptical of whether religious aspects of faith are true or not.[45] Methodological agnosticism, then, means that evidence is approached in such a way that supernatural and divine agency is assumed to be unknowable and therefore must be overlooked for the sake of study. Such a concept is similar to the phenomenology of religion notion of *epoche*, which encourages researchers to approach religious traditions with an open mind and suspend personal judgments about any religion.[46] Today, the question about methodological atheism and methodological agnosticism in the study of religions is still very much debated.[47] However, the similarities in the types of discussions, both by those in religious studies and those in biblical studies, concerning the ways in which neutrality can or cannot be achieved in the academic study of religion and what constitutes academic religious studies versus theological studies, are unmistakable. The discussion on these issues by scholars in each field respectively are similar and in need of further interaction. Certainly, it would be beneficial for those working in biblical studies to be more engaged with some of these new approaches within the academic study of religion and vice versa.

The position put forth by this paper, though not entirely analogous to methodological atheism or methodological agnosticism, nevertheless endorses a degree of scholarly detachment from the object of study. While such neutrality might entail a certain hermeneutical naïveté—to claim that a scholar can be completely objective and impartial—it is clear, as mentioned, above, that this objectivity need not be ideal objectivity. Rather, it is one where the scholar is self-conscious, self-aware, and modestly admits that one cannot see everything. Of course, where the proposed position of this paper differs significantly is in its exception with respect to religious violence.

---

44. Berger, *Sacred Canopy*, 100; See also Berger, *Heretical Imperative*, 133.
45. See Smart, *Science of Religion*.
46. See Amanze et al., *Biblical Studies*, 266–269.
47. See Cantrell, "Must a Scholar of Religion;" Fitzgerald, *Ideology of Religious Studies*; McCutcheon, *Critics Not Caretakers*; McCutcheon, *Insider/Outsider Problem*; Porpora, "Methodological Atheism."

Religious Texts & Violence Today

While the proposed neutral and objective stance on the value of religious texts is how biblical scholars should carry out the field of biblical studies, there is an important exception when scholars need to step in and publicly disavow the use of religious texts in the modern world. That exception, I believe, is in cases when they are used to promote, incite, or justify violence. Academic scholars of religion do not always take the problem of religious violence as seriously as they ought to.[48]

This is where the work and research of Avalos has been very important, in particular his work on the scarce resource theory of violence.[49] In the world today, we find that people are not just reading ancient religious texts like any other literary work or simply as a guide for their lives; rather, many people have and continue to use religious books and/or ideas in order to promote or incite violent acts.[50] There is a sense that much of what is currently transpiring in the world today—such as the continued international terrorist attacks, the news of people being recruited to support, join, and/or fight in religious wars, ongoing struggles for land in Jerusalem, and so forth—all deal with violence and religion in some form or another. While all violence in general can be seen as problematic and in need of consideration, it is religious violence that continues to be especially troubling. As Avalos asserts, religions can be understood as having created a more tragic source of violence than other scarce resources because many of its scarce resources are unjustifiable and/or altogether false.[51] This essay advocates that it is certainly the role of biblical or religious scholars to publicly denounce the use of religious texts and ideas when, as a result of reading or hearing these, people initiate violence in our communities and in the world at large. Scholars and biblical scholars must adamantly denounce such atrocious and dreadful uses of biblical or religious texts. They must not stand neutral in this regard; rather, they must actively and publicly protest and object to those who use religion and religious texts in order to harm others.

---

48. This may be due to the fact that some scholars still question what exactly constitutes religious violence and whether or not religion even has a role to play in said violence. See Allen, "New Scholarship has Emerged;" Cavanaugh, *The Myth of Religious Violence*; Armstrong, *Fields of Blood*. For a response to these views see Avalos, *Fighting Words*; Avalos, "Religious Violence is not a Myth;" Avalos, "Response to Professor Paul Allen."

49. Avalos, *Fighting Words*.

50. My understanding and definition of violence follows that of Avalos. See Avalos, *Fighting Words*, 19–20.

51. Avalos, *Fighting Words*.

While the article advocates for a neutral and objective stance on the role of the biblical scholar when it comes to avowing or disavowing the value of religious texts for modern audiences, it fervently promotes an exception to the rule when it comes to religious violence. Scholars need to be proactive in dispelling religious violent actions. This understanding of the role of the scholar is not novel. It is well known and widely accepted that scholars and academics have a social responsibility to the public because, in many cases, professors and researches are publicly funded by taxpayers' money.[52] Therefore, there is a responsibility to work towards helping the public be that through teaching, research, publications, social media, etc. As Avalos states in regards to conducting academic research, "Knowledge for knowledge's sake is useless. It's about helping the world."[53] Biblical scholars should not study the Bible simply for the sake of knowledge; though that is certainly a part of the equation, the objective and mission should be to give back to the community, be it in teaching courses, giving public lectures, and also speaking up when tragic violence unfolds.[54]

Conclusion

In conclusion, the role of the academic biblical scholar, then, should *no longer be* to maintain the value of the biblical texts, or any religious texts (ancient or modern), for people living in the world today. At the same time, it is not the goal of the biblical scholar to disavow the value of such works regardless of personal opinions on whether or not people today should re-appropriate these ancient texts and use them as guides for their lives. The biblical scholar should study religions from as objective and neutral a stance as possible. Like the ideal historians, psychologists, sociologists, and anthropologists, biblical scholars must position themselves on the outside looking in. Where the scholar does need to interject is in those cases when these texts are used to promote or incite violent acts or harm others. In such cases, it is the ethical responsibility of the scholar to try to help end such uses of biblical or other religious texts. Those working in the field of academic biblical studies should strive to be detached, non-partisan, and independent as much as possible.

---

52. Even in cases where they are not, it remains the duty of those working in the academic field to promote the betterment of humanity by resisting those who would use religion or religious texts for violence.

53. Avalos, "In Conversation."

54. For a view on the religion scholar as a public intellectual see Tite, "Sacred Violence," 3–10. For an alternative view see Wiebe, "Politics of Wishful Thinking," 7–38.

Bibliography

Allen, Paul. "New Scholarship has Emerged to Challenge the Myth that Religion is Violent." *Montreal Gazette*. June 16, 2015. http://montrealgazette.com/news/world/opinion-new-scholarship-has-emerged-to-challenge-the-myth-that-religion-is-violent.

Amanze, James N., et al., eds. *Biblical Studies, Theology, Religion and Philosophy: An Introduction for African Universities*. Eldoret, Kenya: Zapf Chancery, 2010.

Armstrong, Karen. *Fields of Blood: Religion and the History of Violence*. New York: Knopf, 2014.

Avalos, Hector. *The End of Biblical Studies*. Amherst, New York: Prometheus Books, 2007.

———. *Fighting Words: The Origins of Religious Violence*. Amherst, New York: Prometheus Books, 2005.

———. "Philip Davies on the End of Biblical Studies." *Debunking Christianity*. July 16, 2009. http://debunkingchristianity.blogspot.ca/2009/07/philip-davies-on-end-of-biblical.html.

———. "Religious Violence is not a Myth." *Montreal Gazette*. June 22, 2015. http://montrealgazette.com/news/world/opinion-religious-violence-is-not-a-myth.

———. "A Response to Professor Paul Allen: The Supposed Myth of Religious Violence and Religionism in Secular Academia." *Debunking Christianity*. June 29, 2015. http://debunkingchristianity.blogspot.ca/2015/06/a-response-to-professor-paul-allen.html.

———. "In Conversation with Hector Avalos (Part 2)." Inquisitive Minds Podcast Interview. August 3, 2015. http://inquisitiveminds.podbean.com/e/in-conversation-with-hector-avalos-part-2/.

Berger, Peter Ludwig. *The Heretical Imperative: Contemporary Possibilities of Religious Affirmation*. New York: Anchor, 1979.

———. *The Sacred Canopy: Elements of a Sociological Theory of Religion*. New York: Anchor, 1990.

Berlinerblau, Jacques. *The Secular Bible: Why Nonbelievers Must Take Religion Seriously*. New York: Cambridge University Press, 2005.

Boer, Roland. "Elitism, Colonialism, and the Independence of Biblical Studies: Reflections on the Lemche-Avalos Debate." *The Bible and Interpretation*. November 2010. http://www.bibleinterp.com/articles/art11358010.shtml#sdfootnote1sym.

———, ed. *Secularism and Biblical Studies*. London: Equinox, 2010.

Bulkeley, Tim. "The No-man's-land of Biblical Studies: Isn't it Odd?" *The Bible and Interpretation*. December 2010. http://www.bibleinterp.com/opeds/noman358028.shtml.

Cantrell, Michael A. "Must a Scholar of Religion be Methodologically Atheistic or Agnostic?" *Journal of the American Academy of Religion* (2015) 1–28.

Cavanaugh, William T. *The Myth of Religious Violence*. Oxford: Oxford University Press, 2009.

Davies, Philip R. "Whose Bible? Anyone's?" *The Bible and Interpretation*. July 2009. http://www.bibleinterp.com/opeds/whose.shtml.

———. *Whose Bible is it Anyway*? 2nd Edition. London: T & T Clark, 2004.

Davis, Gary. "Academic Freedom and the Teaching of Religion." *Improving College and University Teaching* 32 (1984) 76–80.

Dessì, Ugo. "Objectivity and Belief in the Academic Study of Shin Buddhism." *The Pure Land* (*New Series*) 25 (2009) 57–70.

Fiorenza, Elisabeth Schüssler. *Democratizing Biblical Studies: Toward an Emancipatory Educational Space*. Louisville, Kentucky: Westminster John Knox, 2009.

Fitzgerald, Timothy. *The Ideology of Religious Studies*. New York: Oxford University Press, 2000.

Gross, Rita M. "The Place of the Personal and the Subjective in Religious Studies." Pages 163–178 in *The Researcher Experience in Qualitative Research*. Edited by Susan D. Moch and Marie F. Gates. California: Sage, 2000.

Hendel, Ronald S. "Farewell to SBL: Faith and Reason in Biblical Studies." *Biblical Archaeology Review* 36 (2010) 28–29.

Johnson, Luke Timothy. *The New Testament: A Very Short Introduction*. Oxford: Oxford University Press, 2010.

LaFargue, Michael. "Are Texts Determinate? Derrida, Barth, and the Role of the Biblical Scholar." *Harvard Theological Review* 81 (1988) 341–357.

Legaspi, Michael C. *The Death of Scripture and the Rise of Biblical Studies*. New York: Oxford University Press, 2010.

Lemche, Niels Peter. "Guns do not Kill, People do!" Pages 52–58 in *Secularism and Biblical Studies*. London: Equinox, 2010.

Levine, Amy-Jill. *Short Stories by Jesus: The Enigmatic Parables of a Controversial Rabbi*. San Francisco: HarperOne, 2014.

McCutcheon, Russell T. *Critics Not Caretakers: Redescribing the Public Study of Religion*. Albany, New York: State University of New York Press, 2001.

———., ed. *The Insider/Outsider Problem in the Study of Religion: A Reader*. Controversies in the Study of Religion. London: Continuum, 2005.

Morrow, Jeffrey L. "The Enlightenment University and the Creation of the Academic Bible: Michael Legaspi's The Death of Scripture and the Rise of Biblical Studies." *Nova et Vetera* 11 (2013) 897–922.

Porpora, Douglas V. "Methodological Atheism, Methodological Agnosticism and Religious Experience." *Journal for the Theory of Social Behaviour* 36 (2006) 57–75.

Rogerson, J. W., and Judith Lieu, eds. *The Oxford Handbook of Biblical Studies*. Oxford: Oxford University Press, 2006.

Simkins, Ronald A. "Biblical Studies as a Secular Discipline: The Role of Faith and Theology." *Journal of Religion and Society* 13: (2011) 1–17. http://moses.creighton.edu/JRS/2011/2011-23.pdf.

———. "Scientific Nonsense, Historical Fiction, and Biblical Authority: The Historical Adam and Other Misguided Dogmas." Pages 31–45 in *Religion and the Sciences: Opportunities and Challenges*. Edited by Ronald A. Simkins and Thomas M. Kelly. Journal of Religion & Society Supplement Series 11. 2015. https://dspace.creighton.edu/xmlui/bitstream/handle/10504/65501/2015-4.pdf?sequence=3.

Smart, Ninian. *The Science of Religion & the Sociology of Knowledge: Some Methodological Questions*. The Virginia and Richard Stewart Memorial Lectures. Princeton: Princeton University Press, 1973.

Tite, Philip L. "Sacred Violence and the Scholar of Religion as Public Intellectual." Pages 3–10 in *Religion, Terror, and Violence: Religious Studies Perspectives*. Edited by Bryan Rennie and Philip L. Tite. New York: Routledge, 2008.

Waardenburg, Jacques. *Classical Approaches to the Study of Religion: Aims, Methods and Theories of Research*. Religion and Reason 3. Berlin: Walter de Gruyter, 1973.

West, Jim. "The Sackgasse of A-theistic Biblical Studies." *The Bible and Interpretation*. June 2010. http://www.bibleinterp.com/opeds/sack357908.shtml.

Wiebe, Donald. "The Politics of Wishful Thinking? Disentangling the Role of the Scholar-Scientist from that of the Public Intellectual in the Modern Academic Study of Religion." *Temenos* 41:1 (2005) 7–38.

Withrow, Brandon C., and Menachem Wecker. *Consider no Evil: Two Faith Traditions and the Problem of Academic Freedom in Religious Higher Education*. Eugene, Oregon: Cascade Books, 2014.

8

Secularized Theology and the Propensity for Violence in the Modern State

Derek Bateman

This paper demonstrates the relationship between religious violence and political violence in the twentieth and twenty-first centuries. The secularization of Western culture saw transference of theological discourse from the absolutism of monotheistic concepts to the absolutism of political ideologies where the "godhead" was now realized in the person of the political leader. Carl Schmitt, in his discussions regarding political theology stipulated, "the omnipotent God became the omnipotent lawgiver."[1] The divisive and violent rhetoric of non-rational religious absolutism is embraced by political ideologues as a means to maintain power through the "us/them" paradigm that encourages the subjugation and/or eradication of the perceived enemy through acts of violence. The decontextualized interpretations and manipulation of Scripture allowed for pseudo-justifications and a perverted legitimization of violence as a perceived necessity related to communal preservation. This is a relative and essential polemic regarding the historiography of power struggles within the church and the evolution of temporal concepts of state sovereignty. The tension between church and state regarding authority transformed during the post-Enlightenment age of "reason" culminating in a hybridity whereby the state absorbed the theological pedigree and exploited its potential for indoctrination and power through coercion that blended the fear of violence and punishment with soteriological concepts ingrained with the promise of redemption and emancipation thus maintaining a foundation of "hope" amidst the crumpling of religious certitude.

---

1. Schmitt, *Political Theology*, 36.

The debate regarding the inherent violent nature of religion has spawned a plethora of politically situated camps that are seemingly as entrenched in their belief as any conflicting faith driven religious groups involved in oppositional interpretations of divine cosmological purpose. Much of the contentious flavor of the debate revolves around the idea and definition of religion and the distinction between divine violence and secular (state) violence. A common component involved with this distinction pertains to the idea of authority. Who has the authority to sanction and promote violent behavior? Of course this does not necessarily apply to acts of violence by individuals (lone wolves) who engage in violence solely on their own authority. They may, indeed be drawing upon their interpretation of institutional mandates that could be promoting violence, but they are not directly involved in the organizations that they are claiming to represent. Often they are disavowed by those very same organizations, accused of misinterpreting or misunderstanding the particulars of the message that they claim authorized their violent acts. My interest is with acts of violence that are sanctioned by religious or state authorities and how such acts differ in kind. In order to fully grasp this dichotomy between religious and state violence, or to determine if the distinction between the two is as wide as is often suggested, a brief review of the history of the relationship between the church and state within the political realm of the development of Western culture is necessary. Such a review allows for a closer critique and understanding of the concept of political theology as that term has come to be understood in the twentieth and twenty-first centuries, in large part influenced by the writings of Carl Schmitt.

The relationship between church and state during the inception of what was to become Christianity is rife with contradictory statements in Scripture that have been endlessly interpreted and debated. How does one read Matt 22:21, Luke 22:38, or Paul in Rom 13? How much weight should scriptural passages is to be given when pursuing a historical survey due to the susceptibility of Scripture to non-literal interpretation? I would argue that the understanding and importance of the church and state relationship, in the context of Judeo/Christian culture, can only be engaged after the doctrines of the ecumenical councils had been established and the subsequent rapid growth of Christianity. It is only once the church has power that it impacts the politics of its time.

The history of this power relation is vast and I can only touch upon it very briefly. I want to frame it, however, within the context of Schmitt's political idea regarding the "state of exception" and the two centers of authority that competed to decide on what constituted an exception to the rules and laws in place and any subsequent actions (often violent) that would then be authorized to supersede the understood rule of law.

The Middle Ages saw an intense struggle between church and state that exemplified the importance of theology in the political machinations of European society. While the Donation of Constantine is recognized as a forgery, it had a long life as a believable contract rendering the temporal authorities subservient (to a large degree) to the pope. The details of its creation are well documented and its use during the Investiture Controversy was impactful and revealing in so far as the authoritative powers of the church over temporal matters were consolidated in large part in the Concordant of Worms in 1122 CE. What is significant here is the overtly political nature of the papacy and its investment in temporal political developments. This is important to the current situation in so far as it is a brief encapsulation of the sustainability of the church within the political realm and the strength of the papal mandate within all aspects of society. Even the monarchs who opposed the popes acknowledged their authority as direct representatives of the ultimate authority of the unchallenged and unquestioned power of God.[2] The issue was not so much about challenging the religious authority as much as it was about who would represent and speak for the universally accepted authority of God. The political aspirations of the papacy are a far cry from the eschatological understanding of early Christianity that was predicated on the idea of the immanent Parousia. By the time of Augustine's reassessment of the "new kingdom" being a spiritual/inner transformation as opposed to the apocalyptic physical destruction of the world and the realization that temporal life was continuing, the theological dimension of societal growth had to work within the parameters of the political developments that required decision makers with the authority to implement policy. The fusion of religion and politics was the norm and it was inconceivable to implement policy without taking into account the theological implications. The problem remained, however, that the dualistic authority paradigm (pope/monarch) would inevitably lead to conflict as the history of the Middle Ages demonstrates.

This separation of the temporal authority (king) and divine authority (pope)—both working for political gain—was a constant issue of contention that had a direct bearing on the doctrine of the divine right of kings. Approaching the Reformation, the church experienced a number of problems regarding internal divisions and papal defeats including theological disagreements, the great schism, and the Cathar heresies. This all occurred

---

2. For a thorough investigation of the relationship between the church and state during the Middle Ages see Kantorowicz, *King's Two Bodies*.

in conjunction with the rise of the nation-state as the church center of power was diminishing while the power base within individual states was increasing.

The Reformation exposed the discontent with papal authority and the subsequent rupture in Christian unity left a vacuum regarding the seat of divine authority. Without the undisputed seat of church authority in Rome, the reform churches tended to gravitate toward the state apparatus as the authoritative institution for policy determination. Luther's emphases on the individual's direct relationship with the transcendental and his emphasis on the "kingdom of God," removed the need for the authoritative mediator regarding scriptural interpretation and weakened the status of the "church" *per se*.[3] Matters of the transcendental and the divine are left in the hands of the individual's literal interpretation of Scripture and, as a result, the priest no longer has the ability to engage in absolute decision-making. This removal of papal authority from the temporal/secular sector of political and societal decision-making opened the door for the state rulers to extend their power base. Luther's faith in the individual regarding spiritual matters and acceptance of the state authority (divinely granted) on temporal matters gave the state "the freedom to go from the dominant to the controlling and SOLE institutional authority."[4]

This situation paved the way for the introduction of the theory of the divine right of kings, proposed by Jean Bodin, giving the king absolute authority over both temporal/state and spiritual matters.[5] The "King's two bodies" allowed for the absoluteness of his authority through the "grace" of God, a temporary condition that was initiated through the anointing process and remained in place throughout the king's reign. This consolidation of power with the state has a direct correlation to the theories of Schmitt that trace the evolution of the political from this particular point in history.

Schmitt's ideas regarding sovereignty and the "state of exception" grabbled with the substantial changes in the post-Enlightenment political developments. The diminishment of religious and theological power within the political system, stemming from the Reformation and broadly impacted by the secularization process that followed, continually questioned the seat of authority. Through most of the Middle Ages the concept of the Christian God and the absolute authority over all things temporal and divine related to that God was unquestioned. The divine right of kings was unsustainable

3. The impact of the Reformation on the relationship between church and state is aptly explained in Gray, "Political Theology."

4. Ibid., 189.

5. Bodin's royalist ideology which insists that state power (sovereignty) remain indivisible is developed in his *Six livres de la république*. See Bodin, *On Sovereignty*.

as the progress in technology and science pushed theological influences into the background of political development. Doctrinal Christianity weakened and ethical humanism and liberal democracy emerged as the dominant forces in Western politics. This, in turn, led to an emphasis on the "human" ability to maintain sovereignty and political authority. For Schmitt, this secularized concept of the state still maintained (or at least should maintain) and was driven by transcendental theological concepts that had mutated and been absorbed into the political apparatus. He famously claimed that, "All significant concepts of the modern theory of the state are secularized theological concepts."[6] He proposed that they needed to be excavated from their mutated and subordinated position and be restored in so far as they give a certain transcendent authority to state leadership. This, in turn, enables such a leadership to move beyond "discussions" that are so prevalent in liberal democracy, to decision making abilities that can supersede the limitations of the check and balance democratic system when it comes to times of crisis and the ensuing state of exception that requires immediate action.

What must be remembered is that the religious tendency towards violence maintains the same fundamental impetus towards a consolidation of power; in this way, it has a direct correlation to all acts of secular/political acts of power. While the acknowledgement that the "scarce resources"[7] that pertain to the acts of religious violence are often unverifiable promotes the distinction from secular notions of "scarce resources," the limits of verifiability within the secular/political paradigm can also be observed when the idea of nationalism adopts similar ideologies as that of religion. Resources such as freedom and democracy—resources that are perceived as being threatened by alternative political or religious ideologies—are verifiable only through the shared indoctrination of a social system that insists on a concrete understanding of what those resources constitute. Cultural/social/political differences reflect the contradictory understandings of what resources are and which resources need to be preserved and fought for. If there is not a consensus regarding what freedoms are essential, then the verification of that freedom becomes unstable; empirical evidence needed to solidify the verifiability of the resource is tainted by the interpretative approach of any given society. Absolute freedom is untenable in any functioning society as there are always necessary limitations imposed that serve to protect the individual as well as the functionality of the governing parties.

---

6. Schmitt, *Political Theology*, 36.

7. For a thorough discussion of the importance of scarce resources within the context of religious violence see Avalos, *Fighting Words*.

SECULARIZED THEOLOGY AND THE PROPENSITY FOR VIOLENCE

As such, the preservation of freedom and the secular acts of governmental violence to maintain that freedom are predicated on an unstable premise that is promoted as an absolute "right" and allow for violent reactions if perceived to be threatened.

Western governments often reference the protection of national interests as a justification for acts of violence. These national interests often encompass the notion of freedom and the need to preserve a certain way of life that does not entail a universal consensus. The empirical evidence does not reveal an "absolute" since it is disputed by opposing nationalists who draw upon their own set of empirical data to promote an alternative understanding of nationalism, freedom, and way of life. These secular confrontations are inevitably rife with the same sense of sacred absolutism predicated on the interpretations of constitutional laws. These laws, in turn, adopt the same sacred privileging as the religious texts that are essential to the theological justifications for acts of violence. But, they are both dependent upon interpretation. The right to "bear arms" becomes a sacred resource because it is embedded in the constitution, despite the contentious debates that address the potential negative results of gun laws in the United States. Violence is justified through the constitution if the "resource" (guns) is threatened. The point here is that Hector Avalos rightly recognizes the scarce resource as a prime component of violence justification among religious practitioners, but he does not fully consider the similarities of this proposal with the non-religious entities and their propensity towards violence. This polemic revolves around the attempts to clearly distinguish a difference between religious and secular violence. Insisting that religious violence is distinct because of its embrace of non-empirical and irrational cosmological views fails to acknowledge equally irrational concepts within the political and nationalistic perspectives of so-called secular societies. Furthermore, these shared interpretations that cross over indicate the inseparability of the religious and the secular and demonstrate that the violence attributed to both are securely entwined. The sacred is not the sole domain of the religious. Secular ideologies elevate their resources to a sacred status in the same way as the religious and are equally guilty of allowing unverifiable concepts such as freedom to control the trajectory of their beliefs and violent actions.

The attempts to enforce this distinction are often compounded by the numerous attempts to define religion and to situate it as a separate entity removed from secular societal ideology. Sifting through the plethora of definitions related to religion instills a sense of uncertainty and confusion. New definitions are consistently being developed adding to the difficulties of clarity and infuse the discussion with rhetorical intrusions that often border on propaganda. This problem of definitions involves the attempts to understand religion's relationship to the modern political/secular state. A key component of this issue revolves around the concept of the "absolute." Most definitions of religion include the paradoxical relationship between non-verifiable concepts of the supernatural with and the belief in absolutes.[8] The insistence on a concept regarding the destiny of mankind being non-negotiable and the embrace of an entrenched position regarding what is "right" permeates religious thinking. It is also an ideological position adopted by most secular political movements. What separates the religious notion of the absolute is related to the concept of authority. The acceptance of a supernatural being that has the status of the "creator" will trump any corporeal authority with the understanding that the supernatural creator has, by nature, a greater awareness of the human condition and that the creations (humans) can never usurp an authority that is predicated on the divine. Belief in this divine authority creates a situation whereby any perceived threat to that authority must be eradicated. Human life becomes a secondary concern to the divine life that is responsible for not only the existence of all human life, but for the "existence" of the afterlife as well. Acceptance of this proposition requires an absolute belief in such a divine existence and will propel the believer to grasp on to non-verifiable concepts and mold them into propositions that conform to the absolutist notions involved with the insistence of a divine presence. Once this divine presence is accepted and unchallenged, then empirical evidence that questions the idea is not persuasive since the ultimate belief is itself a non-empirical reality.

The debate revolving around the attempts to come up with a definitive definition of religion continue to unfold and the necessity of a deity is now a contentious subject.[9] This dilemma is relatively new insofar as the premodern world rarely questioned the existence of a deity. State violence was inseparable from religious violence since the state incorporated religious sensibilities in their governing mandates. The protection of the state was the protection of the state religion and the decisions to engage in violence to preserve either were basically one in the same. The resources that were deemed essential to the state were not split between the sacred and political. Unquestionably, those resources were seen to be worth protecting and the use of violence was condoned as a means of survival. The absolute belief in a deity was tied into the absolute belief in the righteousness of the state. Myths evolved and deities were molded to conform to the political realities that shaped the trajectory of the states' development. The need to keep the

---

8. For an overview of recent definitions of religion see: Cavanaugh, *The Myth of Religious Violence*. Particularly relevant to the variety of definition is chapter one.

9. Ibid., 19.

myths central to governmental policy relates to the need to keep the masses under control and to manipulate those masses in such a way to ensure that they would be willing to engage in acts of violence to preserve the status quo. Human decisions could be questioned and opinions challenged, but the proclamations of a deity were absolute. When the state claims to be speaking in the name of an absolute authority—an authority that transcends human sensibility—then that which could be challenged (human authority subject to error and multiple interpretations) is blindly accepted since the belief in the divine subverts rational thinking and encourages violent behavior as a necessity in adhering to and preserving the will of the power (deity) that shaped and shapes the essence of human consciousness. A political or societal system that has no deity removes the idea of absolute authority and subsequently will no longer engage in violence to preserve sacred resources. They will, however, continue to wage war and other violent acts to preserve those secular resources that are deemed essential to the state apparatus. Of course, which resources are deemed essential will then be open to debate unless the state institutes a dictatorial mandate whereby the absolute authority of the divine is replaced with the absolute authority of the state. This trend in the modern world to remove the divine from the policies and politics of the state has spawned both liberal democracies and fascist/authoritarian regimes. These diametrically opposed systems of governments are seemingly removed from religious authority if the idea of religion insists upon the existence of the supernatural/divine deity. As such, the violence attributed to these secular states is not driven by an irrationality predicated on superstition and myth; rather, it is violence that claims to emanate from an empirically based assessment of a situation that poses a direct threat to the interests of that state. The state will present its empirically collected data and argue their reasons to engage in violence and proclaim that the sustainability of the nation is in jeopardy and that action must be taken. But, of course, how that data is analyzed and interpreted will determine the level of threat. Furthermore, how that interpretation is presented will influence its reception and will shape the response of the populace that, in both a democracy and an authoritarian government, is essential in order to maintain the support of the masses. Interpretation and presentation, however, circumnavigates absolutes, but allows for the suggestion of "truth" which can then be embellished in such a way as to galvanize the population and bring them to a level of "faith" in that truth so that they believe it to be absolute in the religious sense of the word.[10]

10. Two examples of such a procedure are the pseudo-scientific conclusions of the Nazis regarding race and the Bush administration's conclusions regarding weapons of mass destruction in Iraq and the way both regimes presented their empirical evidence.

Simon Critchley, in his book *The Faith of the Faithless*, draws on Rousseau's *Social Contract* (1762) to demonstrate how the "question of sovereignty was translated from the divine to the civic" and proposes that Rousseau "believed that the general will, like the divine will, cannot err."[11] Critchley goes on to demonstrate (in accordance to the Schmittian ideal) that the liberal democratic system has transferred the mythological quality of theological discourse to the civil perspective where the myth of heavenly afterlife is replaced by the utopian belief in universal peace. Civil law replaces divine law and the subsequent reliance and "faith" in that civil law explains the liberal democratic system's adherence to and reliance on the judicial branch of government (supreme court). This conforms to the idea of the separation of church and state; all decisions must run through a civil process with its checks and balances giving ultimate authority to the people who elect their representatives and can dismiss them at the next election. For Schmitt, however, the true sovereign is he who "decides on the state of exception;" he who will suspend the operation of law and that decision maker represents the state and that the state must stand higher than the law.[12] Here, we see the transcendental and theological dimension of liberal democratic politics. There still has to be a quality that can supersede the civil apparatus if the threat to the overall system is perceived to be immanent. For Schmitt, this state of exception is analogous to the theological miracle—it is something that transcends the temporal political system and is necessary to preserve that system. This dictatorial concept seems anathema to the principles of liberal democracy (and probably is). The point is, however, that Schmitt saw the liberal constitutionalism of Weimar Germany as weak and subject to collapse due to its insistent "discussions" that curtailed action to combat the immanent economic collapse.

This concept of a theological component to liberal democracy resonates in the actions taken by numerous American presidents. The language employed by liberal democrats may be imbued with secular imagery, but the content of that language maintains the transcendental utopian aspirations that are essential to theological discourse. Where we see the most obvious difference is in the democratic fidelity towards the "nation" as opposed to the theological fidelity towards "God;" but even in this worshipping of reason/science/technology/civil law, there is a mythological impetus that has the same flavor as religious worship. What is commonly considered to be religious violence is violence that uses Scripture (or interpretations of Scripture) as a justification. This usually takes the form of the need of violence

---

11. Critchley, *Faith of the Faithless*, 103.
12. Schmitt, *Political Theology*, 5–10.

to oppose an existential threat to the religious principles that govern the theocratic society (in whatever manifestation that takes). This is the classic us/them dichotomy that drives the rationalization for protective violence. The history of religious violence bears this out (for example the French wars of religion 1562–1598 CE) where each religion feels threatened by the other and proclaims a war of survival. Up until the Enlightenment, with the non-contested "truth" of a Christian God, scriptural justification for violence was unquestioned. But again, theological concerns were part and parcel of the entire political process (regardless of who had the "authority"), so these wars were political in nature given the inextricable theological component of that political system.

The age of reason has led to a dismissive attitude towards such overt religious displays, exposing the irrational logic of theological discourse and the archaic/non-scientific nature of religions that are dependent upon scriptural mythologies that have little empirical substance. The demise of a divine authority left a gaping hole in the functionality of political development that was filled with the "religion" of nationalism. Rousseau's general will of the people and the concept of the nation state became the focus of communal worship.[13] But, this undercut the sense of absolutism and placed faith at the mercy of humanism, with all the deficits that are part of the human psyche. This is a core concern for Schmitt who draws heavily upon the concept of "original sin;" the belief that the masses are predisposed to error and the sovereign who engages the state of exception embraces the old idea of absolute authority (benevolent dictatorship) as the only means of preserving that state society from destruction by adversarial forces.

Other cultures have refused to subvert the religious component of their political system and have maintained the sense of absolutism in the guise of the mythological "god." Their belief that the temporal can never take an absolutist role drives their insistence on the divine presence and the overt display of that "power" that infuses their entire political agenda as it did in Western civilization up to the advent of the modern secular age. The perceived threat to that absolute that the Western form of liberal democracy poses (in their minds at least) drives the propensity for violence as an act of preservation. The societal, political, and cultural practices employed by some of these theocratic states is seen in the West as a threat to the core belief in the utopian universal love myth that underlies liberal democracy. The us/them paradigm is established and violence ensues with both sides insisting on the necessity of that violence. But, the West places the violence that is deemed religious in a very different category; it is "irrational" because

---

13. Rousseau, *Social Contract*.

it is predicated on the irrationality of scriptural dominated theological discourse that is grounded on archaic ideals that have been decimated by the advent of science and reason. Our use of violence is in accordance with the age of reason and is based upon a legal system that embraces Rousseau's general will of humankind; ethical humanism that demonstrates our sophistication and "fairness" in matters of violence. This is what drives much of the current discussions regarding the conflict with religious fundamentalism—from the new atheists and their condemnation of any religion that draws upon mythological arguments for violence and repression to the Christian apologists (Karen Armstrong, et al) and her thesis that the violence of the fundamentalist is not caused by their religion, but by our disdain and oppression of their "way of life."[14] What I think is missing from this debate is the recognition of the homogenized theological aspect of the liberal state. John Gray points out that the faith of liberal humanism in "human progress" resulting in universal peace and harmony is the barely secularized version of the Christian belief in providence.[15] The concern with transcendental/mythological (religious) ideas is still in place within the secular society. Even the overt display of religious belief maintains a presence in this liberal society (the pledge of allegiance, "in God we trust," etc.). But, it is the masked transcendental aspect that is still a driving force. Despite the checks and balances of the three branches of American government put in place to combat and prevent any form of tyranny, Schmitt's "state of exception" and the theological absolutism of the decision maker plays out in American politics. To preserve the utopian/mythological goal of human progress, the laws can be circumnavigated in order to enact violence on the "other" whose initial violence is so "obviously" irrational.

The decision to execute Osama bin Laden bypassed due process—it was a "state of exception" whereby the executive branch of government in the guise of a single authority with absolute power (Obama) authorized the most extreme act of violence (death) without challenge or dispute. The ongoing drone strikes are at the discretion of the commander-in-chief and have resulted in numerous civilian casualties. We do not condemn these acts of violence (and often praise them) because they are deemed "rational" even though they are carried out outside the normal channels of our liberal democratic system.[16] On the other hand, acts of violence initiated by the fundamentalist are often condemned as barbaric and inhumane because

14. Armstrong, *Fields of Blood*.

15. For a more thorough understanding of John Gray's thesis see: Gray, *Black Mass*.

16. For an assessment of the "war on terror" and the particulars involved in the logistical manoeuvrings and contentious military decisions involved see: Bergen, *Longest War*.

they are seemingly overtly religious. If we accept the proposition that our liberal system is still infused with theocratic/theological qualities that are hidden behind the insistence on our secular imperative of "separation of church and state"—a separation that arguably does not exist—would we be as harsh in our criticism of our own acts of violence as we are of the fundamentalists since what seems to be most unacceptable is the religious dimension? I am sure they see our drone attacks as "evil"—the indiscriminate killing of innocent people by the "great Satan"—in much the same way that we see their acts of violence as "evil." But, in both cases, is not the real driving force behind the violence political, whether it is a political system that is overtly religious or a system that has allowed the theological to be absorbed in a language of secular humanism? It seems to me that an argument can be made that what we designate as religious does not have to be in adherence to archaic mythologies; it can also be a belief in the perfectibility of humanity through faith in concerted human action that will lead to a utopian universal peace. Such a utopian vision, or even the atheistic concept of nothingness, is as inconceivable or conceivable as any idea of heaven. If we are committing violent acts in the name of any of these possibilities, possibilities that can only reside in the imagination, are they not all equally condemnable or equally allowable? The only way to avoid such blatant cultural judgments is to remain focused on the political agenda of the violence while recognizing that all political entities contain some theological/religious residue. But, their ultimate concern is always about power; power by any means necessary including the exploitation of the inherent superstitions that are part of the human struggle to understand the unknowable.

Bibliography

Armstrong, Karen. *Fields of Blood: Religion and the History of Violence.* Amherst, New York: Knopf, 2014.

Avalos, Hector. *Fighting Words: The Origins of Religious Violence.* Amherst, New York: Prometheus Books, 2005.

Bergen, Peter L. *The Longest War: The Enduring Conflict between America and al-Qaeda.* New York: Free Press, 2011.

Bodin, Jean. *On Sovereignty: Four Chapters from The Six Books of the Commonwealth.* Translated by Julian H. Franklin. Cambridge: Cambridge University Press, 1992.

Cavanaugh, William T. *The Myth of Religious Violence.* Oxford: Oxford University Press, 2009.

Critchley, Simon. *The Faith of the Faithless: Experiments in Political Theology.* London: Verso, 2012.

Gray, John. *Black Mass: Apocalyptic Religion and the Death of Utopia.* London: Penguin Books, 2007.

Gray, Phillip W. "Political Theology and the Theology of Politics: Carl Schmitt and Medieval Christian Political Thought." *Humanitas* XX:1–2 (2007) 175–200.

Kantorowicz, Ernst H. *The King's Two Bodies: A Study in Mediaeval Political Theology.* Princeton: Princeton University Press, 1957.

Rousseau, Jean-Jacques. *The Social Contract.* Translated by Maurice Cranston. London: Penguin Books, 1968.

Schmitt, Carl. *Political Theology: Four Chapters on the Concept of Sovereignty.* Translated by George Schwab. Chicago: University of Chicago Press, 1985.

9

The Global Impact of Religious Violence

A Response

Hector Avalos

Tip O'Neill, the famous Speaker of the United States House of Representatives (1977–1987), is often credited with popularizing the phrase, "All politics is local."[1] In the case of religious violence, it is particularly difficult to say that "all violence is local." The shootings in Orlando, Florida in June of 2016 are related, even if indirectly, to the airport attacks in Belgium and Istanbul. In turn, these events are related to the American invasion of Iraq and Afghanistan, and to the dissolution of the Ottoman Empire in the early 20th century. Indeed, religious violence can easily transcend geography and locality because its actors live all over the globe and/or can travel seamlessly across many borders. More importantly, the mentality that accompanies religious violence is not restricted to any locality.

The essays in this volume rightly emphasize the global nature of religious violence. The global dimensions of this volume are evident in the treatment of violence in Africa, the Middle East, Europe, and the Americas. But the volume also marks some new milestones in the research on the role of religion in violence. One is that the volume seeks to avoid the religionist traps in which much of the research on religion and violence is conducted.

By religionism, I refer to the idea that religion is beneficial for humanity, and so it should be protected and preserved. Religionist scholarship is marked by exculpating or minimizing the role of religion in violence. It is also marked by definitions of religion that claim that religion either cannot be defined or that it is so interlaced with politics and economics that one cannot attribute any violence to it. The work of William T. Cavanaugh,

---

1. See O'Neil and Novak, *Man of the House*, 6.

author of *The Myth of Religious Violence* (2009), would be an example of a scholar who denies the existence of religious violence.[2] Other scholars, whether religious or not, claim that religion is no more prone to violence than the reification of the nation-state or other ideas such as "freedom" or national identity. The scholars in this volume are aware of these disputes between religionists and secularists, and that is a welcome development in the study of religion and violence.

Another welcome feature of this volume is that most of the scholars belong to a younger generation. That means that some areas that older generations of scholars did not deem to be "research-worthy" now have made a strong case for inclusion. Thus, we have comic books and graphic novels as part of the cultural data that we can study seriously for what they reflect about society and violence. We have a clearer consciousness of the anthropocentric nature of research on violence, and this volume turns our attention to violence toward non-human animals.

Since many of the essays in this volume involve a discussion of my theory of religion and violence, it may be useful to summarize the theory that I fully laid out in *Fighting Words: The Origins of Religious Violence* (2005):

1. Most violence is due to scarce resources, real or perceived. Whenever people perceive that there is not enough of something they value, then conflict may ensue to maintain or acquire that resource. This can range from love in a family to oil on a global scale.

2. When religion causes violence it often does so because it has *created new scarce resources*.

I define religion as "as a mode of life and thought which presupposes the existence of, and relationship with, unverifiable forces and/or beings." This theory allows for a clear ethical distinction between religious and non-religious violence. I specifically argue that religious violence is always immoral, but secular violence is only sometimes immoral. Within a moral relativistic frame that accepts empirico-rationalism as providing reliable data, our argument that religious violence is always immoral begins by positing the seemingly obvious proposition that what exists has more value than what does not exist. Only what exists can be said to have any ethical value, if it has any value for us. If that is the case, then life, as an existent phenomenon, must have more value than what does not exist. We can schematize our rationale as follows:

1. What exists is worth more than what does not exist.

2. Cavanaugh, *The Myth of Religious Violence*.

2. Life exists;

3. Therefore, life is worth more than what does not exist.

We may deem immoral any action that places the value of life as equal or below the value of nothing. Therefore, it would always be immoral to kill for something that has no actual value because it does not exist.

We can also extend this argument to what cannot be proven, on empirico-rationalist grounds, to exist. For example, if I were to say that I am killing because undetectable Martians have declared it obligatory to kill, the argument would be considered rightly as absurd. But, the fact is that the *possibility* of undetectable Martians existing is not what would declare such a statement absurd. It is perfectly possible that undetectable Martians exist and order people to kill other people. The main reason that we do not accept this rationale as moral is that we, as observers, cannot verify that undetectable Martians exist, and so we would regard the perpetrator's claims as absurd.

In fact, we can argue that killing because undetectable Martians said so is equivalent to killing for no reason or to killing for nothing, even if the person killing believes himself or herself to have a just reason. Here, we as observers and members of the larger society are judging the perpetrator based on the empirico-rationalist verifiability of the claim. Since we cannot verify that undetectable Martians exist, we judge the perpetrator's claim to be without merit, and so the killing would be unjustified. Any act of killing not justified or authorized is called a "murder" in our society.

Accordingly, we can propose that, just as it is always immoral to kill for something that does not exist, killing for something that cannot be proven to exist is equally immoral. And since religion is, by our definition, a mode of life and thought premised on the existence of, and/or relationship with, unverifiable supernatural forces and/or beings, then it follows that killing for religious reasons is always immoral. We can make a similar argument for any act of religious violence. Therefore, we recapitulate our proposition as follows: *It is always immoral to commit any act of violence for religious reasons.*

We can also make our case against religious violence within the framework of scarce resource theory. When religious violence is compared to secular violence due to scarce resources, the *a fortiori* argument would be as follows:

> If acts of violence caused by actual scarcities are judged as immoral, then violence caused by resources that are not actually scarce is even more immoral.

Any act predicated on the acquisition or loss of a non-existent resource is morally wrong because a loss of life was traded for a non-existent gain.

We may illustrate this with a more concrete, if fanciful example. Suppose that male twins, who are otherwise equal, were the sole survivors of a boating accident. The twins are fortunate to encounter a helicopter with room for only one person to be rescued. The scarce resource is space on the helicopter. The choices that either of these twins might encounter would logically include:

- One twin gives up his life for the other; or
- One fights the other for the space in that helicopter.

Since either combatant did not cause the scarcity, then fighting for one's life may be considered tragic, but justifiable.

However, let us say that it was not true that there was only room for one more person on that helicopter. In that case, the loss of life would be wasteful. That is to say, the loss of life was sustained on a false premise. But, while this violence may be wasteful, it still might be justified if the killer did not know that there was, in fact, room for both twins.

The situation would be different if the killer could have verified that there was room, but did not. In this case, we may hold the killer to be unjustified. If one has the ability to verify that the seat on the helicopter was available, then one should not kill another person without making such verification. The reason, again, is that a life would be traded for a non-existent scarcity. And what exists is always more valuable than what does not exist.

But, let us say now that the only reason that one twin killed the other is that the killer claimed that an invisible Martian had told him that only one seat was available or that only one twin had the privilege to enter the helicopter even if two seats were available. In this case, we would hold the killer to be unjustified, if we did not hold him to be mentally ill.

The reason is that we cannot verify that invisible Martians exist or communicate with any individual. Just as a jury in Texas convicted Andrea Yates in 2002 for killing her children, even as she claimed it was on God's orders, we would not allow the perpetrating twin to claim communication from an undetectable Martian as justification for his killing.[3]

We can extend this argument to religious beliefs. Let us say that Population X has declared that god, who only communicates with members of population X, gave a certain bounded space to them. While there may be enough physical space, the space has now been made scarce solely because of the belief that a god has declared it to be his property. Any loss of life now

---

3. For an overview of the Andrea Yates case, see O'Malley, *Are You There Alone?*

would be completely wasteful if indeed that god did not exist. Any violence due to this belief would be judged wasteful and/or immoral.

If the morality of any act of violence is measured in proportion to verifiability, then we can judge some specific acts of historical violence as more immoral than others. To begin with, any acts of violence based on scarcities that do not actually exist would be more immoral than any acts of violence based on scarcities that actually do exist. Likewise, any killing by Muslims, Christians, or Jews based on scriptural commands would be immoral as opposed to any killing done because of any resources that actually were scarce. In the latter cases, it may sometimes be immoral to kill for resources that are actually scarce, but it may not always be so (e.g., if there were only one seat on that helicopter).

With these prefatory remarks in mind, I now turn my attention to examining how the different essays in this volume address the idea that scarce resource theory is useful in explaining violence. In some cases, the essays confirm and expand the idea to other areas (e.g., comic books, animals). In other cases, they integrate data from the natural sciences to complement sociological theories of violence. Yet, other writers challenge specific aspects of scarce resource theory or explore the question of whether biblical scholars should be activists against preserving biblical authority in the modern world in light of the violence endorsed in biblical texts. But, all of the essays agree that we must actively strive to understand the role of religion in violence.

André Gagné

The volume's first chapter ("Tyranny of Political Correctness and Religious Violence") addresses an issue of great importance in how modern scholarship approaches violence. Criticism of religion is normally not accepted in Western societies, even among many non-religious individuals. However, within this general reluctance to criticize religion, there is also a specific resistance among many scholars to criticize Islam. Gagné attributes this to "political correctness," which he defines as "the practice of being careful not to use speech and/or engage in actions that could offend a particular group of people" (p. 5). He notes this tendency among some of the best-known writers on violence, including William T. Cavanaugh and Karen Armstrong. Gagné rightly argues that any effort to address the problem of violence will need to involve criticism of religion and of specific religions. One cannot say, for example, that Christianity or Islam are essentially peaceful or that

ISIS is not really "Islamic." Those are theological judgments and should not be represented as historical or scientific ones.

I certainly agree that one should not be labeled an "Islamophobe" for pointing out the issues and problems of violence within certain segments of Islam or within Islam itself. Unfortunately, the issue of whether this should be attributed to "political correctness" has been muddled by the origin and the diverse usage of the phrase "political correctness" and "politically correct." Although Gagné points to one usage, there are opponents of political correctness who are religionist in orientation insofar as they deem criticizing religion to be precisely an instance of "political correctness." This is the case, for example, with the works of Dinesh D'Souza, who helped popularize the war against political correctness. One of his recurrent complaints was that the universities were hostile to religion and he complained about the hostility that evangelical Christians felt in academia.[4] Jonathan Wells and other Creationists often attribute their exclusion from scientific discussion in academia as a case of "political correctness."[5] Roger Kimball, who is also credited with being a leader against political correctness, viewed the introduction of gay and feminist themed courses into academia as an instance of "political correctness."[6]

That is why I prefer to attribute the resistance to criticize Islam or any other religion to "religionism" because political correctness can change depending on who has the power to regulate discourse. Religionism is a more stable category that refers to those who think religion is valuable or necessary for human existence, and, therefore, to be preserved and/or protected. Of course, religionists are also selective. Usually, American religionists strive to protect their own religion, Christianity. These Christian religionists may even be enthusiastic about characterizing other religions as violent, while ignoring that Christianity has been as violent or even more so throughout history. Indeed, Tom Sizgorich, among others, has striven to show how early Islamic war practices were borrowed or adapted from Christian and biblical sources.[7]

Gagné is definitely in accord with the idea that scholars should be activists. Scholars should attempt to speak out against the role of religion in violence, and to repudiate openly any of the theological concepts or

---

4. D'Souza, *Illiberal Education*, 84, 302, and 226, where he speaks of how evangelicals find the atmosphere of Harvard to be "intolerant" to them. For the role of D'Souza in popularizing the war against Political Correctness, see Williams, *PC Wars*, 1, 11, 24, 26, 52, 58, 72–73, 87, 90, 97–98, and 100–01.

5. Wells, *Politically Incorrect Guide*.

6. Kimball, *Tenured Radicals*, 7.

7. Sizgorich, *Violence and Belief*.

scriptural warrants used to foment violence. His main goal is, as it is mine, to use education as one of the main methods to combat violence. As he phrases it: "We need to target the ideology; this means that education has to be at the forefront of debunking dangerous and harmful ideas" (p. 9). I could not agree more.

Jennifer Tacci

For an example of the younger generation of scholarship on religious violence, one should look to Jennifer Tacci's "Apocalypses and Superhero Mythology: The Scars of Crisis and the Remnants of Outbursts between Reality and Imagination." Tacci issues a much-needed corrective on the previous hesitation to use popular mythology, here in the form of comic books and graphic novels, as a source to analyze religious violence. In this case, comic books can be a primary source that simulates and echoes ancient apocalyptic literature. Tacci follows John J. Collins and others in defining "apocalypses":

> By Apocalypses I am referring to the texts which belong to the genre according to the well-known scholarly definition: "a genre of revelatory literature with a narrative framework, in which a revelation is mediated by an otherworldly being to a human recipient, disclosing a transcendent reality which is both temporal insofar as it envisages eschatological salvation, and spatial insofar as it involves another supernatural world" (p. 20, n. 33).

She explains how comic books and ancient apocalypses are similar: "What do comic books and apocalypses have in common? For starters they both have a tendency to intermingle history and myth" (p. 20). Tacci also notes that "many apocalypses were written during or shortly after a serious crisis" (p. 16). A fascinating portion of Tacci's analysis is how comic books have reacted to 9/11 and how prescient some of them appear to be concerning 9/11.

The core of my work on violence has been to identify and clarify the ethical distinctions between religious and non-religious violence. Tacci shows similar concerns. She specifically analyzes Frank Miller's *Holy Terror* (2011), a graphic novel that was viewed as a screed against Islam.[8] She then compares *Holy Terror* to the book of Revelation, the paradigm of apocalyptic literature in the Bible. According to Tacci, "Revelation is much more dangerous than *Holy Terror* because the biblical text is held by some as truth" (p. 23). Indeed, *Holy Terror* is not being used as a sacred text to authorize any

---

8. See Miller, *Holy Terror*.

behaviors depicted. Even if others may mimic the ideas in *Holy Terror*, one does not usually encounter people saying that we must fight Islam because Frank Miller says so.

Tacci's work should inspire others to undertake similar explorations of how modern media perpetuates ideas found already in ancient biblical texts. One desideratum is to elucidate further the extent to which, not just comic books, but also how all sorts of media (film, video games) view violence as the primary solution to the problems of human conflict. How many comic books or video games, for example, are dedicated to alternatives to violence in solving world problems? The fact that violence so predominates in all forms of media as a "solution" is surely one of the most important questions our culture can raise about itself.

Costa Babalis

A different angle on the issue of religious violence is outlined by Costa Babalis's essay, "The Common Good Gone Bad." Babalis accepts the concepts that scarce resources are a key to explaining violence. He also recognizes the difference between scarce resources that actually exist and those that are unverifiable supernatural ones. Babalis seeks to show that an appeal to the common good often conceals a hegemonic ideology. He raises the following question:

> How many times have religious authorities invoked the common good, which in itself suggests the well being of the individual, the community, and ultimately humanity, only to persecute and obliterate their opponents? (p. 40).

This is a good question, and I hope Babalis will elaborate further with more detailed and concrete historical examples. For example, Babalis mentions the Thirty Years War. However, it is very important to note that there are scholars of that war that deny that it was mainly a religious conflict. Peter H. Wilson's treatise on that war explicitly states that "it was not primarily a religious war."[9] Indeed, one of the most salient problems is that many scholars of violence (e.g., Cavanaugh on the St. Bartholomew's Day Massacre) do not consult the primary sources thoroughly before issuing judgments on causation.

---

9. Wilson, *The Thirty Years War*, 9.

Spyridon Loumakis

Spyridon Loumakis's chapter ("Genocide and Religion in Rwanda in the 1990s: 'What Weapons Shall We Use to Conquer the *Cockroaches* Once and For All?'") is a very impressive piece of historical research. Loumakis has sifted through personal testimonies, media accounts, and judicial records. The genocide in Rwanda is certainly one of those tragic human events that should never be repeated. In fact, Rwanda shows how easily a nation can devolve into genocidal frenzies in full view of the world. Loumakis seems very familiar with the primary source materials, and broader methodological and theoretical issues in the study of religion and violence inform his analysis. The chapter certainly exemplifies the global nature of religious violence highlighted in this volume. According to Loumakis:

> The present work seeks to establish the connection between the violent events of the 1994 Rwanda genocide and the Christian religion as experienced and lived by the people of this country, influencing each other, both top-down and bottom-up, in the everyday interactions and everyday aspects of their lives; from high politics and decision making to bloody roadblocks in a small village in the countryside (p. 49).

Loumakis argues that "[r]eligious violence goes beyond the Church or the Bible, penetrating deep into the Rwandan society. It makes horrible actions—such as those committed during genocide—justifiable and acceptable" (pp. 50–51). Loumakis does note how Justin Mugenzi, a Minister of Trade and Industry in the Interim Government in Rwanda until 1994, used the Bible to promote his agenda. Mugenzi is quoted as stating: "I used the Bible citation which in our context, the Bible was well known to Rwandans" (p. 61). The Hutu published their version of the Ten Commandments (pp. 62–63).

The rationales used by the Hutu in their genocide of the Tutsis are ones we have seen before. For example, the idea that victory over enemies is a sign of a God's favor is certainly documented among the Hutu. However, those killed on the side of the ones committing genocide are "martyrs," while those on other side are sinners and transgressors who received just punishment. Some of the rationales seem perfectly rational if one accepts certain dogmas about God's omnipotence and omniscience. As Loumakis observes: "a genocide unfolding under his assumingly all-seeing capability, without hindrance, leaves *génocidaire* Hutu believers room for only one explanation: God's approval" (p. 73).

The conclusion reached by Loumakis is that *"the 1994 Rwanda genocide was religiously violent"* (p. 77). Nonetheless, Loumakis adds:

> In conclusion, the evidence available for studying the 1994 Rwanda genocide demonstrates that Avalos's theory is in need of some expansion. His arguments are often text-based and overemphasize examples about how people read and interpret their sacred books or how they act according to what they think is the right interpretation of said writings. . .The use of biblical motifs, as well as religious motifs in general, in the way that a religion is experienced in everyday life, even during a genocide, has much less to do with sacred books and their systematic interpretation than with their vague invocation or with general claims tentatively based on a shared religious background that people should have in a certain culture at a given time and place. (pp. 77–78).

I agree with Loumakis in affirming that we must go beyond texts to explain religious violence. My theory allows for this, and does not say that religious violence is only generated by religious texts. Rather, it says that religious thinking can create scarce resources, one of which is inscripturation—the idea that God reveals himself/herself in a limited set of texts. However, other scarce resources, including group privileging, which are an important factor in explaining the genocide in Rwanda, need not invoke Scripture to be "religious." To be "religious" the group privileging must be based on the notion that such a privilege was given by a supernatural being. Overall, Loumakis provides the sort of detailed historical investigation that one must undertake before declaring the extent to which a specific act of violence was religious or non-religious.

Marion Achoulias

Another excellent example of a younger generation of scholarship on religion and violence is Marion Achoulias's "Discourse of Sacrifice: Religious Studies and Violence against Animals." Achoulias rightly challenges the anthropocentric tradition found in so much of the scholarship about violence, including mine. In *Fighting Words: The Origins of Religious Violence* I had a very anthropocentric view, which privileged harm to human beings. In that book, I defined violence as *"the act of modifying and/or inflicting pain upon a human body in order to express or impose power differentials."*[10]

---

10. Avalos, *Fighting Words*, 19.

It is when I began to work on *The Bad Jesus: The Ethics of New Testament Ethics* that I realized how much I had ignored violence against animals. I began to explore how many times biblical texts endorsed all forms of violence against animals, including in the Flood Story (Gen 6–7), sacrificial legislation (Exod 13:13–15), and even in Jesus's attitudes towards dogs and swine (Mark 5:11–13; 7:27). I have since changed my definition to the following: *"Violence is the act of modifying and/or inflicting pain upon a living body in order to express or impose power differentials.*[11] In any case, Achoulias describes her purpose as follows:

> This author proposes that the careful application of Avalos's theory of religious violence to the situation of the animals we eat, wear, and use might bring about a much needed shift in perspective *vis-à-vis* other animals. In the framework of scarcity theory, religious violence is understood as avoidable conflict between competitors over valuables that only exist in the imaginary and is thus inherently unethical (pp. 84–85).

Achoulias, here, understands the ethical distinction between violence generated by scarce resources that actually exist and scarce resources that are unprovable or "imaginary." She recognizes that group privileging is one of the scarce resources that routinely generates violence towards animals because human beings reserve for themselves the right to life that they do not accord to animals.

Achoulias signals her support for an activist stance in scholarship: "With Avalos's critique as starting point, religion scholars can do much to contribute to a better understanding of the religious/ideological aspects of structural violence against animals" (p. 86). While Achoulias indicates that we should not exaggerate the gap between the secular and the religious, that statement still presupposes that the religious and secular can be separable. Yet, Achoulias also sees how complicit scholarship can be in denying rights to animals, and she includes the work of Jonathan Klawans and Kimberley Patton.[12]

It may be useful for Achoulias to clarify some aspects of her terminology and argumentation. One example is her use of the word, "artificial," in phrases such as "Carnism produces an artificial scarcity of arable land, clean water, grain, as well as inequities based on climate change. . .(pp. 89–90)." This might lead some readers to conflate her use of "artificial" with what I would call unverifiable, fictional, mythical, or non-existent resources. In my

11. Avalos, *The Bad Jesus*, 91.
12. Klawans, "Sacrifice in Ancient Israel," 65–80; Patton, "Animal Sacrifice," 391–405.

theory, the scarcity of arable land can be real, even if human beings manufacture it. This would be unlike a religiously generated scarce resource such as "heavenly rewards," which are also artificial, but not "real."

Achoulias's efforts to formulate new frameworks to analyze how biblical scholarship addresses violence toward animals are informed by ideological and Marxist theory. I cannot phrase the agenda any better than Achoulias:

> Now, in the twenty-first century and at the brink of global environmental destruction, it seems high time to systematically challenge the sacrificial taxonomy, to question inherited ideologies that harm human relations to the nonhuman world, and to think through the implications of the Darwinian realization that we all share ethically relevant features with those other animals we routinely exploit and kill (p. 109).

It will be interesting to follow how this work develops and challenges anthropocentric biblical scholarship, which still either neglects the issues of animal rights or tries to mitigate biblical ideas and teachings about animals.

Marc-André Argentino and Dalia Sabra

Soon after Omar Mateen was identified as the shooter in the Orlando massacre, reports began to circulate about his violent tendencies as a child.[13] This raised the question of whether Mateen is simply using Islam or religion as an instrument to exercise violent tendencies, or whether religion generated the specific violent behavior in which Mateen allegedly engaged. This is why the question raised in the chapter "Is There Such a Thing as a Radicalized Brain?" is so important. It brings new light to an old argument about the role of nature versus nurture in behavior and it has much relevance for ascertaining solutions to violence.

Argentino and Sabra argue that there is much neurobiological evidence that some people may be genetically prone to commit violence given the right environmental factors. However, they also rightly emphasize that genes cannot be the entire explanation. As they phrase it: "By itself, the genetic makeup of an individual is only a small proportion of the risk involved in violent behavior. The interaction with other biological, neurobiological, sociobiographical, and environmental factors is crucial" (p. 119). Indeed, the essay by Argentino and Sabra shows how difficult it is to ascertain causality even when we apply our strictest scientific methods. In particular,

---

13. For one report, see Zavadski et al., "Omar Mateen."

consider the study by Avishalom Caspi and his coworkers that is cited by Argentino and Sabra. The objective of Caspi and his co-researchers was to determine why some children who were maltreated grow up to develop antagonist behavior, whereas others do not. Their findings concluded that a polymorphism in the MAOA [monoamine oxidase A enzyme] gene was found to moderate the effects of maltreatment. Thus, children who were maltreated and had a genotype consisting of high levels of MAOA were less likely to develop aggressive behavior. MAOA is an enzyme that "metabolizes neurotransmitters such as norepinephrine (NE), serotonin (5-HT), and dopamine (DA), rendering them inactive."[14] Deleting the gene encoding for the MAOA enzyme results in increased levels of those three neurotransmitters observed in a line of transgenic mice. The increased levels of those neurotransmitters, in turn, are associated with increased aggression in the mice. Restoring MAOA expression of the corresponding gene normalized the aggression. Caspi then tried to show how maltreated children might later engage in aggression depending on their expression of the MAOA gene. However, Caspi notes how difficult it is to then transfer these results to human aggression. Caspi says that "[e]vidence for an association between MAOA and aggressive behavior in the human general population remains inconclusive."[15] Caspi adds that "no study has ascertained whether MAOA plays a role" in determining whether maltreatment has persisting neurochemical correlates in human children, even it has an affect on the neurotransmitters (e.g., dopamine, serotonin) being studied.[16]

Although I am by no means qualified to evaluate the neurochemistry discussed, it is important to note that Caspi uses *The Statistical Manual of Mental Disorders* (DSM-IV) published in 1994 to assess what is called "adolescent conduct disorder." However, it is well known that DSM has had a history of changing criteria or eliminating "disorders" (e.g., homosexuality). Some of the criteria for determining whether someone has "Adolescent Conduct Disorder" require some critical analysis. Terrie E. Moffitt has argued that some of the age-of-onset subtyping used by DSM-IV may still be useful (e.g., differentiating between childhood and adolescent on-set behaviors), but we need more comparative studies and longitudinal studies from different cultures.[17]

In 2014, Courtney A. Ficks and Irwin D. Waldman published meta-analysis of violence association studies that included the MAOA gene. One

14. Caspi et al., "Role of Genotype," 851.
15. Ibid.
16. Ibid.
17. See further, Moffitt et al., "Research Review: DSM-V Conduct Disorder," 3–33.

observation related to the location of the MAOA gene on the X chromosome, and men only have one X chromosome. This can result in gender bias in some studies. According to Ficks and Waldman,

> Because females have two X chromosomes whereas males have only one, heterozygosity may be present in females but not males. As MAOA expression for heterozygous allele carriers remains unclear, many investigators have selected all-male samples or eliminated heterozygous females from their samples...[18]

At the same time, a study of 500 violent offenders in Finland by Jari Tiihonen and his co-workers found that childhood maltreatment did not really affect the behavior of those with the MAOA genotype.[19] Although Tiihonen and his co-researchers believe there is a correlation between the MAOA genotype and violence, they also conclude that: "a conservative estimate implies that 5–10% of all severe violent crime in Finland is attributable to specific MAOA and CDH13 genotypes."[20] In other words, we are still a long way from explaining the mass bulk of violence in the world by looking at the MAOA genotype.

Argentino and Sabra also discuss the role of humiliation in generating aggression. Humiliation is about lowering social status, and so it can be explained by scarce resource theory. The scarce resource would be "status," and when people do not feel they have enough of it, then, they will try to acquire it just like any other resource deemed to be valuable. What is needed in the studies cited by Argentino and Sabra is recognition of how and why any particular ethnic or national status became valuable.

Sometimes religious factors have created the status ("group privilege") deemed valuable. For instance, according to biblical accounts, the creation of the Hebrew ethnic group is traced to the calling of Abraham to form his own separate lineage (Gen 12:1–7), even though he was not different "ethnically" at that point from the rest of his kinship group. Adhering to monotheism further differentiated Abraham's lineage; adding some religiously mandated practices (endogamy, circumcision) that set it apart from neighbors (see Gen 17:12; 24:3–4). A similar phenomenon occurred between Christians and Jews. The initial conflict was between Jews who accepted Jesus as the Messiah and Jews who did not (see John 5:18, Acts 17:2–5, Gal 2:11–16). Such Jews did not really differ "ethnically" from each other. While

---

18. Ficks and Waldman, "Candidate Genes for Aggression," 429.

19. Tiihonen at al., "Genetic Background," 790: "Our results, from over 500 offenders, showed a strong main effect for this genotype, but maltreatment did not modify the risk in any way."

20. Ibid.

it is clear that some persons in the New Testament regarded themselves as both Jewish and Christian, eventually "Jews" became those who retained the traditional religion of their ancestors without accepting Jesus as the Messiah. The Catholic Church then reinforced the separate religious identity of the Jews through marriage laws, professional restrictions spatial separation in ghettos, and distinctive garb, which made Jews even more different and more identifiable targets for humiliation and violence. Yet, it was perceived Jewish antagonism to Christ that was stated as a reason for violence against Jews. Thus, when Pope Paul IV issued his bull, *Cum nimis* (1555), which established a ghetto for Jews, his introductory rationale was that the "Jews' own guilt has consigned them to perpetual servitude."[21] Thus, one cannot always divorce humiliation of one ethnic group by another without analyzing how religion made them different ethnic groups, with different statuses in the first place. Overall, Argentino and Sabra are on the right track. We need to consider any effects of genetics and neurochemistry on violence. This idea, of course, is not new. I discuss some biological theories of violence in *Fighting Words*.[22] However, with the new biomolecular and genomic tools at our disposal we can make new attempts. I concur with the conclusion of Argentino and Sabra: "A multi-disciplinary approach is the only solution that is viable, as there is a multiplicity of causes and consequences that can lead to one same result: violence sourced by a particular religious belief or ideology" (p. 130).

Calogero Miceli

Calogero Miceli's chapter, "Religion and Violence: Rethinking the Role of the Biblical Scholar in the Contemporary World," is very engaged with various aspects of *The End of Biblical Studies* (2007) which argues that the only mission of biblical studies is to end biblical studies as we currently know it. As we currently know it, biblical studies is a religionist apologetic enterprise centered on preserving and expanding the value of biblical texts. Biblical studies is still situated within an ecclesial-academic complex that has no analogue in other areas of the humanities. While not advocating that we end the study of the Bible, *The End of Biblical Studies* argues that we must re-purpose biblical studies. That new purpose is to end the authority that the biblical texts wield in modern society. We would still study the Bible as a relic of ancient culture. That new purpose involves some level of "activism"

---

21. Stow, *Catholic Thought*, 295; Latin (p. 291): *quos propia culpa perpetua servituta submissit*.

22. Avalos, *Fighting Words*, 55–58.

that centers on undermining the authority of biblical texts in the modern world. That is to say, a biblical scholar would now seek to explain to the public why this text should not be used as a moral authority to set any sort of legal or social policies in modern societies. Miceli disagrees in part with this new mission. He says that the Bible and other religious texts "can be academically studied and critiqued without necessarily being promoted or rejected" (p. 135). However, Miceli is willing to make some exceptions:

> The chief exceptions to this tenet, I argue, are in cases when religious texts are used to promote, incite, or justify forms of violence in the world. In such instances, the duty of the biblical scholar must unreservedly be to intervene and strongly disavow the use of religious texts in such deplorable manners (p. 135).

In general, Miceli's "article advocates for a neutral and objective stance on the role of the biblical scholar when it comes to avowing or disavowing the value of religious texts for modern audiences, it fervently promotes an exception to the rule when it comes to religious violence" (p. 150). Accordingly, my aim here is to show that:

a. Objectivity and activism are compatible;

b. There is no reason why the exception should be restricted only to violence;

c. There is no such thing as neutrality.

Let me address first the claim that there is compatibility between objectivity and activism. Miceli seems to view objectivity and activism (either as promotion or rejection) as opposing categories. However, objectivity and activism, whether it involves promotion or rejection of biblical texts, are compatible. The reason is that knowledge has consequences, and beliefs have consequences. Therefore, any piece of knowledge that is consequential for our society must obligate a researcher to either promote what is deemed true or oppose what is deemed untrue.

Consider the history of science. At one time, most people thought that disease could be caused by supernatural beings called demons. Then, science discovered that microbes or other natural causes actually cause many of the diseases attributed to demons. We could demonstrate that administering certain drugs or vaccines could cure disease where prayer had no effect. The discovery is as "objective" as anything else in science. Microorganisms can be correlated with certain diseases and one can conduct experiments to verify that certain microorganisms can cause specific diseases.

Now, should scientists promote this discovery and work against the idea that demons cause diseases? Should scientists not divulge that discovery for fear of upsetting the authority of clerics who pray for the sick? Should scientists not work to undermine beliefs in supernatural causation of disease when they know that vaccines will save millions of lives? What if these scientists started a campaign that said that one should not put their trust in prayer or the demonic theory of Polio because we had objectively found what really caused Polio and had a better alternative? Would these scientists not be objective anymore? Not at all. Objectivity has really nothing to do with whether one will advocate for the beneficial consequences of any discovery, and the harmful consequences of maintaining some false theory of illness.

There is no reason scholars in biblical studies, religious studies, and other areas of the humanities cannot be just as vocal and objective as in science when the results of their research have crucial consequences for humanity.[23] Restricting the exceptions to violence also overlooks many other areas in which religious beliefs can do harm to a society. Consider the claim that one must legally mandate a one-man-and-one-woman marriage because that is the only marriage that has ever been accepted in human history.[24] The Supreme Court of the United States actually discussed this sort of claim, and accepting could mean denying millions of people the right to marry the persons they love when they are of the same sex.[25] But, historians know that human beings have had a diversity of "marriage" arrangements.[26] So, should they divulge their discovery and say that certain historical claims about marriage practices are false? Their argument may be objective (based on documents showing the diversity of marriage practices) and activist at the same time. There is compatibility.

What about creationism, which undermines genuine scientific education? Scientists have actively challenged creationism for decades by testifying in federal court cases in the United States, and opposing legislation that aims to introduce it as science in classrooms. In 1983, Laurie Godfrey published an anthology called *Scientists Confront Creationism*, which featured many prominent scientists trying to undermine a literal understanding of Genesis.[27] Would that mean those scientists were not objective? Many bibli-

---

23. See also, Donovan, "Neutrality in Religious Studies."

24. See Coontz, *Marriage*.

25. Most recently in Supreme Court of the United States, "Obergefell et al. v. Hodges," which declared as unconstitutional prohibitions against same-sex marriages.

26. Coontz, *Marriage*.

27. Godfrey, *Scientists Confront Creationism*.

cal scholars (e.g., Peter Enns) have actively undermined the whole idea that Genesis is a scientific account of our origins, and say so.[28] Are these scholars not being objective insofar as they base their arguments on empirical data? If their arguments are based on objective empirical evidence, their advocacy of what they have found objectively should not be viewed as a transgression.

We could compile a long list where most biblical scholars might say that researchers have an obligation to reveal what they have learned and to advocate for the practical results of those investigations. I could mention climate change, which might destroy our biosphere if not checked in time. Biblical scholars might support fighting anti-vaxxers, whose beliefs could result in millions of deaths if left uncontested. Indeed, almost anything that harms human beings or living beings can be seen as a type of violence, and, therefore, it can be included even by the exemption that Miceli himself advocates.

And, of course, there is no such thing as neutrality because knowledge and "truth" are not neutral. Aristotelean logic affects all of our beliefs so that if you assert that X is true, you must be asserting that its opposite is not true; nothing neutral about that. If you say that germs cause disease, you automatically are in opposition to those who say germs do not cause disease. If you say that marriage has had many forms in history, then you are saying that a one-man-one-woman marriage is not the only form of marriage in history. Science and all good research are meant to discriminate between good theories and bad ones; between true and false claims.

The End of Biblical Studies also claims that activism can help biblical studies remain relevant. Biblical scholars are often not viewed as solving any problems akin to what scientists solve. That endangers their employment and relevance in academia. However, that view is partly the result of the silence and passivity of biblical scholarship in divulging the significance of its discoveries. If biblical scholars were more activist in informing the world of the dangers of biblical beliefs for modern society, then perhaps we could have people pay more attention to what biblical scholars have discovered about the true nature of the societies that produced the biblical texts. Activism, in other words, may be what saves biblical studies from total irrelevance. There are degrees of activism and many forms of it. Perhaps Miceli is actually protesting those who conduct their activism in unseemly fashion. They might shout insults or personally degrade those who do not believe likewise. However, the world needs all sorts of activism, and activism is determined by context and the imminence of any threat, as it does in the rest of life. Some activist scholars can write articulate essays to express

---

28. Enns, *The Evolution of Adam*.

themselves in a respectful fashion, and others may want to protest with pithy slogans outside of a congress.

In addition, Miceli raises the important issue of the role of activism in teaching in the classroom. I, for one, don't usually advocate for any particular political or secularist stance in classrooms. I simply report what different viewpoints believe. My personal views are revealed on the last day of class for those who wish to know them. My approach, as far as students and peers have evaluated it, has not impeded the objectivity with which I can report different viewpoints. I make a distinction between being a reporter of many viewpoints in a classroom and engaging in activism and advocacy for my viewpoint in the broader public arena.

In sum, Miceli and I disagree only on the extent to which one should be an activist. He restricts activism to violence, and I favor activism in all cases where harm or death to human beings or our biosphere can be the result of silence. Indeed, at some level, the negative consequences of some biblical teachings can result in harm or death to human beings that reach beyond the violence of an interpersonal or inter-state nature. If you believe climate change is not real because of certain biblical teachings, then harm may come to human beings and to life on earth, and that harm is no less painful or tragic than that of other actions we classify as "violence." If children are left to die of horrible diseases because parents believe that the Bible favors prayer only, and not medical treatment, that can also be a type of "violence" suffered by that child. Indeed, there is no reason to restrict activism to just classic forms of "violence" if the assistance of biblical scholars can help ameliorate the plight of human beings who will suffer some sort of injury or death because of the attempt to preserve some biblical beliefs.

Derek Bateman

The paper by Derek Bateman raises a perennial issue in the study of violence—namely, the relationship between religious and non-religious violence. This is very important because William T. Cavanaugh and other theorists go so far as to say that religious violence is a myth. Some scholars claim that religious violence is really political violence that uses religion as a tool. The idea that religious violence is not really *ethically different* from non-religious violence is perhaps the primary target of my theory. Bateman rightly notes that "[m]uch of the contentious flavor of the debate revolves around the idea and definition of religion and the distinction between divine violence and secular (state) violence" (p. 155). Bateman affirms that non-religious scarce resources can create violence that simulates the scarce resources created by religion. As he phrases it:

> The point here is that Hector Avalos rightly recognizes the scarce resource as a prime component of violence justification among religious practitioners, but he does not fully consider the similarities of this proposal with the non-religious entities and their propensity towards violence. . .Insisting that religious violence is distinct because of its embrace of non-empirical and irrational cosmological views fails to acknowledge equally irrational concepts within the political and nationalistic perspectives of so-called secular societies (p. 159).

Bateman regards "freedom" as one of those non-religious yet unverifiable concepts: "Secular ideologies elevate their resources to a sacred status in the same way as the religious and are equally guilty of allowing unverifiable concepts such as freedom to control the trajectory of their beliefs and violent actions" (p. 159). Although there may some points of agreement, there are a number of reasons why I disagree with at least some of Bateman's analysis.

First, he is not addressing where the fundamental distinctions between religious and non-religious violence lie in my theory. According to Bateman, I apparently deny that non-religious entities can create violence similar to the violence created by religion ("he does not fully consider the similarities of this proposal with the non-religious entities and their propensity towards violence" p. 159). However, Bateman here displays some misunderstanding of my theory. My proposal affirms that "[m]ost violence is due to scarce resources, real or perceived. Whenever people perceive that there is not enough of something they value, then conflict may ensue to maintain or acquire that resource. This can range from love in a family to oil on a global scale."[29] The latter certainly acknowledges the ability of non-religious scarcities to cause violence. I have repeatedly stated the not all violence is caused by religion, and I do not regard religion as the only cause of violence.

Indeed, Bateman overlooks the fact that I do not make a distinction in the *ability* of religious and non-religious factors to generate similar acts of violence. It is scarcity, religious or not, that I deem to be the underlying cause of violence, whether secular or not. Furthermore, I argue that the mechanism that leads to violence is the same in religious and non-religious violence: *The effort to acquire or maintain Scarce Resource X.*[30]

---

29. Avalos, *Fighting Words*, 18.
30. See Avalos, *Fighting Words*, 22.

What I do make is an *ethical distinction* between verifiable and unverifiable scarce resources that Bateman does not fully recognize or address. Despite the same basic mechanism (*The effort to acquire or maintain Scarce Resource X*) behind violence, there is an ethical distinction in trying to acquire or maintain a resource that exists and trying to acquire or maintain a resource that does not exist or cannot be proven to exist. Here is a simple illustration:

a. I will commit violence because I want to acquire the water my enemy is denying me.
b. I will commit violence because I want to acquire the reward called eternal life.

I argue that if killing for a resource we can prove to be scarce is bad enough, then killing for a resource that cannot be proven to exist is worse. As mentioned, committing acts of violence for something that does not exist or that cannot be proven to exist is always immoral in my theory. The reason is that in the cases of unverifiable scarce resources one is harming beings that do exist in return for rewards that do not exist or cannot be proven to exist. What does not exist has no ethical value, while that which exists can or does have ethical value. Therefore, trading something ethically valuable for something of no ethical value is always immoral. The same is not the case with resources that actually exist. If someone wants to take my life, and I commit an act of violence to save my life, then I am trying to maintain a resource (life) that has ethical value. In the latter case, I am not trading real lives for unverifiable resources or rewards. In order to truly understand the ethical distinctions I make, Bateman would have to answer clearly the question of *whether there is an ethical distinction between violence committed for a resource that exists and violence committed for a resource that does not exist or cannot be proven to exist*. He needs to address the specific example I offered above or others I discuss elsewhere.

Second, Bateman substitutes other terms for the ones I am using, and thereby addresses arguments I did not make. For example, one main distinction I make is between verifiable and unverifiable when speaking of resources created by religious versus non-religious factors. Bateman sometimes substitutes a different category of "rational/irrational" ("fails to acknowledge equally irrational concepts within the political and nationalistic perspectives of so-called secular societies," (p. 159). I do not use "rational/irrational" in quite the same way. For example, I have argued that if a person believes a god hates homosexuals then it may be "rational" for a believer in that god to commit an act of violence against homosexuals. In another instance, he states that "[t]he sacred is not the sole domain of the religious" (p. 159). However, here he is substituting his own definition of "sacred" for mine. I only use the term "sacred" when it is related to something religious. But, even if we used "sacred" for what we might value most, there is still an ethical difference in my theory between valuing things whose existence is verifiable and valuing things that do not exist and cannot be proven to exist.

Third, Bateman conflates general abstract categories with specific categories and thereby creates asymmetrical comparisons. For example, he contends that the concept of "freedom" is "unverifiable" (". . .unverifiable concepts such as freedom. . ." p. 159), and then equates this abstract concept of freedom with specific unverifiable scarce resources generated by religious thinking. But, my theory does not say that "the concept" of religion is unverifiable. That is to say, we can verify that the concept called religion does exist just as does the concept of freedom. Beliefs exist and concepts exist in my theory. As long as I can verify that Person X believes Y or has a Concept Z, then beliefs and concepts exist and are verifiable.

Moreover, the unverifiability of the scarce resources that generate violence does not lie so much in the abstracted genus ("religion" or "freedom"), but in the species of scarcity ascribed to that genus. Carl Schmitt, the scholar upon whom Bateman relies for some of his arguments, actually makes a similar observation when speaking about "sovereignty":

> About an abstract concept there will be in general no argument, least of all in the history of sovereignty. What is argued about is the concrete application and that means who decides in a situation of conflict what constitutes the public interest or interest of the state, public safety and order, *le salut public*, and so on.[31]

Accordingly, we certainly can verify the existence of specific freedoms. For example, I can verify that I have the "freedom to vote in an election." I can verify that I have the "freedom of movement in a particular territory." I can verify that I have the "freedom to worship a particular god as I wish." Once one identifies specific freedoms, then verifiability can enter our ethical evaluation. Those who have those freedoms and those who do not can verify that any particular Person X has those specific freedoms. These specific types of freedoms are resources that can be made scarce or abundant in a real way.

The same is not true with religious scarce resources. Believers in a heavenly reward cannot verify that they have such a reward, and neither can non-believers. These resources cannot be made more abundant by simply

---

31. Schmitt, *Political Theology*, 6.

THE GLOBAL IMPACT OF RELIGIOUS VIOLENCE   189

believing that they are more abundant. On the other hand, I can increase the amount of freedoms I grant to others in a real and observable manner.

Fourth, Batemen is relying heavily on Carl Schmitt's flawed analogy between religion and a nation-state. Carl Schmitt (1888–1985) was a political theoretician active in Germany during the Weimar, Nazi, and Post-World War II periods.[32] Schmitt had a very complicated relationship with Catholicism and Nazism that I will not detail.[33] Scholars of Schmitt have debated whether he was a Catholic in the late Weimar period that shifted away from Christianity during the Nazi period, and then reconciled with the Church in order to distance himself from Nazism in the post-War period.[34]

For my purposes, it is important to point out that Bateman is primarily relying on Schmitt's *Political Theology*, which was first published in 1922, during his pre-Nazi period. Bateman actually is using George Schwab's 1985 translation of the 1934 German edition, which was published during the Nazi period.[35] By Schmitt's own account, this second edition remains "unchanged" from the first.[36] Bateman quotes Schmitt's famous declaration that "[a]ll significant concepts of the modern theory of the state are secularized theological concepts. . ." (p. 158)[37] However, Bateman quotes only part of Schmitt's sentence, as translated by Schwab, which I reproduce here in its entirety:

> All significant concepts of the modern theory of the state are secularized theological concepts not only because of their historical development—in which they were transferred from theology to the theory of the state, whereby, for example, the omnipotent God became the omnipotent lawgiver—but also because of their systematic structure, the recognition of which is necessary for a sociological consideration of these concepts.[38]

32. For some basic studies of Schmitt, see Balakrishnan, *The Enemy*; Bendersky, *Carl Schmitt*; Schwab, *The Challenge of the Exception*. For a recent assessment of his relationship to Christianity and the Catholic Church see Roberts, "Carl Schmitt—Political Theologian?"

33. See further Bendersky, *Carl Schmitt*.

34. For some comments on this evolutionary view of Schmitt, see Roberts, "Carl Schmitt—Political Theologian?"

35. Schmitt, *Political Theology*.

36. Ibid., 1.

37. Ibid., 36.

38. Schmitt, *Political Theology*, 36. Schmitt, *Politische Theologie*, 43: "Alle prägnanten Begriffe der modernen Staatslehre sind säkularisierte theologische Begriffe. Nicht nur ihrer historischen Entwicklung nach, weil sie aus der Theologie auf die Staatslehre übertragen wurden, indem zum Beispiel der allmächtige Gott zum omnipotenten Gesetzgeber wurde, sondern auch in ihrer systematischen Struktur, deren Erkenntnis

Given the centrality of Schmitt's claim for Bateman's chapter, my aim is to show that:

a. Schmitt is wrong historically;

b. Schmitt's claims do not invalidate the ethical difference between religious and non-religious violence;

c. Schmitt is probably engaged in crypto-Christianity and is actually applying a biblical principle at the time he made this claim.

Schmitt does not provide any thorough defense of his claim beyond some analogies he observes. On a historical level, his claims are outdated and refuted by not only historical, but also anthropological research. Human organization preceded any elaborate theology to justify or explain that organization. If one looks at the ancient Near East, one sees that pantheons are pervasively organized as families so that one could just as well make the case that theology simply replicated human organizations, not the other way around. "Custom" (e.g., Gen 29:26) can be cited as a reason for a legal or social decision in the ancient Near East, and that is analogous to impersonal "law" that is often cited in modern times. Therefore, an impersonal institution called "custom" that governs behavior was perfectly compatible within monotheistic and polytheistic systems of law of antiquity, and is not a modern development. Much of the juridical and governing apparatus of the Catholic Church was explicitly simulating the Roman Empire (e.g., the title of Pontifex for the Pope), and Jesus himself is often portrayed as another version of the Roman emperor.[39]

Philosophically, the analogies contain some crucial differences that Schmitt and Bateman overlook. For example, even if "the law" or "a human lawgiver" is just secularized theology, the fact remains that those entities are verifiable, whereas a divine lawgiver is not. Thus, if I commit an act of violence because a human "omnipotent" lawgiver told me to do so, then I am choosing to follow the will of a real existent being. The reasons of that human lawgiver may be flawed, but that lawgiver does exist. The same applies if we say we commit violence because of "the law" or some set of laws that guide our policies. Those laws do express the will of real entities.

The same is not the case with "God." He either does not exist or cannot be proven to exist, and so he is not analogous to a human lawgiver or to an institution we call "the law." Thus, there is no real or verifiable "will" of God that is being reflected by any "God-given" law as far as we can determine,

---

notwendig ist für ein soziologische Betrachtung dieser Begriffe."

39. See Fantin, *The Lord of the Entire World*.

whereas the will of a real entity is being reflected in "the law" or a human lawgiver. Harming or injuring another human being because of the will of a non-existent or unverifiable being will always be ethically objectionable, whereas that is not always the case of following the will of "the law" or a human lawgiver, who might have empirically verifiable motives to engage in violence (e.g., we are about to be attacked). That is why a nation-state cannot be considered the same sort of entity as "God" or some similar supernatural entity. A nation-state usually consists of a bounded space that has a human hierarchy that exercises power within it. The boundaries and the hierarchy all can be verified to exist. It may be artificially and arbitrarily constructed, but it exists to the extent that it is composed of a group of individuals who make up the government or rulership. It exists to the extent that it can control its borders and enforce its will on its subjects.

True enough, there may be people who do not "recognize" the nation status of a particular territory or organization, but there still may be a real organized or territorial entity that is not receiving that recognition even in the eyes of the deniers of that status. The ISIS state or "caliphate" may not be recognized by Western powers, but those same powers recognize that there is a group of people who call themselves ISIS who control a particular territory. Real military operations are organized to root out real people from a real territory.

Moreover, there remains a strong demarcation between religious and non-religious state violence. Any state that says, "We will commit Violent Act X because a belief in a supernatural being leads us to do so," is engaging in religious violence if those beliefs are sincere. A state that says "We will commit Violent Act X in order to Acquire Freedom to extract oil from Location Y" is not engaging in religious violence.

In contrast, God exists only by virtue of belief in that entity, and God has no verifiable existence beyond the mind of believers. Therefore, we can still make an ethical distinction between violence committed by believers in a real entity like a nation-state, and violence committed by believers in an entity that does not exist or cannot be proven to exist. Believers in a nation-state may sometimes be unjustified in their violence, but not always. If a nation-state is attacked, for example, it is usually deemed justified to defend it because it is composed of people whose lives are real. On the other hand, violence committed because of the belief that one is defending God's honor or will is always immoral because real lives are being killed or harmed for the honor or will of an entity that does not exist at all or cannot be proven to exist. Bateman also raises the issue of the relationship between "consensus" and "verifiability."

> If there is not a consensus regarding what freedoms are essential, then the verification of that freedom becomes unstable; empirical evidence needed to solidify the verifiability of the resource is tainted by the interpretative approach of any given society (p. 158).

However, "consensus" does not really affect verifiability in that fashion in my theory. If people cannot agree on what freedom means or what a national state's powers should be, that does not render any specific powers held by humans or freedoms allowed less verifiable. It only means that consensus itself becomes a scarce resource that can generate violence, and so it is perfectly consistent with my theory. That is to say, the lack of consensus is itself a scarce resource that is subject to the same mechanism: "Effort to acquire or maintain Consensus X may generate violence."

The lack of consensus about a general resource ("gender equality") will not affect the verifiability of the specific actions or resources that derive from that general category. For example, let us say that we cannot agree on what "gender equality" means. Some might say that it means only allowing women to vote in elections, and others might argue that it means that women can serve in any political office held by men. Will the lack of consensus on "gender equality" really mean that we cannot verify whether women serve in the same political offices as men or whether women can vote or not? Again, the issue revolves around how Bateman views the verifiability of an abstracted genus ("gender equality") versus the verifiability of the specific actions or behaviors associated with that general category.

Finally, one must look at Schmitt's own context and biography more critically to understand why he was making the claim.[40] As mentioned, some scholars have viewed Schmitt as a religionist and a devout Catholic early in his career (or even throughout his career). His interest in Catholicism's place in society is illustrated by his book, *Roman Catholicism and Political Form* (1934). Consider Schmitt's essay "Die Sichtbarkeit der Kirche: Eine scholastische Erwägung" ("The Visibility of the Church: A Scholastic Consideration") published in 1917–1918. Therein, Schmitt states that "[w]hen the Christian obeys authority, he obeys God and not authority because it [authority]—[in its] foundation and limits—is from God."[41] In other

---

40. See Roberts, "Carl Schmitt—Political Theologian?" especially 462.

41. Schmitt, "Die Sichtbarkeit," 74: "Wenn der Christ der Obrigkeit gehorcht, weil sie—Grund und Grenze—von Gott ist, so gehorcht er Gott und nicht der Obrigkeit." It is uncertain what biblical translation Schmitt was referencing, but the words of Luther's translation also use "Obrigkeit" and "von Gott" in Rom 13:1: "Jedermann sei untertan der Obrigkeit, die Gewalt über ihn hat. Denn ist keine Obrigkeit ohne von Gott; wo aber Obrigkeit is, die ist von Gott verordnet."

words, Schmitt was echoing the Pauline declaration in Rom 13:1: "Let every person be subject to the governing authorities. For there is no authority except from God, and those that exist have been instituted by God."

Not long after that, in 1922, Schmitt wrote his more famous declaration about the main concepts behind the state as being "secularized theology." A plausible case can be made that Schmitt's *Political Theology* was attempting to retain God's place in a secularized world or trying to expose the illusion of secularization when he believed that God is really in control of all government, secular or not. But, whether such an interpretation of Schmitt is correct or not, it will not support the conflation of supernatural beings and nation states.

In short, Schmitt's claim about states being secularized theologies was one that he never worked out in detail in *Political Theology*, and it should not be used without far more historical and anthropological study of human organizations and state formation. It is especially important to observe that Schmitt's Germany followed one of at least five nationalist paths identified by Liah Greenfeld, and they should not all be equated either.[42] National ideologies can produce violence as much as any religious ideology. But, the ethical distinction will remain in the difference between fighting for entities that exist and fighting for entities that do not exist or cannot be proven to exist. Nations, laws, and human ideologies, even if arbitrarily constructed, have a verifiable existence. Gods and supernatural resources do not. Therefore, it will always be immoral to trade real human lives for entities whose existence is unprovable and so have zero ethical value.

Conclusion

The essays in this volume have explored a number of issues, and raised important questions. In general, the volume illustrates the necessity of approaching the issue of violence, and particularly religious violence, by using a multidisciplinary approach. The volume reflects part of a shift to activism in the scholarship of religion and violence. That is to say, at least some of the authors advocate that scholars actively repudiate and challenge religious ideas and texts that can lead to violence. I think most of the essays also illustrate the utility of scarce resource theory in explaining religious violence, even if there are further clarifications and elucidations that should be made. The main issues that need to be settled or clarified include:

– **Causality**: Clearly, a recurring issue has been how we differentiate violence attributed to religious factors from violence attributed to

---

42. Greenfeld, *Nationalism*.

non-religious factors, or even if such a differentiation can be made. Too much of scholarship is still content with simply asserting that politics use religion or that religion is concealing the role of economics without any rigorous empirical or historical research to justify those conclusions. We must insist on more philosophical and historical rigor when we assign causality. That means that we need more scholars willing to master the primary sources when discussing specific conflicts (e.g., Thirty Years War) in order to make judgments about causes.

– **Definition of religion**: In some ways the issue of causality is related to the issue of the definition of religion; the very strict definition versus the very broad one. I certainly do not espouse Jonathan Jong's recent argument that it is useless to define religion.[43] The fact is that the usual arguments against defining "religion" would apply to virtually any other word or category we use. Perhaps the best we can do is simply to be transparent about the definition we are using. If one believes that committing violence to maintain or acquire resources that exist as opposed to committing violence for resources that do not exist, then a definition of religion that focuses on a relationship with supernatural beings and/or forces can still be useful in illuminating an ethical distinction that otherwise would be missed. In my case, I would urge a commitment to reject any and all modes of thinking that are based on supernatural entities. If we can eliminate violence based on the will of invisible beings, we would have eliminated at least one substantial source of violence.

– **Activism**: The extent to which scholars believe that their findings have consequences and are relevant to humanity is the key to encouraging scholars to be activists. There is no reason that scholars of religion cannot be just as activist as scientists when they discover that a disease is caused by a microorganism, not some demon. Similarly, if scholars find that religion and religious factors are correlated with religious violence repeatedly, then they have a moral obligation to say so. They have a moral obligation to undermine the authority and relevance of those religious beliefs. Such criticism of religion and specific religions should not be viewed as cause for accusations of racism or ethnocentrism concerning corresponding believers (e.g., as Islamophobia).

Finally, the recognition that religious violence is global can bring both advances and frustrations in minimizing violence. Advances may result in forging broader coalitions of scholars across the world to address the issue. Frustration will continue insofar as one cannot contain religious violence by defeating it in any particular territory, especially with the power of

43. Jong, "On (Not) Defining (Non)Religion."

social media to incite individuals anywhere at any time. Whatever differing viewpoints there may be among the contributors as to the diagnosis and prognosis of global religious violence, the questions and issues raised in this volume should set the agenda for how one studies religion and violence from now on.

Bibliography

Avalos, Hector. *The Bad Jesus: The Ethics of New Testament Ethics*. Sheffield: Sheffield Phoenix, 2015.

———. *Fighting Words: The Origins of Religious Violence*. Amherst, New York: Prometheus Books, 2005.

Balakrishnan, Gopal. *The Enemy: An Intellectual Portrait of Carl Schmitt*. London: Verso, 2000.

Bendersky, Joseph W. *Carl Schmitt: Theorist for the Reich*. Princeton: Princeton University Press, 1983.

Caspi, Avshalom, et al. "Role of Genotype in the Cycle of Violence in Maltreated Children." *Science* 297:5582 (2002) 851–854.

Cavanaugh, William T. *The Myth of Religious Violence*. Oxford: Oxford University Press, 2009.

Coontz, Stephanie. *Marriage, A History: How Love Conquered Marriage*. New York: Penguin, 2005.

Donovan, Peter. "Neutrality in Religious Studies." *Religious Studies* 26:1 (1990) 103–116.

D'Souza, Dinesh. *Illiberal Education: The Politics of Race and Sex on Campus*. New York: Free Press, 1991.

Enns, Peter. *The Evolution of Adam: What the Bible Says and Doesn't Say About Human Origins*. Grand Rapids: Brazos, 2012.

Fantin, Joseph D. *The Lord of the Entire World: Lord Jesus, a Challenge to Lord Caesar?* Sheffield: Sheffield Phoenix, 2011.

Ficks, C. and Irwin D. Waldman. "Candidate Genes for Aggression and Antisocial Behavior: A Meta-analysis of Association Studies of the 5HTTLPR and MAOA-uVNTR." *Behavioral Genetics* 44:5 (2014) 427–444.

Godfrey, Laurie R., ed. *Scientists Confront Creationism*. New York: W. W. Norton, 1983.

Greenfeld, Liah. *Nationalism: Five Roads to Modernity*. Cambridge: Harvard University Press, 1992.

Jong, Jonathan. "On (Not) Defining (Non)Religion." *Science, Religion & Culture* 2:3 (2015) 15–24.

Kimball, Roger. *Tenured Radicals: How Politics Has Corrupted our Higher Education*. 2nd Edition. Chicago: Elephant Paperbacks, 1998.

Klawans, Jonathan. "Sacrifice in Ancient Israel: Pure Bodies, Domesticated Animals and the Divine Shepherd." Pages 65–80 in *A Communion of Subjects: Animals in Religion, Science, and Ethics*. Edited by Paul Waldau and Kimberley Christine Patton. New York: Columbia University Press, 2006.

Miller, Frank. *Holy Terror*. Burbank: Legendary Comics. September 2011.

Moffitt, Terrie E., et al. "Research Review: DSM-V Conduct Disorder: Research Needs for an Evidence Base." *Journal of Child Psychology and Psychiatry* 49:1 (2008) 3–33.

O'Malley, Suzanne. *Are You There Alone? The Unspeakable Crime of Andrea Yates*. New York: Simon and Schuster, 2004.

O'Neil, Thomas P. and William Novak. *Man of the House: The Life and Political Memoirs of Speaker Tip O'Neil*. New York: Random House, 1987.

Patton, Kimberley. "Animal Sacrifice: Metaphysics of the Sublimated Victim." Pages 391–405 in *A Communion of Subjects: Animals in Religion, Science, and Ethics*.

Edited by Paul Waldau and Kimberley Patton. New York: Columbia University Press, 2006.

Roberts, Aaron B. "Carl Schmitt—Political Theologian?" *The Review of Politics* 77 (2015) 449–474.

Schmitt, Carl. *Political Theology: Four Chapters on the Concept of Sovereignty.* Translated by George Schwab. Chicago: University of Chicago Press, 1985.

———. *Politische Theologie: Vier Kapitel zur Lehre von der Souveränität.* 8th Edition. Berlin: Duncker & Humblot, 2004.

———. "Die Sichtbarkeit der Kirche: Eine scholastische Erwägung." *Summa: Eine Vierteljahresschrift* 2 (1917–1918) 71–80.

Schwab, George. *The Challenge of the Exception: An Introduction to the Ideas of Carl Schmitt between 1921 and 1936.* New York: Greenwood, 1989.

Sizgorich, Thomas. *Violence and Belief in Late Antiquity: Militant Devotion in Christianity and Islam.* Philadelphia: University of Pennsylvania Press, 2009.

Stow, Kenneth R. *Catholic Thought and Papal Jewry Policy, 1555–1593.* New York: Jewish Theological Seminary of America, 1977.

Supreme Court of the United States. "Obergefell et al. v. Hodges, Director, Ohio Department of Health, et al." April 28, 2015–June 26, 2015. https://www.supremecourt.gov/opinions/14pdf/14-556_3204.pdf.

Tiihonen, Jari, et al. "Genetic Background of Extreme Violent Behavior." *Molecular Psychiatry* 20 (2015) 786–792.

Wells, Jonathan. *The Politically Incorrect Guide to Darwinism and Intelligent Design.* Washington: Regnery, 2006.

Williams, Jeffrey, ed. *PC Wars: Politics and Theory in the Academy.* New York: Routledge, 1995.

Wilson, Peter H. *The Thirty Years War: Europe's Tragedy.* Cambridge: Harvard University, 2009.

Zavadski, Katie, et al. "Omar Mateen 'Lacked Remorse' as a Kid and Grew More Violent in School." *The Daily Beast.* June 16, 2017. http://www.thedailybeast.com/articles/2016/07/21/trump-rape-accusers-turn-on-each-other.html.

www.ingramcontent.com/pod-product-compliance
Lightning Source LLC
Chambersburg PA
CBHW060609230426
43670CB00011B/2039